ENGINEERS IN POWER

Engineers in Power

Judy Slinn

LAWRENCE AND WISHART
LONDON

Lawrence & Wishart Limited
144a Old South Lambeth Road
London SW8 1XX

First published 1989
© Judy Slinn

Photoset in North Wales by
Derek Doyle & Associates, Mold, Clwyd,
and printed in Great Britain by
Billings & Sons Ltd, Worcester.

Contents

Illustrations

Preface

The Association's National Executive Committee decided to commission a history of the Association because it believed that the history is worth telling, and recording. The first 75 years of the Association seemed a convenient span to cover. I have no doubt that those who read the following pages will conclude not only that the story is interesting, but that it has a number of lessons which are of value today – and tomorrow. It is, too, a part of the richly complex social and industrial history of our country over the last 75 years. I believe that past and present members of the Association will read it with pride; and that those who read it among the wider public will feel they have learnt something rewarding and enriching about this country's history.

John Lyons
General Secretary

Introduction

When the EPEA celebrated its 50th anniversary in 1964 it was suggested that to tell its story would be largely to tell the story of the electricity supply industry. To an extent that is so, but the Association has a rich and varied life of its own both within the industry and outside; some impression of that is, I hope, conveyed by this history.

The status and position of electrical engineers have always presented problems and for the 75 years that this history covers the Association has worked to improve them. In 1919 one of the founder members wrote that within the industry, 'The obscurity which enshrouds the power engineer would seem to have a direct bearing on the rate of remuneration paid him for his important services to the community', while for the general public the 'sole conception of an engineer is a grimy individual in a suit of overalls, strolling around with an oilcan, or making an unpleasant noise with a hammer on a piece of refractory metal.' It was that image that the Association set out to change.

But in the course of organising to do so the Association has consistently found itself caught in the conflict between on the one hand the objectives and standards of its members as professional people and on the other the aims and ideals of trade unionism. Irreconcilable in theory, in practice a solution to the conflict has to be and is found, as the EPEA's history shows.

Many people inside and outside the Association have contributed to the research and writing of the history. I would like to thank all the EPEA's officials, honorary and permanent, and all the members of Divisions and Sections who welcomed me so hospitably to their meetings. From

Elgin to Belfast, Cardiff to Hythe and Berkeley to Drax, they are too many to be named individually; as also are all the members who have talked and written to me about events and people in the industry and the Association. Special thanks must go to Bill Bradley, whose interest in the EPEA's history led him to preserve some of the vital early archival material and to start writing about it until his retirement activities took up most of his time. He generously gave me the fruits of his work. I have benefitted much from Arthur Palmer's long involvement with, and knowledge of, the industry and the Association and I am most grateful to him for the time he has spent with me and his helpful criticisms and comments on the text. For reading the draft history and making many helpful suggestions I would like to thank John Lyons and Harry Page, while Pat Battams' interest and help with both the text and the illustrations has been invaluable.

John Lyons has ensured that I had access to all the material I needed at Chertsey and the Association has given me every facility combined with freedom of choice as to what to include in the history. The EPEA staff at Chertsey have all helped greatly, particularly Jill Harlow, and my gratitude to June Blake for dealing so efficiently with my drafts and alterations is considerable. Lawrence and Wishart have been considerate and long-suffering editors. Any mistakes of course are mine.

Judy Slinn, January 1989

Chapter 1
Origins and Early Years

'A new Association has been formed'
Electrical Review, 21 February 1913.

The birth of the Association for Electrical Station Engineers, parent of the Electrical Power Engineers' Association, was announced in the columns of the *Electrical Review* in 1913. It was greeted with pleasure by that journal, for it had been,

> ...as a result of a discussion ... often somewhat irrelevant and sometimes bitter, but always turning on the grievances of the junior staffs of the electricity works ...(that) the members of those staffs have been brought into touch with one another and a new Association has been formed to voice their views and to safeguard their interests.

> ...we trust that, under wise and discreet management, it will soon establish itself on a sound basis and become a prosperous and beneficient institution.[1]

The electricity supply industry in the early days

It was apparently only through the press that the members of the technical staffs of electricity undertakings were able to communicate with one another. This reflected the fragmented structure of the electricity supply industry at that time. The industry was also small, both in national terms and by comparison with the supply industry in other countries, particularly those of Britain's greatest industrial competitors, Germany and the USA. Although Faraday

1

had discovered the principles of generation of electricity by mechanical means in 1831, it was not until some fifty years had elapsed that machinery and apparatus were developed to make possible the production of electricity on a commercial scale. The first application of electricity was to the telegraph and its practitioners called themselves 'telegraph engineers': the term electrical engineer came haltingly into use in the 1870s. Even in 1879, the Playfair Committee concluded that the time had not yet arrived when 'the progress of invention brings a demand for facilities to transmit electricity as a source of power and light from a common centre for manufacturing and domestic purposes...'[2]

In the 1880s however there was rapid change, both legislative and technological. The Electric Lighting Act of 1882 laid down procedures for establishing electricity supply undertakings both by municipal and private enterprise, at the same time giving the former the option of purchasing the latter after 21 years. It was held by many that this 21-year rule inhibited private enterprise but there was no sign of this in the brief boom in electrical companies on The Stock Exchange, which followed the passage of the Act. Rather the technical problems still unsolved and the industrial recession of the 1880s were responsible for the slow development of most of that decade. However in 1888 a new Electric Lighting Act was passed which, although still giving local authorities the right to buy out private enterprise extended the time period to 42 years. This, combined with improvements in filament lamps and generating machinery, stimulated more rapid growth of the electricity supply industry.

By January 1889 there were 26 central generating stations operating in Britain, with 17 more under construction. A year later the number had grown to 46 and by January 1891 to 54, of which 17 were in London.[3]

The significance of the development of the electrical engineering industry, in both the supply and the manufacturing sectors, was recognised when, in 1887, the Society of Telegraph Engineers changed its name to the Institution of Electrical Engineers. By 1891, of its nearly 2,000 members, 6% were engaged in electricity supply, not a large proportion but enough to show the growth of the industry; in 1881 the proportion had been negligible, less than 1%.[4]

For domestic use, mainly for lighting, electricity in the 1890s was expensive. In Leeds, where a new central station (the term then used for power station) was opened in 1893, the quarterly cost of lighting a terrace house was estimated to be £1.15s (£1.75) (discounted to £1.13s.3d (£1.66) if paid promptly!). That would be far beyond the means of the occupants of such a house and more expensive than the alternatives of gas or candles. Until after the first world war electricity in the home remained a luxury.[5]

In 1910 less than one in twenty homes had electricity supplied. But as the use of electricity for transport and industry expanded, the 1890s and the first decade of the 20th century saw a considerable growth in the supply industry. There were improvements in machinery and innovations, particularly in the 1890s – the introduction of polyphase alternating current, the use of paper insulated cables, and the development of Parsons steam turbine. Over two hundred new electricity generating under-takings started operations between 1900 and 1913 and, as the load on the early stations grew, it began to make economic sense for undertakings to build larger stations away from the centre of towns and cities and transmit at high voltages. This avoided the kind of problems faced for example by the British Electric Light Company who installed their generator behind Savile Row. Local inhabitants took the company to law in 1882 for 'nuisance' on two grounds, '...first by causing the exhalation of gases which were believed to be injurious, and secondly, by the noise made by the engine of the company, which it was said worked both day and night.'[6]

Even so the average size of the central stations remained small. Excluding the Newcastle-on-Tyne Electric Supply Company (NESCo), which with Charles Merz as its adviser had a pioneering record second to none, the average power company in 1912 had a capacity of about 10,700kW and the standard large turbo-alternator being installed was about 5,800kW.[7] With 391 undertakings in 1912, only

34 of them of 10,000 or more kilowatts the electricity
supply industry in Great Britain resembled a 'patchwork
quilt' of operations, varying in size, technology, ownership
and practice.

While some undertakings were privately owned, others
were municipal enterprises : the latter sold more electricity
more cheaply and with lower capital and working costs
than the former. In 1910-11 municipalities charged an
average price of 1.7 old pence per kWh compared with the
average 2.5 old pence charged by private companies.[8] By
that date the question of the merits of municipal or private
enterprise had become clouded by politics, particularly in
London, which was the only area where undertakings
were allowed to compete and 12 local authorities and 14
private companies supplied distribution systems. A
scheme to rationalise London's supply was proposed in
1905, but foundered in what Hannah has described as the
'Byzantine complexity' of London's politics.[9]

Each of the nearly four hundred undertakings
employed only a small number of men. In particular there
were very few qualified electrical engineers and they made
their own arrangements for salaries, frequently relying on
the advice or dictate of the chief engineer. Typical of such
arrangements was that made by one Council which
minuted in 1897:

> Recommendation by the Electrical Engineer as to the staff he
> would require to commence operations, with the salaries to be
> paid such officials. Chief Assistant £120 to £150 per annum.
> Three Assistants, in charge of an eight hour shift each, £78
> rising to £104 per annum. Mains Superintendent £100 to
> £120 per annum. One clerk at 25s per week.[10]

The *Electrical Review* found 15 years later that there had
been little change: charge engineers' salaries in small
(1,000-2,000 kWh) power stations ran from £65 to £160
per annum, while in the larger stations (up to 4,000 kWh)
they ran from £91 to £200, the latter regarded in the
industry as a 'princely sum'. Salaries such as these were on
a level with the wages of skilled craftsmen in the
engineering and other industries where skill and a high
degree of unionisation had created the 'aristocracy of

labour'. But they compared unfavourably with the earnings of professional men, for whom something of the order of £500 per annum represented a reasonable middle-class standard of living. In the electricity supply industry only chief engineers could hope for such remuneration; for most of the technical staff earnings in the industry represented a poor return for the time and money they (and their parents) had put into training.

The technical men: poor pay and low status

For electrical engineers, as in other professions, education was based on apprenticeship, which gave the opportunity to learn by doing.[11] Most of the young men who wished to become electrical engineers entered an apprenticeship, either with one of the private supply companies, or with a municipal enterprise, or with one of the companies manufacturing electrical machinery. There were 'premium' apprenticeships, for which parents paid higher fees, their sons being designated for the professional rather than the skilled ranks, and educated and treated accordingly. For theoretical knowledge the apprentices looked to several sources. In the latter part of the nineteenth century some private institutions offering an education in electrical theory were founded. Robert Hammond, an entrepreneur with an unshakeable enthusiasm for the electrical industry, established the Electrical Engineering College in 1882. The College was initially housed in temporary premises at 2 Red Lion Square in London and it offered 'to provide for the training of young gentlemen at Electrical Engineering' through premium apprenticeships with the Hammond Company and 'systematic instruction' at the college, where there was available 'complete laboratory and apparatus of the various systems.'[12] The College later became Faraday House and its courses carried considerable prestige in the industry. That was however only for the few. In London there was also the Central Technical Institution at South Kensington, which became part of Imperial College in 1907.

The majority of the technical men in the industry in the

decade before the first world war (and indeed until well
after the second) received their theoretical knowledge at
one of the new Technical Colleges. The Technical
Instruction Act of 1889 had empowered county and
borough councils to establish technical education for
school leavers and most electrical engineers qualified
through evening study, sometimes day-release, over a
period of years. That they did not all stay the course to the
end is hardly surprising, given the demands of shift work.

It was not until 1913 that the Institution of Electrical
Engineers introduced an examination for candidates
seeking direct admission. With great reluctance the
Council of the Institution accepted the examinations
scheme – British engineers were deeply suspicious of
'book learning' – but it was felt that only by setting such
standards could the professional standing of electrical
engineers be confirmed and publicly acknowledged.[13] In
all of this, it may be noted, university education played
little part. By the turn of the century there were some
degree courses in electrical engineering – Birmingham for
example established a chair in the subject in 1905 – but
graduates in the profession were few and far between.
The cost of a university education was in any case
prohibitive, nor was a degree traditionally part of a
professional training, not only in engineering but also in
other professions such as law and accountancy.

For some there could be a course of full-time study,
followed by apprenticeship of a shorter duration. For
example, William Bleasdale studied first at the ICS School
of Electrical Engineering and followed that with six
months at the MVS College at Bristol University. He then
served a three-year apprenticeship, most of it with the
Penrith Electric Supply Company, with whom he was then
qualified to take a position as chief assistant engineer in
1909.[14] But most found themselves, whatever their
qualifications, in badly paid positions as charge engineers
and sub-station superintendents. Despite the poor
immediate prospects many young men were attracted to
the industry in the first decade of the 20th century. Some
joined for 'love of the game', an interest and even
fascination with what was still a relatively new scientific

discipline, and some because they (or their parents) thought that however poor the pay in the short term, the long term prospects for the expansion of the industry were good. Sebastion de Ferranti's optimism that an 'All Electric' age would be created was reflected in his Presidential address to the IEE in 1910;

> It may safely be said that wherever coal, gas or power are now used, everything for which they are used will be better done when electricity is the medium of application.[15]

If the supply industry was to continue to expand at the same rate – and capital employed in the industry rose between 1899 and 1909 by nearly 500%[16] – there would undoubtedly be more jobs and parents were therefore prepared to support their sons, not only through their training, but also through the early years of working. There were, it was said:

> clever young engineers upon whom their rich and doting fathers had spent anything from £250 to £1,000 plus plenty of pocket money ...supervising extensive plants at a 'salary' of anything from 25s to 35s a week – in fact the drivers got more than they did.[17]

As in many other professions at the time, the hardships of the early years were endured in the supply industry because

> Every young engineer like Napoleon's private, dreamed that he carried a chief engineer's job in his knapsack and that it was only a question of getting a few years training and success would be assured.[18]

Nor were working conditions in the industry easy. Average working hours were 56 a week, higher than in other industries where 50-52 hours became average in the years immediately before 1914. In small power stations where there were less than three charge engineers, working hours could be much longer, rising to 64 a week and more, particularly when the work of sick colleagues had to be covered. Overtime payments were non-existent.[19]

Several factors accounted for the slow realisation by the technical staff that they were being treated as 'sweated labour'. Within the individual power station secrecy was the order of the day as far as salaries were concerned, a secrecy based on the individual engineer's feeling for his professional status in the first instance but fostered by many chief engineers and employers in the undertakings. In later years it was recalled that:

> It was quite a common practice for a Chief Engineer to enjoin upon a charge engineer, who had been granted an advance, that he must not disclose the fact to his colleagues as it was purely out of the goodness of his heart that the Chief Engineer was giving him an additional 2s.6d per week. Little did the poor trusting charge engineer appreciate that the Chief Engineer had already bestowed similar largesse on some other charge engineers and had accompanied it with a similar injunction.[20]

There was little communication between engineers at separate power stations and, because of the lack of standardisation in the industry, it would in any case have been difficult to make comparisons between jobs carrying the same titles but involving the operation of widely varying equipment, systems and technology. Of the supply industry its historian has written:

> It is difficult to understand why the voltages and frequencies adopted by ....undertakings should have exhibited such a rich variety, except in terms of the individualism of British engineers.[21]

That individualism had been stimulated by, and was a response to the attitude of British society to engineers. While the older established professions of medicine and law secured their positions at the top of the hierarchy in the second half of the 19th century, the engineers, first the 'civils', then the 'mechanicals' and later still the 'electricals' had to fight for their professional status. Traditionally an interest in scientific and engineering activities was acceptable as a part-time occupation for gentlemen, but as a full-time occupation it meant getting your hands dirty and that was no calling for a gentleman. Much has been written in recent years to show how 'Victorian values' played an important part in the British failure to innovate in the late 19th and early 20th century and the loss of British industrial supremacy to Germany and the USA.[22] For the electrical engineers, the low regard in which they were generally held by society accounts for what may seem almost the obsession with status and gentlemanly behaviour which dominated their thinking in these years and for many after. But despite the problems of pay and status the supply industry attracted many new recruits in the years around the turn of the century, to the point when it was claimed that because so many were eager to join the industry, they were depressing salary levels.[23]

The relatively slow growth of the electricity industry (due in part to its failure to compete with gas on prices between 1880 and 1900) and its relatively poor record of profitability in those years, left a legacy of, if not miserliness, certainly cheeseparing caution. The private power companies had found it difficult to borrow the money needed to finance expansion both because the losses and failures of the early days had made investors more wary and because of the long period of time which must necessarily elapse before the investment showed any return. Municipalities, where much of the development came in this period, were anxious to keep down costs in the interests of the ratepayers (and their own survival). Their success in supplying electricity at lower prices was achieved partly at the expense of their employees: municipal engineers were usually paid less than those employed by the privately owned undertakings.[24]

The discontent surfaces

From the industry's point of view there was every incentive to keep operating costs to a minimum. Nevertheless the manual workers in the industry, organised since 1889 by the Electrical Trades Union had had their wages kept at a reasonable level. The 1906 census showed them, with an average weekly wage of 31s.7d as being 'reasonably well paid' by comparison with other manual workers.[25] By contrast, engineers and technical staff, who had no organisation to represent them, were in many cases earning less than the manual workers. By 1912 the long simmering grievances of the engineers started to surface. The struggle to live on low salaries had been exacerbated by the steady erosion of real wages in the preceding fourteen years. The purchasing power of the pound fell from 20 shillings in 1896 to 16s.3d (£1 to 81p) by 1912, a loss of nearly 19%. It was 'the most frequently identified industrial irritant'[26] in the years between 1911 and 1914, a period marked in Britain by industrial unrest on a scale not seen since the early 19th century. The number of days lost in stoppages climbed to a new peak, and the public airing of grievances no doubt helped to give the electrical power engineers new comparative information which enhanced the growing realisation among them of exploitation. It was not only industrial unrest which grew in the years before the outbreak of war. There was also social unrest, as the suffragettes embarked on a campaign of civil disobedience and there were troubles in Ireland. It is still a matter of debate whether these were all 'manifestations of a common social malaise' or mere coincidence.

Among the technical staff in the electricity supply industry that discontent surfaced near the end of the year in the correspondence columns of the *Electrical Review*. Some of the letters published contained a simple recital of the facts already discussed above and the need for better salaries. Others, writing under pseudonyms such as 'Booster', 'Motor-Generator' and 'Turbo-Alternator' – clearly intended to disguise their owners from colleagues as well as employers – expressed their feelings in a remarkably tactless manner which left them open to charges of snobbery and class consciousness of the worst kind. The correspondence, some of which is quoted below says much about the attitudes prevailing in the industry at the time. Although the writers all made calls for organised action, there was no consensus as to the form the action should take. One suggestion made was that the Institution of Electrical Engineers should be approached, but others dismissed it as inappropriate. Certainly such an approach, if made at that time, would not have been entertained; the

IEE in 1912-3 was dominated by a clique of engineers and scientists who wanted to see it function only as 'a society for the advancement of knowledge'.[27] They viewed with horror any idea of acting either as a trade association or a trade union.

The Electrical Trades Union watched the correspondence with interest; in a letter published on 3 January 1913 from one of the ETU's District Secretaries, J Potter was brisk.

> The more one reads this correspondence, the more apparent does it become that, however well-intentioned the writers may be they lack a true appreciation of the factors which govern the wages and working conditions of any industry and the sooner they get rid of the shibboleth 'profession' and the snobbishness attaching thereto the better it will be for themselves. The 'Chief' is merely a deputy for the employer and, from the nature of his position, has to show a return on the undertaking and the price of labour, unorganised, is more easily squeezed than the price of Osram lamps.

Mr Potter concluded by mentioning how well-organised the ETU was and how it welcomed recruits![28]

The letter provoked a number of indignant replies. Motor-Generator, while disclaiming 'personal abuse' denounced 'common wiremen' and demanded to know

> ...how would it possibly be practicable to be a member of the same Trade Union as the wiremen who are working under our direction in the stations? There would be no respect for us ... and discipline would be all awry. Another reason is that if we started an ordinary Trade Union we should be just as ordinary tradesmen (not that that is a disgrace to any men) but we hope ... that we are a step above the average tradesman.

Snobbishness he said, was to be found in all classes – it was born in all men 'and even electrical shift engineers are no exception'.[29]

Booster (L M Jockel, then working in Bradford – he identified himself to the *Electrical Power Engineer* in 1960!) went even further:

We unfortunates in sub-stations are badly enough off without putting ourselves on the same level as tradesmen; in the first place the average shiftman is a man of some education and a very large number of them are gentlemen. They have some technical training and they are socially well above the average wireman. The average wireman, on the other hand, is usually a man drawn from the lower classes; he has practically no education worth talking of, he does his work no doubt all right but the most elementary question in electricity would stagger him. ....Mr Potter accuses us of snobbishness; but, personally I fail to see how we are guilty in that respect. It is no crime for gentlemen to keep apart from men who do not enjoy the same social position as they do even if it is their misfortune to be 'shiftmen'. How many of us, I should like to know, would like to get our start in life again at any of the other professions which, at least, protect their men if we only knew then what a miserable business was in store for us, where money and influence, not brains was the principal road to success.[30]

Extreme as they may sound, the views expressed by 'Motor-Generator' were, to judge by the letters, shared by many in the industry; on the other hand there were also those who found them repugnant. G F Sullivan wrote from Birkenhead in the next issue of the *Review*, repudiating the charges:

A shiftman receives his salary in exchange for what he accomplishes or should accomplish. As regards shiftmen being gentlemen, there are gentlemen in all walks of life... If 'Motor-Generator' and his colleagues wish to advertise the fact that they are gentlemen, let them adopt the principles of such. Putting on a superior air, boasting of their University education, and the amount of money their deluded parents have spent on the same, are items which they should keep in the background, for, in the writer's opinion a man with University and shops' experience should be able to obtain a healthier and more lucrative position than that of shiftman.

Sullivan went on to refute the suggestion that only wiremen behaved badly:

...I suppose he has never heard the tale of the shiftman who used to stop the battery discharge meter and pump the battery dry to get a low coal consumption on his shift leaving nothing for the next man on, or of the sub-station attendant who burnt out the transformer by taking the shift on the seat of his pants instead of the soles of his feet. Alas! there are fallen brothers in all professions... I knew one wireman, a doctor's son who used to come to work in a cab. Another was a clergyman's son, who in addition was a fluent linguist; also two who had been 150-guinea premium pupils to a pioneer firm of electrical engineers, and were working under a foreman who had been yard-boy in the days of their pupilage.

He finished with a plea for an examination to be set for all would-be electrical engineers, without which they could not take charge.

This would eliminate the caste question and also weed out the purely University-trained men who will take a job at any price to gain experience.... We should then have common-sense men.[31]

In the same issue 'Switchboard' wrote in to say that qualifications should count for something,' although Chief Engineers of supply undertakings consistently refuse to pay living wages for them'. Though he held no brief for the ETU argument he went on to say:

I must register a mild protest against your correspondents who seem to have a horror of being thought 'tradesmen'. Surely to be a tradesman is nothing to be ashamed of, but rather something to be desired. No higher praise can be given to a man than to say that he is a good tradesman, whether he be draughtsman, fitter or sub-station attendant.

His conclusion – 'It is what a man is, not who he is, which counts in engineering nowadays' - was applauded in a note from the editor, who had, it seems, found himself so embarrassed by the 'irrelevant discussion of social position not unmixed with personalities verging upon abuse' unleashed, that he put in a plea for letters on a 'higher plane'![32]

An Association emerges

In a letter published in December 1912, W J Ebben, a shift engineer at Poplar power station in East London, suggested that all those interested in forming an association of engineers should get in touch with him. The response, according to Ebben was 'voluminous' and on the strength of it a meeting was swiftly arranged. Held in London on 16 January 1913, the meeting was attended by 21 delegates representing electrical stations, who decided to form an Association, to be called the Association of Electrical Station Engineers. Its objectives, as defined at the meeting were expressed in very general terms:

1. To raise the efficiency and general status of members of the Association.

2. To provide means for social intercourse among its members for their improvement, advancement and recreation.

3. To form an information bureau for the general assistance of members and employers.

W J Ebben was elected Honorary Secretary and Charles F Wade acting Honorary Chairman. The meeting was told by Ebben that from the letters he had already received there was in prospect a membership of at least 1,000 and the meeting decided that the *Electrical Review* should continue to be the means of communication with future meetings advertised in its columns. In line with the very general objectives agreed for the Association at its first meeting, an equally general definition of the qualification for membership was agreed:

prospective members must be qualified for and hold a responsible position in an electrical undertaking for power lighting or traction.

This was amplified in a letter written after the meeting to the *Electrical Review* by the Chairman. In it Wade said: 'As to the grades to be included in the membership of the Association it would seem that those mentioned in the following list would about cover the various positions in whose interest the Association has been formed viz: Station superintendent, Mains superintendent, Engineers-in-charge, sub-station assistants, mains assistants, repairs and construction engineers, boiler house engineers, switchboard attendants, meter room assistants, draughtsmen and outside traction assistants.'[33]

One of the major difficulties in setting up the Association was highlighted in Wade's letter. The AESE, he said,

> will provide also for a social and recreative side for at present this has offered the only solution of the difficulty in getting members to become acquainted with each other so as to render it possible for an open election of officers to be made.

In the three weeks that elapsed between the first and second meetings, however, it seems that those most involved managed to get acquainted and on 6 February 1913 at a meeting attended by 50 representatives, including some from outside London, Ebben and Wade were confirmed in their positions and W Arthur Jones, (later the first General Secretary of the EPEA) was elected as Vice-Chairman. These men formed the nucleus of the organising committee which set about the task of recruiting members vigorously.

A letter from Ebben was published in the *Electrical Review* on 13 February 1913. In it he spoke of the interest which had been aroused among engineers at home and abroad by the formation of the Association. He was now in touch with about 4,000 engineers he said but in his view there were many more possible recruits. The last Census of Production (in 1907) had recorded about 22,000 men employed in the electricity supply industry. He calculated that about a third of these would be eligible for membership of the Association, and allowing for some increase to 1912 there should be about 10,000 men available for membership. (Ebben's figure was probably over-optimistic. When the Association achieved a high density in the late 1930s and the industry was considerably larger, the number fell well short of 10,000.) Some engineers, Ebben admitted, had decided on a policy of 'wait and see' but he concluded:

> Considering that active steps to form the AESE were only taken during the Christmas week of 1912 the results are astounding: but like Oliver Twist, I ask for more ...thus we shall be able to better the conditions of that section of the electrical profession for which the AESE has been formed.[34]

Among those who had not rushed forward to join were men working in undertakings where the chief engineer was hostile to the Association. In the editorial quoted at the beginning of this chapter, (February 1913) the *Review* had stated: 'The Association is in no sense hostile to the Chief Engineers, some of whom we believe have already signified their approval of its aims and have promised their support'; however, there is no doubt that some employers were anything but sympathetic to the AESE. In such undertakings the Association found, in its early years, that fear of incurring disapproval or dismissal was an effective barrier to recruitment. Various subterfuges were used: as one member recalled, 'we were timid about our efforts to improve our conditions. We tried to kid our Chiefs that we were a more or less scientific debating society'.[35] For the moment, however, at least the Association was without competitors: in a letter to the review shortly after the formation was announced, W J Webb, the militant London District Secretary of the ETU, wrote in a conciliatory fashion:

> Allow me, first of all, to welcome the movement to bring together our central station men. Of course I should prefer them to be members of our Union but failing that I hope a good strong organisation will be built up.

Unable to resist a final shot he advised the sub-men to organise, join the Association, try to improve their status and to get a living wage but 'don't be snobs'![36]

In the spring of 1913 the new Association gathered strength outside London. In March a meeting was held at the Exeter Cafe in Manchester at which a branch for Manchester and district was formed. J W Thomas, also to become a stalwart of the EPEA, was elected as Secretary. In the same month branches were formed in Glasgow, Bradford and Liverpool, followed in April by Birmingham and Grimsby and then in June a branch at Newcastle was formed. The delay in forming the branch at Newcastle illustrates another of the difficulties that the new Association faced; there was, it was reported, difficulty in finding anyone prepared to take on the 'onerous duties' of Honorary Secretary and it was not until that problem was solved that the branch could be established. It is unlikely that it was a problem only in the North East, and for the men who were most intimately involved in forming the Association and recruiting members at the national level – Wade, Ebben and Jones – who already had demanding jobs in the industry, the effort, the time and the sacrifices called for were considerable. As well as correspondence and paperwork, both national and in their own branches, the founding officers travelled extensively in recruitment campaigns. In later years Arthur Jones recalled speaking from the 'tail of a cart', trying to persuade men in the industry to join the Association.[37]

There were other problems too sometimes highlighted in the reports of new branches being formed. At Bradford, where the first meeting suggested the incorporation of the AESE, a second meeting discussed how to increase the membership of the branch and it was pointed out that a large number of men in the Bradford district were a 'little perturbed' about the effect of joining on their future prospects. In London, W J Ebben continued to write to the *Electrical Review* letters intended both to keep up the enthusiasm for the Association and draw attention to the grievances of its members. At the end of March 1913 a long letter from him was published:

> One of the most interesting sections in the *Electrical Review* is the "Situations Vacant" columns, which I think are perused regularly by a large number of the profession, from Chief

Engineers down to those young gentlemen who have studied
Ohm's law for a few weeks and wish to become electrical
engineers. These columns of your issue of March 28th are
particularly interesting, and give one much food for thought.
Take the case of a switchboard attendant wanted for an
electricity works in Lancashire with three separate supplies –
high tension, three wire D.C. and traction – 'should have
technical school training', for the magnificent salary of 5s. per
week of 56 hours (presumably seven shifts per week), which
works out at 1d. per hour, with an odd 4d, with which the
successful applicant can purchase the *Electrical Review* to look
for another job. This advertisement must be bad reading for
some of the technical institutions.

Then again, we notice that a Chief Electrical Engineer is
required at £500 per year clear of all expenses, and be it
noted he must not exceed 40 years of age.

Now probably a young gentlemen finishing a course at a
technical school notices these two advertisements, and
immediately comes to the conclusion that he starts at the
bottom at 5s. a week and rises to £500 a year before he is 40.
Perhaps !!! He very likely consults the professor in charge of
the institution at which he studies, and hears the old, old tale
about starting at the bottom of the ladder, and goes
straightaway and takes the 5s. job, and in imagination we can
hear the grunt of satisfaction of the electrical Mephistopheles,
'Another one!'.

The point I wish to impress is that the technical institutions
do little or nothing to advise these young men. They are
allowed to go to their doom without any warning, and they do
not have the least idea of the harm they do to the profession
generally by accepting such low salaries for responsible
positions.[38]

Ebben suggested that all the technical institutions
should make the position in the industry clear to the
young would-be recruits, both by lectures on the subject
and by circulating copies of relevant articles from the
technical press. He went on however to bemoan the fact
that electrical engineers, or at least a large number of
them, continued to be apathetic

> with regard to the future prospects of the profession; this
> applies particularly to Birmingham and the Midlands. When
> some members of the AESE were visiting a number of

electrical stations in the above districts, they found that a good number of the men engaged in them did not read the technical Press, and consequently knew nothing of what was going forward other than in their own little sphere. A few back numbers of the *Electrical Review* were distributed among them and it is hoped that this will rouse these men to take more interest in their profession in the future. The majority are in receipt of very low salaries. Some have even dared to marry and have families. Perhaps they have heard tell of the reply which was given by a chief electrical engineer of a London supply authority when it was pointed out to him that he was paying his labourers as much as, and even more than, his engineers. He said the reason why the labourers were what he called 'well paid', was because a labourer generally had a wife and about 10 children, giving the impression that if his engineers obtained a wife and family each he would pay them a larger salary.

I must point out that any improvement must be initiated by the men themselves, in combination with their colleagues all over the country, and earnestly appeal to all electrical engineers who read this letter to come forward and help in the work that is going on to raise the status of the profession by means of the AESE.[39]

The Association was however making steady progress and in June 1913, barely six months after its formation, a national conference was held in London attended by delegates from Glasgow, Manchester, Birmingham, Liverpool, Bradford and Grimsby as well as the members of the London Organising Committee, as Ebben, Jones and their colleagues now called themselves. The delegates approved a much more specific list of objectives for the Association: these included obtaining 'adequate remuneration compatible with local conditions and responsibility', a six-day, 48 hour week, 14 days annual leave and time off in lieu for public holidays worked, facilities for shift men to attend classes and the abolition of the employment of pupils and apprentices in responsible positions.

The delegates pledged themselves to support the Association in every 'practicable way possible' and passed a vote of thanks to their 'indefatiguable' Secretary and to the chief engineers who had given some of the delegates leave of absence to attend the conference.

The expenses of running the conference, together with the other initial costs – printing, hire of rooms and legal fees – absorbed nearly all of the Association's income in 1913. The annual subscription had been set at 10s. 6d (52.5p) which represented less than 1% of even the lowest paid members' wages or salaries. By contrast average trade union members at that time paid between 1% and 4% of their income to the union, more than half of which was returned in friendly and unemployment benefits.[40] Even though the subscription in weekly terms was, according to one member, 'less than one usually spends on superfluous evening papers', and members were allowed to pay it in two instalments, from the start arrears and non-payment of subscriptions kept the Association's income low. The problem was compounded after war broke out and at the end of 1914 the Association had to write off over £300 of subscriptions due but irrecoverable. Income in 1914 was therefore a mere £156, and in the war years, for which no accounts have survived, probably even less.

Association or Trade Union?

In January 1914 the AESE registered as a trade union; in order to protect its funds (then standing at £29.9s.2d [£29.46]) and its legal status no other course of action was open to it. But for many of the members registration did not mean that the Association had to act like a trade union. As the Manchester branch recorded at its first meeting, 'the Association was something more than a trade union, its main objective being to raise the status of the profession'. Others put the matter more bluntly: '...we will keep as far away from Trade Unionism as possible, even though the House of Commons dabbles in it', Motor-Generator had declared in the *Electrical Review* and no doubt many agreed with him. Militancy and strike action were inextricably associated with trade unions in the public mind and the electrical power engineers were no exception to that. The absorption into the system of what had been regarded early in the 19th century as organisations dangerous to the fabric of society was not yet complete. The respectability and acceptance secured by many trade union leaders in the 1890s through their espousal of arbitration had been damaged by the industrial unrest which had broken out in 1910. The disorder which characterised some of the disputes – seamen and dockers, railwaymen and miners – which took place between 1910 and 1914 had aroused middle class fears. Over the same period trade union membership grew rapidly.[41]

By the beginning of 1914 the outlook was considered to be bleak: one leading journal reported

> A welter of movements is going on within the world of labour, and the only thing certain about them is that they will find some outlet. Perhaps the most salient feature of this turmoil at the moment is the general spirit of revolt, not only against employers of all kinds, but also against leaders and majorities, and Parliamentary or any kind of constitutional and orderly action...[42]

With that spirit of revolt, the militancy and the political action, the electrical power engineers did not wish to be associated. The debate about how to achieve the objective of better pay and conditions and higher status, without the taint of trade unionism or the compromise of professional standing and principles, dominated the early years of the AESE. The inability to resolve it, described by one member as a 'deplorable state of affairs', did not help in the struggle to recruit new members. The 'internal friction' crippled the usefulness of the new organisation. Even the most active and stalwart members of the Association were divided on the issue. Arthur O Holt, a founder member and Chairman of the Manchester branch, declared firmly in 1915, 'The AESE must declare itself boldly if it wants members and must say in no halting manner that it is not, and will not be a Trade Union'.[43] In response to this, J W Thomas made an attempt at 'clearing the air'. The AESE, he said, does not claim and has never claimed to be a trade union. But

> this is not to say that it possesses nothing in common with Trade Unionism....Much of the fear of what are called Trade Union methods is ill-founded and is the result either of ignorance or prejudice, often of both.

Thomas suggested that members of the AESE could hardly disagree with the definition of a trade union given by Sidney Webb, the noted Fabian and historian of trade unionism – 'a continuous association of wage-earners for the purpose of maintaining or improving the conditions of employment'; but many engineers, he argued looked upon a trade union as having upon it 'the mark of the beast' for two reasons, the use of the strike weapon and the fear of losing caste and compromising their dignity. The latter he dismissed as both childish and costly: 'Dignity is good ... but, if one had a family to maintain, it may not be the height of worldly wisdom'. The 'bugbear' of trade unionism, the strike, Thomas explained was the weapon of last resource.

> Strikes, like war, can never be absolutely right; they can only be relatively so, in the sense that they are a cruel necessity which had to be faced for the sake of undoing something wrong in the industrial system.

In the fight to achieve its objectives, the AESE should rely on arbitration in the first instance. To help it public recognition was essential;

> the public at large ... are almost entirely ignorant of the fact that it is a set of poorly paid individuals and not a fairy godmother who supply the juice to the wires. The station engineer has played 'possum' too long; he must wake up and beat the big drum.

In his conclusion Thomas wrote that the objectives of the Association

> can only be effected by an Association of men with a true pride of profession, who believe that ability and responsibility should be properly rewarded and that no misplaced dignity should deter them from employing effective methods to obtain such, no matter whether such methods are stigmatised as Trade Unionist or not.[44]

This was by no means the final word on the subject. The debate rumbled on, recurring at intervals as we shall see.

The First World War blights the infant Association

For the AESE, the outbreak of war in August 1914 was disastrous. In the large-scale voluntary recruitment that lasted until conscription was imposed in January 1916, the electricity supply industry lost many of its young men. Acccording to the estimates of the fall in occupied male employees in July 1915, electrical engineers ranked as the second highest group, despite Government certification of the industry as essential for war purposes.[45] Any oversupply of the pre-war years soon disappeared, particularly as the demand for electricity for war-time purposes rose and technical skill was required to coax maximum performance out of aging machinery and with inadequate supplies of coal.

Not surprisingly in these circumstances membership of the Association fell drastically. By the beginning of 1915 there were only 520 members and in an attempt to hearten those who remained and attract new members a monthly journal was launched, under the name of *Progress*. To introduce it W J Ebben wrote that although many would say that it was not a propitious time for such a venture, there were reasons for its production:

> Hundreds of Station Engineers at the close of the war will be asking for a job; some are having their positions held open for them and others not. There will be more men than jobs owing to the great influx of nondescript labour during the past few months into our stations. The law of supply and demand then will tend to reduce salaries to a lower level unless there is an organisation ready and strong to put their weight on the side for a fair and reasonable salary.

In terms reminiscent of the recruitment posters he went on to demand:

> What are you doing to protect your colleague's interests when he returns to civilian work? Your colleague who is fighting to protect you and your home? The very least you

can do is to make sure that your and his Association is
numerically and financially strong.[46]

It was a message constantly repeated in each issue of
Progress. Much of the journal was written by the stalwarts
who had been most active in establishing the AESE –
indeed it seems that under various pen-names, Ebben
himself as editor had to write anything up to three-
quarters of each issue.[47] In 1915 he was cheered by the
activities of the 100-strong Newcastle branch who
successfully demanded a war-bonus payment from
NESCo. War-time inflation, which by 1919 would reduce
the value of the pound to a third of what it had been in
1914, was starting to bite into the already low incomes of
station engineers.

War-time conditions also made it difficult if not
impossible for the technical staff to change jobs, although
there were vacancies advertised. In July 1915, to prevent
strikes, the 'poaching' of labour and, most important of all
for the Government, to keep the munitions factories
working at full capacity, the Munitions of War Act was
rushed through Parliament. It laid down that a munitions
worker could not be taken on by another firm within six
weeks of leaving his last job, unless he had a leaving
certificate from his previous employer.[48] Although the Act
applied only to firms already declared controlled by the
Government – electricity supply companies and borough
councils did not come into that category – it soon became
apparent that the Act was being used by Chief Engineers
as authority to prevent staff from moving within the
industry. The AESE sought legal advice on the matter but
the position of electricity supply authorities remained
obscure. Ebben wrote,

> It almost seems that there is a mutual arrangement amongst
> Chief Engineers not to embarrass each other by taking on
> men who are already employed in the industry. I have no
> evidence that there is a mutual arrangement but it certainly
> seems that they are all of one mind in the industry.[49]

Ebben was not slow to use this situation to point the
moral to those working in the industry who had not joined

the Association. The Munitions of War Act, he noted, had been passed after consultation with the trade unions. As a *quid pro quo* for trade union acceptance of the lifting, for the duration of the war, of restrictive practices in force, the employers had agreed to limit profits. Had the AESE had enough members to be a significant force in the industry it would have been consulted and similar arrangements could have been made for the electricity supply industry. He pressed home his message:

> The industries of this country are becoming more and more dependent on electricity supply engineers but again I say the country is not aware of us.[50]

Although conscription (for unmarried men aged 17 to 41) was not introduced until January 1916, the high rate of voluntary enlistment had left industry short of skilled workers, particularly in engineering. The Government sought to 'dilute' the labour force by the introduction of the less-skilled and also the employment of women, and hoped that by so doing the skilled would be freed to operate where they were most needed. It was not a policy which appealed to the trade unions and to ensure its acceptance the Government had to carry out lengthy negotiations with them and eventually accept amendments to the Munitions of War Act. Here again the workers in the electricity supply industry found themselves at a disadvantage. With no recognised union to voice their views, they were not consulted about dilution in the industry. Advertisements started appearing such as the one in the *Manchester Evening News* on 8 April 1916: 'Wanted, smart intelligent girls age 20 to 30 to be trained as switchboard attendants in power stations and sub-stations. Wages during training 20s. per week, to be increased according to ability.' This prompted an immediate meeting of the Manchester branch where an 'animated' discussion on the introduction of female labour into electrical stations was held. Three resolutions were passed and sent to the Honorary General Secretary and the London Committee (appointed in January to manage the day-to-day affairs of the Association) who were instructed to seek from the authorities guarantees of the kind granted to other protective associations in industries where female labour had been introduced.

The resolutions made clear both the seriousness with which the step was regarded and the anxiety about its effect, both immediate and long-term. They resolved:

1. That this branch views with extreme disapproval the introduction of female labour into electrical stations unless convinced by the authorities that the same is a military necessity.

2. that the wages paid to female labour be the same as that paid to the man displaced.

3. that guarantees be obtained that the positions shall be restored to the men displaced at the termination of the war.[51]

But despite the importance of these issues membership of the Association continued to fall during 1916; indeed the year saw the nadir of its wartime fortunes. A net loss of more than 150 members meant that by January 1917 there were only 215 paid up members; only two branches, London and Manchester, were still functioning. To those who had worked unceasingly for four years to build the Association it seemed that war, apathy and fear were killing it. In later years Arthur Jones recalled the pessimism of the time:

> On one occasion on a propaganda foray Mr. Jones was accompanied by a colleague who had assisted him to explain the Association's aims and objects to such effect that a one-shilling entrance fee had been gathered from a new adherent. Returning homewards in the train, Mr. Jones' fellow missionary expressed serious conscientious doubts as to whether it had been fair to take the man's money while the likelihood of his ever getting any return for the shilling was so nebulous![52]

Even the Honorary General Secretary 'got the hump' : in one of the last issues of *Progress*, his leader column echoed his own disillusionment.

I find it difficult to write calmly on station engineers and their ways at times. Recently I met an old colleague who naturally, after the usual enquiries asked after the health of the A.E.S.E. When I replied that we could do with more members, he replied that it was snobbishness that kept them out. Remembering that he was not a member, I tactfully suggested that perhaps he was of a snobbish persuasion. This was stoutly denied. It was the others who were snobbish (always the others). He could give no sound reason for not joining and he has not joined yet. There are thousands of such men. They like the A.E.S.E. because they think it will do good. They think every other engineer ought to join but themselves. They can give no reason for not joining. They are not satisfied with their present conditions and they are extremely critical. ... Those of us who strive and work to persuade these men to help sometimes wonder if it is all worth while.[53]

In the first six months of 1917 it seemed that the AESE was, to all intents and purposes, dead.

Notes

1. *The Electrical Review*, 21 February 1913.
2. Cited by B Bowers, *A History of Electric Light and Power*, Peter Peregrinus 1982, p 154.
3. *Ibid.*
4. W J Reader, *A History of the Institution of Electrical Engineers, 1871–1971*, The IEE, London 1987, p 29.
5. L Hannah, *Electricity Before Nationalisation*, MacMillan 1979, p 34.
6. *The Times*, 6 April 1882, quoted in Z Schonfield, *The Precariously Privileged*, OUP 1987, pp 49–50.
7. I C R Byatt, *The British Electrical Industry. 1975–1914*, Clarendon Press, Oxford 1979.
8. Hannah, *op cit*, pp 39, 50.
9. *Ibid*, p 48.
10. *Electrical Power Engineer (EPE)*, August 1920, p 32–3.
11. W J Reader, *Professional Men*, Weidenfeld and Nicholson 1966, p 117.
12. *The Times*, 2 May 1882, quoted in J D Poulter, *An Early History of Electricity Supply*, The IEE, 1986, pp 32–3.
13. Reader, *History of the IEE*, *op cit*, p 70.
14. EPEA records.
15. Quoted in Hannah, *op cit*, p 34. See also J F Wilson, *Ferranti and the British Electrical Industry 1864–1930*, Manchester University Press 1988.
16. Reader, *op cit*, p 62.

17. *EPE*, August 1920.
18. *EPE*, March 1949, pp 181–2.
19. *Ibid*.
20. *Ibid*.
21. Hannah, *op cit*, p 50.
22. See e.g. D C Coleman, *Gentleman and Players*, Economic History Review, 2nd series, 26 (1973), M J Wiener, *English Culture and the Decline of the Industrial Spirit 1850–1980*, Cambridge University Press 1981. Also N McKendrick and R B Outhwaite (eds), *Business Life and Public policy*, Cambridge University Press 1986.
23. *EPE*, March 1949, pp 181–2.
24. Hannah, *op cit*, p 50.
25. H A Clegg, Alan Fox, and A F Thompson, *A History of British Trade Unions since 1889*, Vol 1, Clarendon Press, Oxford 1964, p 481.
26. H A Clegg, *A History of British Trade Unions since 1889*, Vol 2, 1911–1933, Clarendon Press, Oxford 1985, pp 24–5.
27. Reader, *History of the IEE, op cit*, p 86.
28. *Electrical Review*, 3 February 1913.
29. *Electrical Review*, 10 January 1913.
30. *Ibid*.
31. *Ibid*.
32. *Ibid*.
33. *Electrical Review*, January 1913.
34. *Electrical Review*, 13 February 1913.
35. Letter from T S Wallis, *EPE*, November 1960, p 501.
36. *Electrical Review*, 24 January 1913, p 127
37. *EPE*, December 1945, p 681.
38. *Electrical Review*, March 1913.
39. *Ibid*.
40. Clegg, *op cit*, p 16.
41. *Ibid*, Chapter 1.
42. G R A Askwith, *Industrial Problems and Disputes*, Books for Libraries Press, New York 1920, p 347.
43. *Progress*, May 1915.
44. *EPE*, November 1920.
45. C J Wrigley (ed), *A History of British Industrial Relations*, 1914–1939, Harvester Press 1987, p 24.
46. *Progress*, January 1915.
47. *Progress*, November 1915.
48. A J P Taylor, *English History 1914–45*, OUP 1965, p 36.
49. *Progress*, October 1915.
50. *Ibid*.
51. *Progress*, May 1916.
52. *EPE*, December 1945.
53. *Progress*, March 1916.

Chapter 2

Resurrection and Re-formation: The Electrical Power Engineers' Association

'Today, technically trained staff engineers engaged in the Electricity (Power and Supply) Industry have a protective organisation such as they have never had before.'

The President's letter, July 1919.

The year 1917 was one of the worst of the war: on the military front neither of the major offensives, at Passchendaele and Cambrai, improved the British position significantly and both involved heavy losses. At home, the existing system had broken down while newly introduced controls were barely in place. Food and fuel were in short supply, trains were slow and crowded and queues became a feature of everyday life.[1] In the first six months of the year industrial unrest grew, evidenced in the increasing number of strikes, the most extensive of which took place in May, mainly in the engineering industry. Sacrifices of sleep, leisure and customary working practices to the demands of the war machine, however willingly made in the name of patriotism in the first instance, were becoming a source of resentment, particularly as inflation bit into the value of wages and salaries. With no trade union or association to represent them, the electrical power engineers fared badly.

That in itself however was not new nor, as we have seen, had it been sufficient to keep the Association of Electrical Station Engineers alive. But in the second half of 1917

29

other events combined to provide powerful stimuli to a
resurgence of interest in the moribund Association. Chief
among these were the publication of the Whitley Report
with its recommendation that joint industrial councils
should be formed, the emergence of proposals to restructure the electricity supply industry after the war and pay
claims put forward by the Electrical Trades Union on
behalf of all of those working in the industry including the
technical staff. The need for a voice to represent the
electrical power engineers in all these matters was overwhelming.

The supply industry – the need for change

The industrial demand for electricity increased rapidly
during the war, particularly after the Ministry of
Munitions embarked on its drive to increase the
production of armaments. The coordination of electricity
supply nationally was in the hands of the Ministry until
1916 when a separate Department of Electric Power
Supply was established, run successively by two distinguished consulting engineers, first Charles McLellan of
NESCo and then Arnold Gridley. Both sought to
concentrate output in larger production units, and the
extension of existing undertakings by the installation of
new plant as well as the construction of new power stations
was directed and sanctioned by the Department. New
plant was installed where it was most needed for industrial
purposes – for example at Rotherham, Sheffield and
Coventry – and some of it was larger and more technically
advanced than before. At Rotherham a 25MW set was put
in, then the largest in operation in Britain.[2] Overall during
the war some £23m was invested in the industry nearly
14% of which was provided directly by the Ministry of
Munitions. Some estimates suggest that aggregate sales
doubled between 1914 and 1918 but that was commensurate with the same rate of growth for the industry as had
prevailed in the immediate pre-war years. Hopes of
greater efficiency arising from cooperation between
undertakings were disappointed, for the entrenched
hostility between private and municipal enterprise did not

disappear even under the duress of war.

Professor Hannah has concluded that in the supply industry the achievement of the war years was to squeeze a lot of output from a restricted investment, and to direct that output primarily to the munitions industries. Rather than laying the basis of later expansion, the effect was to compromise the future by short term expedients, forced on the industry by the priorities of wartime.[3] That squeezing was accomplished by improving the load factor on the generating stations. Before the war a load factor of 23 or 24% was the norm but by 1918 the national average was 30% and in industrial areas it was higher; in Birmingham it was up to 39% by 1917. The achievement of such increases placed a heavy burden on the technical staff in the industry, who bore the brunt of running plant on overload and carrying out essential repairs and maintenance in such a way as to avoid, as far as possible, major shut-downs.

The failure to achieve greater cooperation between the undertakings during the war gave added ammunition to those who had long advocated a reorganisation of the fragmented supply industry. The Reconstruction Committee (established in 1917 by the government to plan radical postwar changes in industry and society) delegated the work of investigating the supply industry through Lord Haldane to Charles Merz, a consulting engineer who had been in the industry since 1892 and had family connections with NESCo. The Haldane-Merz Committee interim report was published in April 1917; it recommended a complete and radical change from the past based on a diagnosis that development of the six hundred electricity undertakings in the industry had been not only technically wrong but also commercially uneconomical.[4] Instead, the committee proposed a new system of dividing the country into sixteen districts, each with a super power-station, although it did not commit itself to a particular form of ownership. Even as the critics started to attack the Haldane-Merz Committee, another committee appointed by the Board of Trade and under the chairmanship of Sir Archibald Williamson, a Liberal MP, was considering the reorganisation of the supply industry. It was clear that, despite the vested interests and the difficulties, some scheme of reorganisation for the electricity supply industry would be embodied in legislation at the end of the war. The electrical power engineers realised the need for a representative body to put their views, distilled from their knowledge of the industry, so that any reorganisation did not ignore their interests.

While the future organisation of the electricity supply industry carried important long-term implications for the electrical power engineers, of greater significance to them in the short term in 1917 were the linked problems of remuneration and the activities of the ETU.

Pay claims and the Electrical Trades Union

Apart from the engineering unions, the trade union most heavily involved in the strikes of May 1917 was the Electrical Trades Union; before the war the ETU, with its members drawn in the main from the electrical contracting and engineering industries, had not carried much weight in the trade union world.[5] In 1910 it had less than 2,000 members but it enjoyed a period of rapid growth during the war and by 1920 it was 57,000 strong. As its membership in the supply industry grew with the industry the ETU embarked on a vigorous recruitment campaign which included the technical staff. In 1917 the ETU put forward claims on behalf of *all* the workers in the supply industry.

The Committee on Production, established in February 1915 and headed by Sir George Askwith, a barrister with considerable pre-war experience of industrial arbitration and conciliation, had a wide brief and dealt with many of the wage claims arising during the war, but other Ministries and individuals were also concerned. The Ministry of Labour was established in 1916 as a *quid pro quo* for the Labour Party's support of Lloyd George and it took over some responsibilities for wages from the Board of Trade; the Admiralty and the Ministry of Munitions were involved in wages negotiations and there were individual Ministers who made wage settlements, such as the Coal Controller who, in September 1917, without consultation with anyone, awarded a flat-rate war grant of 1s.6d (7.5p) a day to the miners. Writing in 1920 Sir George Askwith recorded his view that during the war 'in labour matters the Government had no policy, never gave signs of having a policy and could not be induced to have a policy'.[6]

One of Askwith's colleagues noted with regret the lack of coordination and its effects:

> The chaotic, individual and competitive handling of labour pursued by the various departments has resulted in fostering the spirit of unrest; harassing and rendering impotent the employers or management; in addition to vastly adding to the cost of the war and hindering output.[7]

This situation was at its worst in the second half of 1917. Unable to control the inflationary spiral, the Government's response to the industrial unrest and the May strikes was to appoint Industrial Commissioners, charged with investigating and reporting back on the causes, within fourteen days, and recommending remedies. This despite the fact that the Committee on Production had already agreed with both sides of the engineering industry in February of that year that wages in the industry should, in the abnormal conditions of the war, be reviewed at four-monthly intervals, and awards had been made in both March and June.

When the Industrial Commissioners reported back a further committee was appointed to consider what action should be taken; its deliberations were lengthy, lasting from July until October but its proposal, embodied in an Order giving an award of 12.5% to engineering workers on October 14 leaked out well before that date. The Committee on Production was beset with claims from other industries for an increase of 12.5%. Among these were the electricians. The ETU had been pressing for a revision of wages for its members, including those in the supply industry, throughout the summer of 1917 and threatening action if its demands were not met. A dispute had been averted by advances awarded in September and December but by the beginning of January 1918, with the

question of 12.5% still unsettled, an all-out strike was
threatened. Fearful of the effect such a disruption of
supply would have on industrial and particularly
munitions production, now so heavily dependent on
electricity, on January 5, even as the electricians started to
walk out, the Government agreed the 12.5% award and
asked Askwith to deal with the matter.[8]

The difficulties in the industry were considerable, as
Askwith had already noted in his previous encounters:

> The employers themselves were divided into three principal
> sections with divergent views and interests. There were the
> great power companies, municipal and private employers,
> and the electrical contractors. Some of them were under the
> Munitions of War Acts, some were not. Some were
> reimbursed by the Government for extra expenditure, others
> would not be reimbursed. In addition the managers and chief
> officers of all these undertakings were paid on no organised
> scale. Some of them received very low salaries. Borough and
> city councils gave them most varied remuneration. They, too,
> were moving for increased emoluments.[9]

Into this confused and difficult situation, where most of
the employers were resisting the ETU's demands for the
application of the award, there came in 1918 the
resuscitated Association of Electrical Station Engineers.

The emergence of the Electrical Power Engineers'
Association

On 5 September 1917 some of the few remaining
members of the Association of Electrical Station Engineers
met in London, the first of a number of meetings held in
London and elsewhere over the next few months. The
London members agreed to reconstruct their division and
to seek representation at the conference of Local
Authorities on Wages (one of the employers' organisations). On 17 October a similar meeting was held at
Lockhart's Café in Manchester, attended by 35
engineers, with A O Holt in the chair and J W Thomas as
secretary – both stalwarts of the Association since 1913.
The meeting decided to reconstruct the branch and

elected A L Lunn as its Chairman (a year later he became President of the EPEA). In the autumn of 1917 and the early months of 1918 meetings were held in Bury, Stockport, Blackburn, Sheffield and Leeds, the last two attended by chief engineers. Organisations sprang into existence all over the country, some branches of the Association, others having an independent or semi-independent existence; in Birmingham the engineers formed the Midlands Power Supply Engineers Association.[10]

There is no doubt that this flurry of activity was in the main stimulated by outrage on the part of the engineers at the claim of the ETU to represent all workers in the supply industry and its attempt to justify that claim by recruiting technical and supervisory staff, in some cases by methods both unwelcome and unwise. One of the first actions of the London meeting bears out this interpretation: a 'protest memorial' was drawn up disputing the claim of the ETU to represent the interests of station engineers. Signed by the technical staff of 38 undertakings and sent to Askwith, as Chief Industrial Commissioner, the protest gave an indication of the stirrings among the electrical engineers.

At the beginning of February 1918 a national conference was organised and held in London. It was a crucial meeting. Arthur Jones wrote:

> It was always felt ... that the need for an Association such as the A.E.S.E. would eventually be appreciated. Events have justified this optimism and this meeting, together with the present position is a compensation for the dull days of 1915-16.[11]

At the conference delegates from the newly organised branches decided to unite under a new name, the Electrical Power Engineers Association. A National Executive Council, composed of delegates from Divisions (then three in number, London and the South, the Midlands and the North) would be the Association's decision-making body. A new constitution and rules were to be drawn up and the annual subscription was set at a guinea (£1.05). Arthur Jones was elected as Honorary

Secretary, for W J Ebben resigned. No reason for this was
given at the time nor does his name appear again in the
records of the Association; it seems however that,
disillusioned by four years of the struggle to organise the
technical staff, early in 1917 he suggested that the
remnants of the AESE should join the ETU.[12]. The new
name and the resignation of Ebben gave added point to
Jones's judgement of the significance of the conference:

> To those of us who have been members of the AESE since its
> inception this meeting marks the close of one epoch and the
> commencement of another.[13]

By the middle of 1918 the EPEA claimed a membership
of over 1500 and was still growing. Another 'protest
memorial', couched in more definitive terms was drawn
up and the Association regarded it as showing its increased
strength: 1350 engineers representing 152 undertakings
signed it, including 90 chief assistants. In it, as before, the
Association registered its protest against the ETU
representing them. It went on to say:

> The Association desires to impress upon all the Authorities
> that the technical staffs of Electricity Supply Undertakings
> have the strongest objections to being forced to join the ETU
> or any Trade Union other than that of their own choosing.
> Should the Authorities decide against the expressed wish of
> the members of this Association, they must also accept the
> responsibility of any action accruing from such decision.[14]

The events leading to the Stoker Award

In 1918, ETU action in pursuit of its objective of industrial
unionism posed a threat to the EPEA, a threat which had
to be defeated or at the very least contained. The ETU had
the year before introduced its 'green card' scheme, which,
by grading workers gave the union greater control over
pay and conditions for each grade.[15] The scheme was also
used by the ETU to extend its membership into the
supervisory levels. When its members were promoted the
union insisted that they kept their cards and their
membership. This gave the ETU a basis both for claiming

for supervisory grades and recruiting among them; and it became apparent in 1918 that the ETU was prepared to use the strike weapon to force electrical engineers to join. In July 1918 there was strike action by ETU members in Liverpool, aimed at forcing EPEA members, including the chief electrical engineer and his assistant at Harland and Woolf to join the ETU.[16]

In August 1918, at the hearing before the Committee on Production of the ETU claim for wage increases, the employers opposed the ETU's inclusion of the technical grades in their claim. Members of the ETU delegation at the hearing were far from pleased to see EPEA representatives present, apparently at the invitation of the employers. The unions demanded an immediate adjournment and 'heated discussions' took place.[17] The Committee's chairman however ruled, after the meeting resumed, that if the ETU had only one member employed in a grade, the union could legitimately insist on its claim being applied; the ETU promptly noted that it had 42 members who were charge engineers in the London area. But the opposition of the employers and the EPEA ultimately won the day and the increases made by Award 2772 later that month specifically excluded all grades above switchboard attendant.

For the Association it then became imperative, not least to sustain its own credibility, to seek commensurate salary increases for the technical staff. Although work had started on drafting a comprehensive schedule of salaries for all grades of technical staff, it had become clear that this would take some time both to work out and negotiate. In the meantime the technical staff were losing out financially, as inflation reduced the value of money. Although in some areas, particularly London, the Association had achieved war bonuses in its early days of revival in the previous year for local members, they had not been granted country-wide.

On 11 October 1918, therefore, the EPEA submitted its application to all electricity supply undertakings,

For an increase of 20% on present salary plus £90 per annum. Present salary shall be understood to be the salary now paid after deduction of all war wages or war bonuses but

inclusive of all increases received since July 31 1914 not
definitely stated in the salary roll or pay sheet as war wages or
war bonuses.

Although the claim was rushed in for consideration by
the Committee on Production, the latter in fact did not do
so before it was dissolved in December 1918. The
Government intended to introduce legislation to set up an
Industrial Court as the Whitley Committee had recommended (see p 40), but in the interim period the
procedures of the Conciliation Act of 1896 applied.
Although the Standing Conference of Electricity Supply
Undertakings recommended its members to accept and
pay the EPEA claim in January 1919, this did not of course
carry any binding obligation on undertakings to pay up,
as an award from the Committee on Production would
have done. In these circumstances the only way the
Association could get their claim awarded on a statutory
basis was by referring it to an Arbitrator. The claim was
heard on 18 February 1919, before W H Stoker, and
shortly afterwards Award 9281, which became known as
the Stoker Award was made, giving the technical staff of
the electricity supply undertakings in full the 20% on
salary plus £90 for which the Association had applied.[18]
Of greater long term significance was the recommendation added by the Arbitrator that representatives of the
employers and the technical staff should continue to meet
to agree a schedule of salaries for all grades. This
coincided with the Association's wish to establish collective
bargaining machinery on the Whitley model in the
electricity supply industry.

The implementation of the Whitley recommendations

The growth and acceptance of collective bargaining, in the
last two decades of the 19th century was noted with
approval by the Royal Commission on Labour in 1894.

> When organisations on either side are so strong as fairly to
> balance each other, the result ... is a disposition ... to form a
> mixed board, meeting regularly to discuss and settle questions
> affecting their relations.... We hope and believe that the

present rapid extension of voluntary boards will continue. Authoritative and responsible organisations of workpeople could maintain control over their members' behaviour in a way that legal sanctions could not.[19]

In the two decades that followed the Report, the Board of Trade, particularly under Hubert Llewellyn Smith (a protégé of Beatrice and Sidney Webb) who was Permanent Secretary from 1907 to 1919, encouraged union recognition and collective bargaining as steps towards industrial harmony and social progress. Such thinking was not confined to liberals and social democrats; Bonar Law, the Conservative leader, told the House of Commons in 1912, 'I should like to see the trade unions become stronger, because I think that, as a rule, they tend to the diminution of disputes.'[20]

The war strengthened collective bargaining and the centralisation of trade union authority, partly because, as government control of industry was extended, government departments, particularly the Ministry of Munitions, had to make arrangements with trade unionists and preferred to do so on a national basis. Trade union membership grew rapidly during the war and new channels of communication were opened between government and the unions. Even so the pressures of war strained the system, leading not only to a degree of chaos in industrial relations but also to the emergence of unofficial movements.

When the Reconstruction Committee turned its attention to the shape of postwar industrial relations, it established a sub-committee, chaired by J H Whitley (1866-1935), later Speaker of the House of Commons, to consider making 'suggestions for securing a permanent improvement in the relations between employers and workmen'. The trade unionists, employers, economists and social workers who sat on the committee produced five reports designed, if implemented, to create a cooperative as opposed to an adversarial system of industrial relations. The committee's first, best-known and probably most significant report was published in June 1917. Its major recommendation was that there should be

some form of industry-wide regulation of industrial
relations in every industry; in well-organised trades, the
committee suggested that a Joint Industrial Council
should be set up, where representatives of employers and
workers would be able to deal with issues affecting the
whole industry.[21]

The reports of the Whitley Committee went on to
recommend the extension of the JICs to the district level
and to the workplace, with the formation of District
Industrial Councils and Joint Works Committees respectively; it also proposed a permanent court of arbitration
and measures to deal with industries where trade
unionism was not established. As a whole it was 'an
impressive attempt to create a coherent system of
arrangements through which the relations between
employers and workers could be conducted on a voluntary
basis'.[22]

Whitley received a mixed reception; some employers
were hostile and some trade unionists, particularly those
who were well-established, such as the railway unions, felt
that Whitley offered no improvement on their present
situation. Generally though in the TUC trade union
leaders who looked to the future did not wish to return to
industrial warfare, as long as legitimate trade union
interests did not have to be sacrificed.[23] In many
industries Whitley was received enthusiastically and talks
began which were directed to establishing JICs in the latter
part of 1917 and early 1918. By the end of 1918, 20 JICs
had been formed.[24] As the proposals were extended to
government departments and municipal authorities in
1918, the electricity supply industry became an obvious
candidate for setting up a JIC; the electrical power
engineers, however, to secure a role in the negotiations to
establish a JIC, needed an active, organised trade union
with a membership large enough to be claimed as
representative.

By the summer of 1918 when the talks began between
the unions and employers in the supply industry, the
EPEA felt it had a right to be represented. Arthur Jones
and A L Lunn attended, on the Association's behalf, the
preliminary conference held in Manchester in June 1918.

At the conference both J Rowan of the ETU and R Williams of the National Transport Workers Federation questioned the EPEA's presence, suggesting that the Association was not a *bona fide* trade union, recognised by the TUC.[25] On these grounds they were able to exclude EPEA representatives from the meetings that followed the June conference.

Angry and disappointed, the Association appealed to the Ministry of Labour but a meeting with the Ministry's permanent officials in October 1918 gave them little comfort. Trade union claims, they were told, had been difficult to reconcile in other industries, particularly those of the technical workers, and the Ministry had no powers of compulsion nor did it wish for them. In the parlance of the day, the Ministry officials asserted that to give them authority to govern the constitutions of industrial councils would smack of 'Prussianism'; an EPEA delegate riposted that it seemed to him that 'to avert the danger of Prussianism recourse had been had to Bolshevism'![26] The ETU objections to the EPEA, according to the Ministry, stemmed partly from the fact that the Association was not affiliated to the TUC and partly because its members were seen as 'toffs' whose inclusion in a JIC would add strength to the employers' side. The EPEA delegation assured the Ministry that they intended to sit firmly on the side of the workmen and that in their view the expertise and knowledge of the industry of the technical staff would be useful to the manual workers; but there was no real progress at the meeting nor could there be.[27] In the voluntary situation the cards were stacked on the side of the ETU.

By the time the Stoker Award was made, it was clear to the EPEA that the intransigence of the ETU had successfully blocked any possibility of their participating in the Joint Industrial Council. Although the Ministry of Labour had suggested, in November 1918 the formation of a JIC with two sections, one for the technical staff and one for the manual workers, that too had been vetoed by the ETU. The formation of the JIC for the manual workers went ahead in the spring of 1919 and its members assembled for their first meeting on 1 May 1919. For the

EPEA and the employers the only course of action left, in
order both to establish Whitleyism for the technical staff
and to meet the recommendations of the Stoker
Arbitration, was the formation of separate machinery.

In one sense this reflected the comment of the President
of the IEE.

> The Whitley Report most unfortunately recognises only two
> classes : workmen and employers. The brains of manufac-
> turing works and of all technical industries are left out
> altogether. It is a gross injustice and most extraordinary
> oversight.[28]

But the ETU's determination that the EPEA should not be
part of the JIC was based on its conviction that the
Association was the creature of the employers. While it is
clear that the impetus for the formation of the Association
came from the technical staff themselves, it is true that
some employers saw a separate union of the electrical
power engineers as a useful weapon and a counterpoise to
the growing power of the manual workers' unions.

In the autumn of 1919 therefore a series of meetings
between the employers and the Association established a
framework for separate Whitley machinery for the
technical staff. In December 1919 the important decision
to set up the National Joint Board to negotiate the pay and
conditions for the technical staff of the supply industry
was taken.

The growth of the Association

A further spur to the growth of the Association in 1918
was the recognition gained from the Institution of
Electrical Engineers. The ETU's claim to represent the
technical staff had not gone unnoticed at Savoy Place.
Already perturbed by falling membership, C H Wordingham, the President in 1917 and 1918 and 'probably one
of the most active Presidents the Institution has had', was
'outraged' when he heard of the very strenuous efforts
were being made by the ETU to bring within its
membership not only workmen but engineers of all ranks

up to and including chief engineers of central stations.[29]
Prompted by Wordingham, the IEE decided that it must
establish a protective association for the industry, which, it
anticipated, would be joined by what it saw as a number of
small associations already in existence. Wordingham was
appointed as President of the IEE's new association and
meetings were arranged up and down the country. The
Council of the IEE was however ill-informed about the
strength and size of the EPEA. What Wordingham
described as 'very violent opposition' to the IEE initiative
came from the EPEA. It was also a successful opposition;
in the face of it the IEE retreated rapidly, if 'without much
grace' and entered into discussions with the EPEA.[30]

In the consultations that followed it was agreed between
the IEE and the EPEA that all technical staff should be
eligible for Association membership, up to and including
chief engineers, provided that they were not employers or
employers' representatives on an Industrial Council. The
EPEA qualification for membership had so far been
expressed in very general terms: applicants for membership 'must be trained engineers and holding or qualified to
hold responsible positions requiring skill, training and
knowledge of electrical engineering in the electricity
supply industry'. Now it was agreed with the IEE that from
December 1921 all new EPEA members would be required
to have passed the examinations for Associate Membership of the IEE, or its equivalent. Wordingham was much
involved with the EPEA over the summer months in 1918
– indeed he attended the National Executive Council
meeting held in Manchester on July 27, and was duly
thanked by the members for his help and advice. It was
not however until October that the IEE gave its formal
recognition to the EPEA as *the* protective association for
the technical staff. That recognition was a testimony to the
strength and position acquired in a short time by the
EPEA and to its status as a trade union. Wordingham
spelled it out from the IEE point of view:

Now the Trades Union idea was a very bitter pill to most of us
to swallow. I do not pretend for a moment that any one of the
Council, nor in fact many members of the Association itself,

wished to promote or to join a Trades Union, but that is
practically put upon you by the Government. Unless you are
one you are no better than a Mutual Admiration Society. In
order to act effectually you must be a Trades Union, whether
you like it or not. Some of us have gulped at this pill and some
of us have more or less choked over it; but it has had to be
swallowed.[31]

The arrangement arrived at benefitted both parties.
The EPEA always acknowledged the help and support of
the IEE and the official recognition undoubtedly helped
the EPEA to recruit members, particularly those hostile to
trade unionism, in the early years. For the IEE, 'It would
obviate the necessity ... to soil its hands with protective
activities which, in spite of persistent demand from
members, it had always been loath to do.'[32]

The EPEA did not as yet have the field solely to itself: of
the organisations which had sprung up, the Society of
Technical Engineers, with a mainly industrial membership, was a thorn in the flesh to the EPEA as it started to
extend its recruitment into electricity supply. There was
an uncomfortable area of overlap between the two unions,
for the EPEA also had attracted some industrial members
(see p 68) and accusations of 'poaching' of members went
to and fro.[33] But by the end of 1918 the Association's
membership had topped the 2,000 mark, representing,
the officials believed, a 40% density.

The launch of the Electrical Power Engineer

So many issues confronted the new Association in 1918
and 1919 that its own organisation took second place.
Nevertheless the broad shape of the constitution of the
Association with its sections and divisions, a shape still
recognisable today, began to emerge. With only honorary
officials to carry out all the negotiations and paperwork
the burden was heavy on them and more particularly on
W Arthur Jones, the Secretary. In October 1918 it was
noted at the NEC meeting that, in connection with putting
in the claim that led ultimately to the Stoker award, 'In
seven days the Hon. General Secretary had sent out 964

letters [to members], the whole of the work being done, it must be remembered in his spare time.'[34] With important negotiations about the claim coming up, an increasing membership to service, the complex matter of establishing an EPEA presence in the Industrial Council and representations to be made on the proposed legislation on the structure of the electricity supply industry, the NEC recognised that it could not continue on the basis of entirely voluntary labour.

It decided therefore to appoint W Arthur (as he became affectionately known in the Association over the next 30 years) as General Secretary at a salary of £500 per annum. It was recognised in retrospect, if not at the time, that in accepting the appointment, he took a grave risk.[35] Although the Association was attracting a much larger membership than had the old AESE its future was still uncertain. If it were to become impossible for it to sustain a permanent official, Jones might well find it difficult to find employment again in the industry; hostility to the Association was still widespread among the senior managers of the electricity undertakings. But Arthur Jones, then a charge engineer in the London borough of Leyton was a 'dedicated man'. He was to prove the ideal choice for the job; 'calm and collected ... always courteous and reasonable', he soon gained respect from all sides as a skillful negotiator. 'An all-rounder who was equally at home in any company, he detested showmanship, humbug or hypocrisy in any form. He never sought the limelight and did his best to escape from its beams.'[36] For some months Jones continued to run the Association from his home; his salary, it had been decided was to include the rent, rates and taxes of so doing although he was allowed to employ a typist at a cost of £2 a week. It was not until May 1919 that the Association secured proper offices in Chancery Lane.

It had been agreed at the outset that the NEC should meet quarterly but the pressure of business in 1918 was such that it met in both June and July, at Birmingham and Manchester respectively. By October, when it met in Leeds, it was recognised that some provision had to be made for urgent decision-making when matters cropped

up between NEC meetings. It was decided to form an
Emergency Committee to be composed of the President,
the General Secretary and one representative (an NEC
member) from each of the Divisions, the quorum to be
five. At the next NEC meeting in January 1919 it was
agreed to replicate the national Emergency Committee in
each Division, so that decisions could be made both as
speedily and as democratically as possible.[37]

Membership continued to grow, even though the
subscription was raised to two guineas (£2.10) in October
1918; over 1,000 new members joined in 1919 bringing
the total up to 3,415 by the end of the year. New sections
were formed and by the end of 1919 there were 32, the
number at which they then remained for some years. In
August 1919 J W Thomas and A O Holt went from
Manchester to Ireland where there were still members of
the old AESE in Cork and Dublin. Inspired by the visit
they formed a section of the EPEA. In Belfast a section
had been formed in April that year. The three divisions of
1918 were extended to five by 1919 by the formation of a
Scottish Division and by splitting the top-heavy Northern
Division into a Northern and North-Eastern. Divisional
representation on the NEC was based on the numbers of
members in each division. An attempt to secure equal
representation from each Division by the Midlands, itself a
smaller division, was decisively defeated by a vote from all
members in June and July 1918.[38]

Despite the many activities of the Association in 1919
and the fight on which it had to embark to ensure
implementation of the Stoker Award on a national basis
(see Chapter 3), time was found to organise and launch the
journal which was to provide both channels of communication and a forum for members. The first issue of the
Electrical Power Engineer, 'the official organ of the Electrical
Power Engineers' Association' appeared in July 1919. As
its editors wrote:

> One of the most serious handicaps with which the Association
> has had to contend during its period of growth has been the
> difficulty of keeping a considerable proportion of its
> members who, to a large extent, have been isolated from the

centres of gravity of the Sections in intimate touch with the activities of the movement. It will be readily understood that in some cases it is almost impossible for members in outlying districts to attend General Meetings with anything like regularity and as a consequence they are obliged to rely upon the scraps of intelligence that come to them through the corresponding member.

It is not surprising therefore to find some members writing to the Electrical Press seeking information on matters with which they should be fully conversant or querulously criticising the officials for adopting policies on which they themselves have been hopelessly misinformed. It goes without saying that such a state of affairs is very detrimental to the best interests of the Association and does much to create discontent and foster erroneous impressions. The primary purpose of this Journal is to remedy this condition of things and if only for this alone its advent should be heartily welcomed by every member.[39]

The *Electrical Power Engineer* rapidly assumed the format which it was to maintain for nearly twenty years (and some features for longer than that) with its editorials, notes on current topics, members' letters, reports of NEC, Section and Divisional meetings. It soon claimed a guaranteed circulation of 3,000 copies a month; initially offered at 2d [0.83p] per issue, including postage, from October 1919 it was issued free to all members.

The launch of the journal was timely: as A O Holt, described in the journal a year later as 'one of the small band of missionaries which carried the good tidings', wrote in the first issue, under the title 'Thoughts on the Present Discontent':

We must frankly confess that the spirit and the temper of the staffs in Electricity Undertakings throughout the three kingdoms was never more unsettled. Staff engineers exasperated by the complete ignoring of their interests during the war period are seeing that even at this date employers (with a few notable exceptions) are doing nothing to allay their discontent but are rather goading the responsible engineers into adopting the militant methods they profess to so deeply deplore.

But Holt went on to say of the EPEA,

> ... there is a unity of spirit and purpose operating today
> throughout the EPEA which would have been deemed
> impossible two years ago ...We have had our difficulties, we
> have had our set-backs, we expected them, but they have left
> us stronger.[40]

Unity and strength were to be called for in good
measure in the year ahead.

Notes

1. A J P Taylor, *op cit*, p 88.
2. L Hannah, *op cit*, p 59.
3. *Ibid*, p 62.
4. *Ibid*. p 63.
5. Clegg, *op cit*, p 274.
6. G R A Askwith, *op cit*, p 443.
7. *Ibid*, p 443.
8. *Ibid*, p 438-41. War Cabinet Minutes, 5 January 1918, PRO/CAB
2315.
9. Askwith, *op cit*, p 438.
10. EPEA, General Reports, Vol 1, *EPE*, April 1949, p 267.
11. General Reports, Vol 1.
12. Report on negotiations in respect of wages, H H Morton, ETU. I
am grateful to John Lloyd of the EEPTU for the loan of the report.
13. EPEA General Reports Vol 1.
14. *Ibid*.
15. Hannah, *op cit*, p 262.
16. EPEA, General Reports, Vol 1.
17. ETU report, *op cit*.
18. *EPE*, April 1949.
19. A Fox, *History and Heritage*, Allen and Unwin 1985, p 252.
20. Quoted in Fox, *op cit*, p 260.
21. H A Clegg, *op cit*, Vol 2, pp 204–7.
22. B C Roberts, *The TUC 1868–1921*, Allen and Unwin 1958, p 289.
23. *Ibid*, p 288.
24. Clegg, *op cit*, p 248.
25. NJIC Minutes 1918–21. I am grateful to John Lloyd of the EEPTU
for the loan of these minutes.
26. EPEA NEC Minutes, 26 October 1918. Report of meeting held 7
October 1918.
27. *Ibid*.
28. W J Reader, *A History of the IEE*, *op cit*, p 97.
29. *Ibid*, pp 96-8.
30. *Ibid*.

31. *Ibid*.
32. *Ibid*.
33. EPEA NEC Minutes, 27 July 1918.
34. NEC Minutes, October 1918.
35. J W Thomas, *EPE*, April 1964, p 127.
36. George Essex, *EPE*, April 1964, p 127
37. NEC Minutes, 1918–19.
38. *Ibid*, Annual Returns to the Registrar (for membership figures).
39. *EPE*, July 1919.
40. *Ibid*.

Chapter 3
From the Stoker Award to the Schedule

'To uphold the principle of negotiation between employers and employees, and to discourage the use of the strike until other means of settling disputes have been explored.'

EPEA Rule Book 1923.

For almost two years after the armistice of November 1918 British industry enjoyed a period of prosperity and expansion. During the boom, trade union membership expanded rapidly – from 6.46m in 1918 to 8.25m by the end of 1920 – a trend reflected in the EPEA's own membership which peaked at 4,156 at the end of 1920. There was however also industrial unrest and industrial conflict in the two years after the war, much of it related to the change from wartime to peacetime conditions and the reconstruction of industrial relations.[1] Greater expectations on the part of the workforce accounted for some of the conflict, as well as the shift from local to national collective bargaining, which was by no means confined to the electricity supply industry.

The impact of the Russian Revolution and the militancy in some trade unions created a climate of opinion where the establishment and government feared, with no real basis for doing so, that a rising tide of 'Bolshevism' would engulf the country causing industrial chaos leading to revolution. Those fears were enhanced in 1919 by the activities of the Triple Alliance (miners, railway and transport workers) which in 1919 drove the cabinet almost to panic.[2] In the autumn of that year the railwaymen went on strike and the EPEA, following the policy agreed the year before, maintained its distance, instructing its members to carry out their normal duties 'to ensure continuity of supply'. It was a difficult stance to maintain and led to accusations against the Association of black-legging, particularly from the ETU.[3]

But the events of 1920 and 1921 forced many, although not all, of the members of the Association to recognise that there were circumstances in which only the use of the strike weapon would achieve the result they desired.

The fight for the Stoker Award

It was, as the Association realised at the outset, one thing to have achieved the Stoker Award but quite another to ensure that all 600 undertakings paid up. Only 147 of the 600 were parties to the arbitration and therefore bound to implement the award, although they included some of the most influential undertakings in the country, there were still many others which had to be persuaded, cajoled or in some way or another pushed into paying. In some cases further arbitration was agreed – Derby and Sunderland, for example – and a speedy settlement followed. In some cases there were anomalies or difficulties about the date from which payments should be made which the Association was able to settle by negotiation. But as A O Holt wrote in the *Electrical Power Engineer* in October 1919, 'Most undertakings apply the Stoker Award just as it suits themselves, and hope that will be the end of an unpleasant business'[4], and there remained a number of recalcitrant undertakings, mostly municipal, who refused to pay the award to all or some of their technical staff.

Further action was needed, clearly, to enforce payment and in June 1919 the Association balloted its members on whether they would agree to hand in their resignations *en masse* if the award was not paid. Although some 88% of those voting were in favour of the action, they only represented 67% of the membership, falling short of the 70% required by the Association's rules. As a first test of the solidarity of the Association on a 'momentous issue' it was, the *Electrical Power Engineer* claimed, encouraging and reflected the change which had taken place among the engineers given their 'deep-seated repugnance' to 'any idea of extreme action'. To those who had voted against the action, the journal issued a warning:

> They have broken the sword that might have been wielded so effectively by the Executive Council and on them lies the responsibility if the Council finds itself powerless.[5]

At a special NEC meeting in July, convened to consider what to do next, it was agreed that if members of the Association who worked in an undertaking which had not paid up, were prepared to hand in their resignations, they were to be assured of the complete support of the NEC. That included raising a levy on the rest of the membership to pay those resigning full salary for a fortnight and 75% of salary thereafter as long as they were unemployed as a result of the action. This was to prove, as the Association found, quite a commitment. With some undertakings the policy brought immediate results. The threat of 46 resignations brought Sheffield Corporation briskly to arbitration and settlement. There were however two undertakings where the original dispute about payment of the award became inextricably involved with other issues, and the conflicts which resulted at Stalybridge and with the Yorkshire Electric Power Company lasted much longer.

The Stalybridge undertaking belonged to the Lancashire and Cheshire Association of Employers which refused to attend the original arbitration and insisted that it wanted to deal separately on its own account with the EPEA. The problem arose when the chief engineer, Blackmore, did not pay the award in full to his junior technical staff and they came to the EPEA with complaints of their treatment. Their grievances included being paid by the hour, no sick pay and bare-time rates for overtime which they were compelled to work. Investigation by local members of the Association gave added substance to the grievances at Stalybridge. Failure to agree over the matter led to a number of resignations in December 1919, although the station's technical staff was divided and the chief assistant, Lumsden, who supported his chief, resigned from the Association. Blackmore was furious at what he regarded as interference with his management and a deliberate singling out of Stalybridge by the EPEA. He refused to go to arbitration except on his own terms nor would he allow EPEA negotiators access to the directors of the undertaking. Stalybridge therefore was boycotted by the EPEA, with notices in the *Electrical Power Engineer* and the technical press advising electrical power engineers not to apply for jobs there; the boycott lasted until June 1921 when the dispute was eventually settled.

The Yorkshire Electric Power Company (YEP) was controlled by its engineer and manager, W B Woodhouse, 'a ruthless autocrat with sole right of hiring and firing'; although he represented the employers on the newly formed NJIC he was believed to be less than enthusiastic about Whitleyism and was developing a reputation as an anti-union man.[6] Ostensibly about payment of the award which the EPEA claimed had not been made in full, by the summer of 1919 the dispute had, as Arthur Jones acknowledged, 'a very minor connection' with the question of pay. The discontent which erupted at YEP in the shape of the resignation of all the technical staff in May 1919, arose from 'the attitude of the engineer and manager towards his technical staff'. A compromise was patched up in May and the resignations withdrawn but by July matters had again worsened. Two dismissals were followed by 15 resignations from the technical staff.[7]

It seems clear that Woodhouse had not liked his engineers joining the Association. In January 1919 there had been what the Association described as an 'unfortunate episode' between Woodhouse and RCAtkinson,YEP's construction engineer. Atkinson was an active member of the EPEA who had played a major part in drawing up the Rules and in putting forward the claim which resulted in the Stoker Award. In May he was given notice by Woodhouse, the excuse being that the company's construction programme had been curtailed. According to Arthur Jones the treatment of Atkinson together with 'the imputation made by the engineer and manager that his executive officials cannot effectively carry out their duties if they are members of the EPEA' were responsible for the friction at YEP.[8] All attempts to negotiate with Woodhouse failed and, as with Stalybridge, the EPEA successfully imposed a boycott on jobs with YEP which lasted for a year, well after the arbitration had settled the matter of applying the Stoker Award.

One man broke the boycott; a Mr Thomsen accepted a position as Resident Engineer with YEP and, after the rest of the dispute was settled, the EPEA maintained that the embargo must remain until Thomsen was removed. But in August 1920 the NEC recognised the plea of the remaining members at YEP that they were under a very heavy pressure of work because of the company's failure to recruit other staff, and the boycott was lifted. Mr Thomsen remained a thorn in the flesh. The *Electrical Power Engineer* declared him 'a traitor to the Association ... so long as he remains in the Electricity Supply Industry he will continue to be an outcast from the fraternity of engineers and his position will always be a precarious one'.[9] Thomsen was the cause of a further dispute when he was taken on by Coventry Corporation in November 1921.

But even as the Association was endeavouring to make sure that the Stoker Award was paid in all undertakings, work was going on in the newly formed National Joint Board to agree a more permanent schedule of salaries.

The National Joint Board and the first Schedule

The National Joint Board as it was constituted in the early days consisted of eight representatives from the employers, chosen by the associations to which they belonged: on the municipal side, the Incorporated Municipal Electrical Association (IMEA) and on the company side the Incorporated Association of Electrical Power Companies (IAEPC) and the Provincial Electric Supply Committee. At the early meetings the Conference of Chief Officials of the London Supply Companies was also represented but they withdrew in June 1920. On the employees' side the EPEA shared its representation with the Electricity Supply Commercial Association until they were persuaded by the employers to withdraw. The Board was chaired by Alderman William Walker of Manchester who also chaired the National Joint Industrial Council. The Alderman had been instrumental in establishing national negotiating procedures and his firmness combined with tact was widely acknowledged in the industry as an asset in negotiations. An electrical engineer by training hisprofessional involvement was greater than that of most of municipal electricity committee men; Walker's good humour made him popular among his colleagues, despite a tough exterior and sometimes brusque manner with all concerned.[10] For three decades the Alderman was to dominate the national negotiating machinery in the electricity supply industry. Also on the Board, as a company representative, was the man with whom the EPEA were having such difficulties at the Yorkshire Electric Power Company, W B Woodhouse.

The first action of the NJB was to agree a £30 bonus for the technical staff in March 1920: the weakness of the employers' side of the NJB was immediately apparent when a number of undertakings refused to pay the bonus, some on the grounds that they were not directly represented on the NJB and they had not recognised the authority of the NJB to negotiate on their behalf. The change to national collective bargaining was accompanied in other industries too by a reluctance to change and such backsliding was not uncommon.[11] Wimbledon Corporation, however, as a member of IMEA, had not such a leg to stand on, and in the face of a threat from EPEA members to strike, the undertaking paid up. It was an indication of what might be expected when the NJB published on 12 May 1920, the conditions of employment and salary schedule which it was proposed should apply to all technical staff in the electricity supply industry.

The schedule, based on that submitted by the Association, stipulated salaries for 15 grades of technical jobs in undertakings of nine plant sizes, starting with 1,000 KW; by so doing it provided the basis on which salaries for technical staff were to be negotiated for many years. Small undertakings of less than 1,000 KW proved to be an intractable problem, and jobs in them were never

Table 1

The 1920 Schedule of Salaries
Plant Capacity in Kilowatts

Grade	Class A 1,000-2,000	Class B 2,001-4,000	Class C 4,001-5,000	Class D 6,001-8,000	Class E 8,001-10,000	Class F 10,001-30,000	Class G 30,001-50,000	Class H 50,001-100,000	Class J 100,001 and over
	£	£	£	£	£	£	£	£	£
1	538	574	625	657	–	–	–	–	–
2	471	502	547	576	620	–	–	–	–
3	427	455	498	523	564	585	625	670	732
4	371	407	432	469	504	524	575	611	657
5	352	378	411	433	465	499	518	565	596
6	322	354	376	407	426	457	486	516	561
7	293	322	354	371	399	427	442	484	509
8	293	293	322	349	365	392	416	430	467
8a	272	272	298	322	340	365	388	404	436
8b	252	252	275	296	315	339	360	379	406
9	–	–	252	270	291	313	333	354	376
9a	–	–	–	252	271	282	299	319	342
10	–	–	–	–	252	252	266	284	309
10a	–	–	–	–	–	–	252	270	290
10b	–	–	–	–	–	–	–	252	270
10c	–	–	–	–	–	–	–	–	252

Source: NJB document, EPEA archives

scheduled. The Schedule also provided for changes in salaries to be related to variations in the cost of living index; a similar sliding scale agreement was accepted by the manual workers in the NJIC, although not until November 1921.[12]

The EPEA argued that most of its members would benefit from the Schedule but it admitted that it was the lower grades, and particularly the junior staff who stood to gain the most.

> This is as it should be. Generally speaking it is this grade which in the past few years has been so badly paid and as it has been at the basis of the structure it has had the inevitable consequence of depressing the grades above.[13]

Shift engineers of course, as the Association's experiences at Stalybridge and other undertakings had shown, were not only badly paid, but in some places were not even treated as staff. They represented the greater portion of the EPEA membership and held the jobs to which the ETU also laid claim. There were, for the Association, many pressing reasons, not all voiced at the time, for improving the salaries and conditions of junior technical staff.

The Schedule also represented an attempt, most important to the Association, 'to bring some measure of order and justice out of the welter [of chaos]'; indeed the *Electrical Power Engineer* referred to this as the 'outstanding feature' of the Schedule. As the journal wrote in August 1921,

> the charge engineer is the basic grade on which the whole schedule is built up, for the reason that his position is the only one which is strictly comparable in the various undertakings throughout the country.[14]

For those who did not benefit directly from the salaries, the conditions of employment establishing sick leave as of right and holidays would offer some improvement in their standard of living.[15] In many undertakings, the Schedule offered better pay to all grades: that was the case, for example, in Southampton (see Table 2 overleaf).

Table 2

National Joint Board of Employers & Members of Staff
Power of Station – 8,001-10,000 Killowatts (Class 6)

	Total Salary as at 1st March 1920			Grade	Commencing Salary			Maximum Salary			Scheduled Salary 1st October onward		
	£	s	d		£	s	d	£	s	d	£	s	d
J.B. Howat, Chief Asst.	455	0	0	1	657	0	0	675	6	4	683	5	8
E.G. Hooper, Station Supt.	380	0	0	4 rising to 3	504			564			530	4	2
R.P. Avens, Shift Engineer	331	18	8	8	Maximum			365			388	7	2
R.A. Lovell, Shift Engineer	320	4	8	rising to 8	352	2	9	365			374	13	5
A. Terry, Shift Engineer	308	10	8	rising to 8	339	5	5	365			363	13	11
O. Button, Jun. Shift Eng.	247	4	4	rising to 9	271	16	11	271			291	8	5
J. Hooper, Jun. Shift Eng.	229	13	4	rising to 9a	252	11	0	271			270	14	8
S.G. Hodges, Jun. Shift Eng.	235	10	4	rising to 9a	258	19	7	271			277	12	5
H.L. White, Jun. Shift Eng.	229	13	4	rising to 9a	252	11	0	271			270	14	8
J. Shepherd, Mains. Engineer	375	18	4	4 rising to 3	504	0	0	564			530	4	2
F. Lee, Asst. Mains. Eng.	258	18	4	rising to 8	347	2	8	365			372	2	6
S. Kyte, J. Asst. Mains. Eng.	170	1	8	rising to 10	228	0	8	252			244	9	0
T. Brookes, Electl. Tester	273	8	8		366	12	0	—			390	1	2

Source: S.G. Hodges

But, as anticipated, acceptance of the Schedule was slow. Many undertakings adopted a policy of 'shilly-shally and delay'. In line with the rise in prices in the first half of the year, the NJB awarded cost of living increases on the Schedule salaries, to operate from the end of July and again at the end of October, but the latter was the last for some time.

For in October 1920 boom turned to slump, unemployment started to rise and prices began to fall. In the electricity supply industry, demand held up but did not expand as had been anticipated, because ambitious plans conceived during the boom, for example for electrifying the railways, had to be jettisoned. Nor did the radical reorganisation of the industry suggested by the Williamson Committee take place: it was a casualty not of the slump but of determined opposition in the House of Commons to the provisions in the Bill which gave the Electricity Commissioners compulsory powers to impose interconnection schemes. A greatly weakened measure, the Electricity (Supply) Act of 1919 established a new body, the Electricity Commission, which was charged with the responsibility of setting up Joint Electricity Authorities (JEAs) to secure the co-operation of undertakings in operating more efficiently and economically over large areas. But the entrenched hostility between municipal and company undertakings ensured that the Commission made little progress in its first seven years.[16] The employers remained fragmented as ever, enhancing the difficulties faced by the EPEA in the struggle to get the Schedule accepted.

EPEA militancy secures the Schedule

The Association, aware that the economic tide was starting to turn against them, determined to get the Schedule established. At the beginning of November the membership was balloted again as to what should be done and with more than 80% in favour of 'drastic' action, the Association gave notice to all electricity supply undertakings and the NJB that unless the Schedule and conditions of employment were accepted by 27 November

1920, all members of the Association would withdraw their labour on 30 November. It was, as the employers' side of the NJB recognised, a crisis. At a special meeting Alderman Walker persuaded the Association to extend the deadline into December and then he and his colleagues endeavoured to persuade the industry to accept the Schedule.

In a letter to the Association's Technical Representatives, on 23 November, Arthur Jones made clear the NEC's stand.

> The experience of the EPEA in its endeavours to secure the general adoption of the Schedule has forced it to the conclusion that the greatest obstacle has been the lack of organisation on the Employers' side and the indisposition of the Employers to group themselves for the purposes of collective bargaining. Even today many undertakings refuse to acknowledge any allegiance to the National Joint Board, and in fact repudiate the claim of any outside body to represent them on matters affecting their staffs.
>
> They have repeatedly asserted their determination to settle all such questions themselves individually without outside assistance and the problem which has confronted and still confronts the EPEA is the compelling of such Undertakings to group themselves and to recognise the authority of some body acting on their behalf. The Association, therefore proposed to treat all undertakings as a group and to place upon them the onus of achieving a national settlement of a national claim by bringing pressure to bear on the recalcitrant members of that group. The day for dealing with individual Undertakings in turn is past. That method is both wasteful and ineffective as bitter experience has shown. The time has arrived to abandon desultory skirmishing and to close in a decisive battle which will clear up the business once and for all.[17]

There can be no doubt that the firmness displayed by the Association at this juncture won the day for them. The threat of applying national strike action to those who had accepted the Schedule as well as to those who had not forced the former to put pressure on the latter. It also showed how far the Association was prepared to go in establishing national collective bargaining. The struggle to secure the Stoker Award had toughened the members and there were other factors (see p 74-6) which led to a realisation that they could not go on refusing to use the ultimate trade union weapon.

At a meeting of the NJB on 11 December the results of a campaign by the employers' side to gain acceptance for the Schedule were considered. Telegrams flew across the country and some of the replies came in during the course of the meeting. The threat had worked : more than 60 additional acceptances came in, albeit some under protest and pressure. After considerable discussion, the Association agreed to lift the threat of strike from those who had accepted the Schedule, but the threat remained for those who would not accept it by 14 December. When the NJB met again (13 December), with Sir David Shackleton from the Ministry of Labour in attendance, undertakings representing more than 90% of the country's output of electricity had accepted the Schedule and it was agreed that the remainder should be tackled by the Ministry of Labour. The battle however was not yet finished. As the *Electrical Power Engineer* pointed out, 'The Association would indeed have been fortunate if it could have secured a national settlement of the dispute over the Salaries Schedule without a single strike occurring'. By January, Ilford Corporation was still refusing to accept the Schedule without imposing its own conditions. A strike therefore was called, which lasted for five days; with the support of the manual and clerical workers the Association's members refused all suggestions that they might relieve the paralysis of the town which was without light or tramways. Public pressure forced Ilford to negotiate and with the help of the Ministry of Labour, a solution was negotiated and the Schedule accepted by the Corporation.[18]

With Ilford, the struggle was to all intents and purposes over and won, at least for the time being. Some obstinate cases lingered on: at the March meeting of the NJB, Arthur Jones cited Aberdeen and Colchester and at the NEC meeting in May 1921 it was noted that 11 undertakings (mainly small ones) were not applying the

Schedule. The repercussions of the fight were considerable. The employers were forced to recognise their weaknesses both in their own associations and in the NJB and to take steps to remedy them. In July 1921 it was agreed that instead of being elected by IMEA, the municipal representatives should be chosen directly from the District Joint Boards. The employers' representatives on the NJB therefore rose to 26, half from the DJBs and half from the companies. The NJB, which had been criticised and maligned, gained a new and better reputation. Much of this was due to the efforts of Alderman Walker who dashed about the country organising conferences to secure acceptance of the Schedule; by so doing he established both his own and the NJB's credibility and their intent to make national collective bargaining work for the technical staff in the electricity supply industry. For the EPEA the success was a vindication of the more militant policy it had adopted. As the NJB settled into a more normal routine in 1921, the District Joint Boards were developed and the Association turned to look at some of its own more pressing problems of organisation.

The EPEA's national organisation

In the immediate post war years the burden of developing an administrative system as well as running the Association's affairs fell mainly on Arthur Jones, who, as General Secretary, was the Association's only full-time official. In 1920, J W Thomas, an exceptionally able man who qualified as a barrister in his spare time but retained his interest in the Association and the supply industry throughout his life, was appointed as Assistant General Secretary. In July of that year, he and Arthur Jones produced a lengthy document on the Association's organisation. The relationship between the Committees at section, division and national level is indicated in Figure 1.

In the undertakings, the technical representative, the TR, elected annually, was 'the ambassador of the EPEA' and the unpaid shop steward. In the smaller undertakings there would only be one technical representative, but it

Figure 1. The EPEA Organisation: 1920

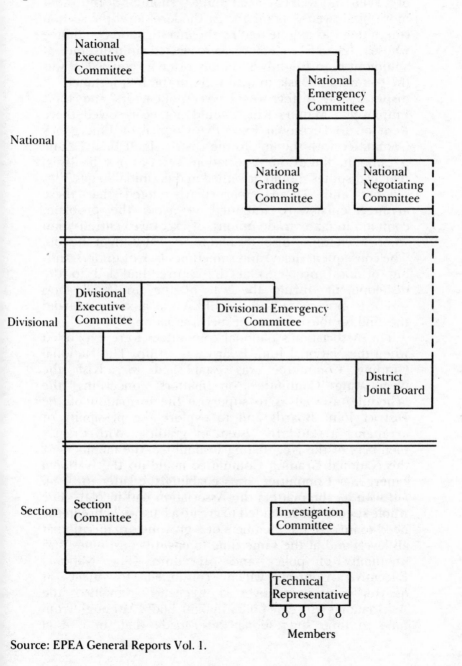

Source: **EPEA General Reports Vol. 1.**

was suggested that one man – and he should be 'possessed of a keen and well balanced mind' – should not represent more than twenty members. At the local level the section committee was augmented by the investigation committee whose three to five members, also elected annually, met, at a minimum, fortnightly and more often if required. It was the committee's task 'to deal with, in the first instance, all disputes and differences between members and their Employers'. Matters which could not be resolved there went on to Divisional Executive Council or Emergency Committee with the link to the District Joint Board. 'The paramount aim of the Association, as far as possible [was] that all disputes should be settled in their initial stages.'[19]

Jones and Thomas particularly noted that these arrangements were intended to avoid the problem, common in many trade unions, of excessive centralisation where even minor disputes had to be dealt with at the top. The consequent delay, and sometimes lack of understanding of local problems at the centre, had led to the development during the war of the unofficial shop stewards movement and the EPEA was anxious to avoid the 'undesirable features' of such a situation.[20]

The Association's national committees were expanded when the National Joint Board was set up. The National Grading Committee was established to advise the Negotiating Committee on matters concerning the Schedule, as well as to supervise the formation of the District Joint Boards and to explore the possibility of arranging a standard system of grading. With the six members of the Negotiating Committee, the members of the National Grading Committee made up the National Emergency Committee, thus enabling the latter to be *au fait* with all the matters the Association had in play. The whole system was intended to create a balance between the need to involve the members of a growing organisation at all levels and at the same time to ensure consistency and unanimity of policy and procedure. The National Executive Council which continued to meet at quarterly intervals, over a weekend, remained the Association's supreme policy making body. Although from time to time suggestions were made that an annual

conference or convention for policy-making, as held by
many other trade unions, would ease the difficulties of
communication which were a continuing problem for the
Association, the suggestion was rejected, not least on the
grounds of expense.[21]

In 1919 and 1920 the Association found itself
hard-pressed to fund its expanding range of activities. Its
income in those years from entrance fees, subscriptions
and an additional levy imposed was around £10,000 which
was adequate but no more. At the same time it became
increasingly difficult for two permanent officials to cope
with the workload from the two tiny offices at Chancery
Lane. In the autumn of 1920 therefore the NEC decided
to increase the subscription to £4 a year, an amount still
considerably less, as the *Electrical Power Engineer* pointed
out, than that paid by members of other trade unions such
as the AEU. At the same time the NEC also decided to buy
the lease of a house at 102, St George's Square, Pimlico,
which would provide not only much more spacious office
accommodation at a price at which it was simply not
available in Central London, but also a flat for the General
Secretary.

The higher subscription brought the Association's
income in 1921 up to £16,000 and separate Unemployment and Benevolent Funds were established.[22] The
NEC also decided that the Association could afford to
employ another – and much needed – permanent official.
As the journal had pointed out the Association relied
heavily – and would continue to do so – on the work of its
honorary officials:

> No tribute of praise and gratitude can be too high for the
> devoted labours of these men. They sacrifice their leisure and
> cudgel their brains without stint ...[23]

The Association had found its first two permanent
officials among its most active members and it found the
third there too. George Essex, who was a member of the
North Eastern Division and had been a member of the
NJB since its inception, was appointed Assistant Secretary
in May 1921. At the time of his appointment he was

Table 3

EPEA Subscription income by division 1921-25

Division	1921	1922	No. of Sections 1922	1923	1924	1925	No. of Sections 1925
Northern	3,522	3,482	7	3,593	3,440	3,274	7
Southern	3,857	3,431	9	3,355	3,021	2,949	8
North Eastern	1,665	1,718	2	1,519	1,300	1,282	2
Scottish	1,601	1,414	4	1,201	1,204	1,107	4
Western	1,017	1,006	4	975	1,016	1,031	4
Midland	1,219	1,076	4	999	993	920	3
Irish	309	310	3	218	181	204	3

Source: Finance Sub Committee minutes.

assistant engineer to the North Eastern Supply Company and he had previously worked, from 1912 until 1920, as a distribution engineer with the Sunderland Corporation undertaking.[24] As Assistant Secretary his was a roving commission, involving a great deal of travel up and down the country.

The widely scattered nature of the membership of the EPEA was (and would remain) a problem. Attendance at section meetings entailed long journeys for many members who did not work in urban centres; for honorary officials required to attend divisional and other meetings the travelling could become an intolerable burden, conflicting with domestic and other ties. These geographical difficulties were particularly acute in Scotland, the fourth largest division (see Table 3), where a return journey of well over 100 miles was not uncommon for attending section meetings. It had proved difficult in Scotland to find men willing to take on jobs as section secretaries and in 1920 the Scottish members felt themselves isolated, as the burden of business and negotiation kept the General Secretary and the national officials in London.

The Scottish Division put forward a demand for a full-time official for their area; when it was not met discontent in the Division grew. Early in 1921 the Scots decided to withhold their subscription money until they got what they wanted. Such unconstitutional action was not well received by the NEC who felt that other areas also had similar problems – the Western division, for example: to give way to the Scots would create a dangerous precedent. Lengthy discussions with a Scottish delegation at the May NEC meeting produced a compromise of sorts. It was agreed that since George Essex was to travel about the country, the Assistant General Secretary, J W Thomas, would spend three months in Glasgow. After that, leaving a clerk in charge of the Glasgow office, he would be based at a strategic centre giving him easy access to the North of England as well as Scotland. Reluctantly the Scots accepted this although they were again disappointed by the base chosen for Thomas: the merits of Newcastle, York and Carlisle were debated but although the Scots argued

strongly for Carlisle, the NEC chose York. It proved
however to be a temporary arrangement. At the end of the
year the Association appointed J F Wallace as Scottish
Divisional Secretary. It was also agreed that the President,
accompanied if possible by the General Secretary, would
undertake a Scottish tour and this became, *de rigeur* an
annual event.

More intractable and continuing problems were presented by the industrial members. From the beginning, the
Association had attracted a number of electrical engineers
who worked on the railways, the tramways, and for other
organisations which generated their own supply. Only in a
few centres – London, Liverpool and Sheffield – were there
enough of them (over 20) to form a separate section. Their
employers were not represented on the NJB and in the
early years it was difficult for the Association to do much for
them. The problem was pointed out in a letter to the journal
from E B Pausey, a stalwart member from the early days,
later (1922-1931) to act as assistant editor of the *Electrical
Power Engineer*. Pausey noted:

> Nobody can claim or maintain that those "industrial
> members" who are engaged in such large, important and
> well-managed concerns such as those belonging to Messrs.
> Boots at Nottingham, Lever Bros at Port Sunlight, the British
> Cellulose Company at Spondon ... in the great railway and
> tramway power stations or the extensive and intricate systems
> belonging to our large asylums and similar institutions are in
> any way whatever inferior to or in a different category from
> those – at present – more fortunate members who are
> engaged in what are classified as "public supply".[25]

The Association, recognising the limitations on what it
could do for the industrial members, kept the subscription
at two guineas when it was raised to £4 for ordinary
members. The fact that engineers outside the supply
industry remained members of the Association is a
measure of the success achieved by the EPEA and the
hope that it might be extended further. But events in 1921
prevented the Association from embarking on wider seas
for the moment.

The attacks on the Schedule

The effects of the collapse of the post-war boom were at their worst in 1921. By the middle of that year industrial production was nearly 20% below the level of the previous year. Unemployment rose from 2.6% to 17.9% of the insured population over the same period. Wholesale prices fell by more than a third and showed no sign of stabilising: retail prices naturally followed suit. In these circumstances wages had to come down and for the new system of industrial relations the negotiation and implementation of pay reductions was a major challenge.[26] In the economy programme which swept (or devastated, as the *Electrical Power Engineer* described it) the country in 1921, the electricity supply industry did not escape unscathed.

In what the Association regarded as an 'economy stunt' the Town Council of Dover (where a recent by-election had returned an anti-waste candidate) decided to break away from the NJB agreement. In June 1921 the technical staff at the Dover undertaking were given notice to terminate their engagements and were offered re-appointment at new and lower salaries. If such a move was allowed to go unchallenged, the Association recognised that 'the salary Schedule would meet its Waterloo'. Dover Corporation was intransigent. It refused either to discuss the matter with the Association or to refer it to the NJB; Arthur Jones therefore gave notice to the Corporation that unless the notices to the technical staff were withdrawn within the week, EPEA members at Dover would strike.

George Essex was sent to Dover to orchestrate the resistance to the attack on the Schedule. It was a baptism of fire for the new official. His first action was to address meetings of the manual workers' unions and to secure pledges of their support. And then, in his own words,

> Moving about in Dover I soon realised that public opinion was in favour of the Council's action and that if our efforts were to be successful it would be necessary to alter this opinion as quickly as possible. Therefore ... I had 10,000

printed pamphlets setting out our case distributed in the town and in addition 15 sandwich men paraded the streets bearing appropriate news sheets ... On Thursday July 14th, I addressed a public meeting in the Town Hall, Dover and placed the whole facts of our case to a crowded audience. This meeting ... was undoubtedly the turning point of our campaign.[27]

The following day a series of meetings started which ended with an agreement on the part of Dover Corporation that it would apply the NJB schedule. The agreement was reached only two hours before the strike notices were due to expire. Although the sandwich-board men caused some raised eyebrows among the membership – they were employed on George Essex's own initiative – the outcome of events at Dover was regarded as a great success.

Similar problems at Perth and Greenock were speedily resolved but it was clear to the Association that many of the employers who had always disliked the Schedule were determined to force a reduction in salaries greater than that provided for by the sliding scale related to the cost of living index. The stage was set for a further confrontation.

Notes

1. H A Clegg, *op cit*.
2. *Ibid*, p 275, pp 290–1.
3. *EPE*, November 1919, pp 70–1.
4. *EPE*, October 1919.
5. *EPE*, June–July 1919.
6. L Hannah, *op cit*, p 269; information from EPEA members.
7. EPEA General Reports, Vols 1–2.
8. *Ibid*.
9. *EPE*, August 1920.
10. Hannah, *op cit*, p 266.
11. Clegg, *op cit*, p 266.
12. Hannah, p 270.
13. *EPE*, June 1920, p 198–9.
14. *EPE*, August 1921.
15. *EPE*, June 1920; for the Southampton information I am indebted to an EPEA member, S.G. Hodges.
16. Hannah, *op cit*, Chapter 3.
17. EPEA General Reports, Vol 2.
18. EPEA General Reports, Vol 2, *EPE*, 1921.
19. EPEA General Reports, Vol 1, 1918–1920.

20. *Ibid.*
21. *Ibid. EPE*, 1920–1922
22. Finance Sub-Committee Vol 1.
23. *EPE*, October 1920, p 62
24. Information from G. Essex's daughter, Mrs Pettitt.
25. Letter in *EPE*, August 1920; *EPE*, February 1948. Obituary of Pausey, who died in December 1947.
26. Clegg, *op cit*, Chapter 3.
27. *EPE*, August 1921, p 30–2.

Chapter 4

Trade Union or Association?

'There is ... no cause for alarm and certainly none for panic but there must be a closing up of the ranks and a determination to insist upon fair and equitable terms.'

Electrical Power Engineer, May 1922.

Between 1922 and 1926 the Association's position in the wider trade union world was the subject of much discussion. Its relationship with the manual workers' unions in the supply industry provoked a crisis in the NJB and there was a continuing debate among the members on the question of affiliating to the Trades Union Congress. At the same time the economic recession caused continual pressure on salaries and the Schedule, stretching the Association's protective activities for its members almost to the limit.

Better relations with the ETU

Hostility from the ETU continued to plague the Association particularly in London where, during the rail strike of October 1919, W J Webb, the militant ETU official, publicly accused EPEA members of 'blacklegging'. After its success in excluding the Association from the NJIC, the ETU was not pleased by the formation of the National Joint Board:

The one fly in the ointment is the formation of the EPEA which has had the effect of splitting the staff and the employees. The work of getting this fly out is one of the most important tasks we must tackle as soon as possible.[1]

72

Two disputes in April 1920, both centring on the disputed grade, the charge engineer, continued the interminable bickering. At Southampton a Mr Hooper, who as a charge engineer had been a member of the ETU, was promoted to Station superintendent; he resigned from the ETU and joined the EPEA. The ETU charge engineers came out on strike and the chief engineer, Ellis, after keeping the station running with the assistance of EPEA members took on new staff in place of the strikers. The local press had a field day, for a play with the title *Who's Hooper* happened to be running and so the headlines screamed 'Who the Ellis Hooper'.[2] Only after a deputation to the Electricity Commission and a series of meetings with Southampton Council was a solution reached; the new men were dismissed and the strikers reinstated. Mr Ellis also resigned. The *Electrical Power Engineer* while describing the dispute as a 'fiasco' which had injured the undertaking, both morally and materially, commended Hooper for his 'firm stand against the outrageous coercion'. It drew the moral that the two unions needed a line of demarcation to prevent the recurrence of such disputes.[3]

But before the dust of Southampton had settled, fresh trouble broke out at Port Sunlight where a new power station was being built for Lever Brothers Ltd. Three new charge engineers were recruited, two of them already members and the third intending to become a member of the EPEA. When the management of Levers refused to give away to ETU demands that the three be dismissed or at least suspended, the ETU members went out on strike.

It was at Port Sunlight that the ETU objections to the EPEA were brought out into the open and clearly stated. The EPEA it argued was not a *bona fide* trade union; it had been formed by employers and chief engineers to combat and break the ETU's solidarity, and the Association's policy towards strikes showed that it was not a genuine trade union. In the negotiations that followed, some conducted on behalf of the ETU by the young Walter Citrine, then Mersey Area District Secretary, the EPEA refuted the charges, pointing out that far from being a creature of chief engineers, it had experienced considerable hostility from them. On the vital matter of strike policy, the Association admitted that it had changed its view since the previous year.

> The EPEA was a young organisation and had much to learn. One conclusion had been forced upon them in their short history, and that was that there were occasions when it was necessary to apply the method of drastic action to enforce their demands. As they accepted the principle themselves they were prepared to uphold it when applied by other Trade unions in a proper manner.[4]

As the Port Sunlight strike moved to a settlement, a meeting was arranged between the ETU and the EPEA in the hope that

> the outcome will be some mutual arrangement based on fundamental principles which will eliminate the hostility and bitterness which has hitherto marked the relationships between the two.[5]

In July 1920 the Association issued its memorandum on policy on industrial disputes (see Appendix at the end of this chapter). The opportunity to put Clause 13 to the test followed almost immediately, when at the engineering works of Cammell Lairds at Penistone, the ETU demanded that a foreman who had left the union on promotion should rejoin or lose his job. The demand was rejected and the Engineering Employers imposed a lock-out, refusing the mediation of a Court of Inquiry for which the ETU then asked. In these circumstances the ETU moved early in September to threaten a strike of their members, which widened the dispute to other industries, including electricity supply.To the surprise, shock and dismay of many, the EPEA announced that they would not, in the event of an ETU withdrawal of labour, do the jobs of the men on strike or supervise blackleg labour. It was, as Arthur Jones pointed out to Association members an entirely logical stance.

> The EPEA is not concerned with the merits of the dispute, nor is it concerned with its origin... The EPEA has only one test which it can apply, viz., which side has refused a

reasonable method of settlement? By that test the Employers' Federation stands condemned, and the line of action of the EPEA is clear. It will instruct its members not to do anything liable to defeat the object of the strike on the part of the ETU. To act otherwise would be to throw overboard a principle which we have stood for and fought for as an Association, and for which we may have to fight very strenuously in the near future. It would be to condone the flagrant repudiation by the employers of reasonable methods of settling disputes, and would render it almost impossible for the Association to insist on the settling of constitutional machinery in the Electricity Supply Industry. Moreover it would be to brand the EPEA as an organisation that varies its principles with the stress of circumstance and would be to forfeit our right forever to the claim to be consistent Trade Unionists.[6]

The impact of the EPEA's position was clear. As the *Daily Telegraph* pointed out bluntly, 'Without them no power-house could carry on'.[7] Soon afterwards the Engineering Employers lifted the lock-out and agreed to a Court of Inquiry; the ETU was forced to withdraw its strike threat.

Logical as the Association's position in defence of constitutional action may have been, the cause of the dispute, the ETU's action at Penistone, was exactly the same as that to which the EPEA itself had taken exception at Port Sunlight – an attempt to control the appointment of foremen. There was little public sympathy for the ETU, which was widely regarded in the industry as the 'stormy petrel of the industrial world', controlled by 'a minority of firebrands'.[8] Opposition to the EPEA's position came from its own members as well as the employers. A letter of protest from 'a Group of Senior Power Engineers', published in the *Electrical Times*, recorded their objection to the Association's 'forfeiture of our independence' while nine members from Norwich wrote to the *Electrical Power Engineer* 'with alarm' describing the action as 'deplorable'; both groups of protesters saw the EPEA's action as a new and radical departure from its established practice and not one which they were prepared to condone again. So too did the Conference of Chief Officials of London Electric Supply Companies who, describing the action as 'suicidal', urged the Association to adopt 'a better and wiser policy of preserving neutrality ...[to] avoid losing the confidence and support of the Employer'.[9]

Nor did the matter go unremarked at the NJB. When the Board met shortly afterwards the EPEA was called upon to explain its position and the employers' representatives 'withdrew to consider the matter'. In the event an anodyne statement reiterating the value of constitutional machinery was issued but there can be no doubt that the employers looked askance at the stand the EPEA had taken. There is however no indication as to whether it prepared them for the greater militancy the EPEA was about to show in pursuit of securing the acceptance of the Schedule (see Chapter 3) or for the rapprochement developing between the EPEA and the manual workers' unions in the industry.

The NJB crisis

In the battle for the Schedule ETU members had helped the EPEA at several undertakings, including the particularly recalcitrant cases at Colchester and Aberdeen and in the strike at Ilford. The talks which started after the Port Sunlight dispute continued and early in 1921 the ETU suggested an amalgamation. That the ETU could even make such a proposal indicates a total failure to understand the thinking of the Association. It is clear that in 1920 'the whole orientation of the Association policy appeared to be changing definitely "Leftwards" '. Increasing numbers of members recognised that the Association could no longer 'plough the lonely furrow, a solitary staff organisation, dignified and somewhat helpless'.[10] But while the Association sought better relations with the manual workers' unions to promote industrial harmony and peace, amalgamation was not on the EPEA's agenda; manual workers and 'brain workers' had different interests which required separate representation. Firmly rejecting the ETU suggestion, the EPEA made proposals for greater co-operation and prepared an agreement which would clearly define each's responsibilities.

At its meeting in May 1921 the NEC had, as one of the

chief items for consideration, the draft agreement with the ETU. Although the agreement provided only for mutual support, the very suggestion of working with the ETU aroused considerable emotion. A L Lunn, a Manchester member from the beginning and first President of the Association, argued that many members would see a binding agreement with the ETU as the beginning of the end – affiliation leading to amalgamation and loss of the identity of the Association. It would moreover, Lunn argued, offend the senior men in the industry who had been so difficult to recruit. Finding the right balance between the claims and attitudes of chief engineers at one end of the spectrum and switchboard attendants at the other was a perennial problem for the Association (see p 89)

Lunn's arguments reflect the attitudes of one who had for four years been obliged to regard the ETU, as much as the employers, as the enemy. But he was persuaded by NEC members like J N Waite (see p 132) who recognised the changing times, and the case succinctly put by T A Margary (then Chairman of the Midland Division and in 1924 President):

> We have used these Trade Unions and we go on using them. There are many places where we cannot do things off our own bat. We have to be honourable. We must not use them when we are in trouble and leave them when they are in trouble. Therefore as honourable men we are bound to put our cards on the table and on some straight agreement...[11]

J H Parker, who as President the previous year had been intimately involved in the struggles for the Schedule, stated the case even more bluntly:

> ...the people with whom we are dealing are only too pleased to pit the two conflicting Unions in the Industry against each other. Our salary was got through because they were afraid of the workmens' union... If they could have relied on the workmens' unions being hostile they would have fought us and they would have won.[12]

Although the agreement with the ETU was approved by the NEC, the negotiating parties failed in the autumn of 1921 to find a solution to the problems of demarcation and no formal agreement was ever signed. But before that deadlock was reached, news of the proposed agreement leaked and the employers at the NJB meeting in October 1921 expressed concern. Although the EPEA had failed with the ETU, in the following year it was able to come to terms with two other manual workers' unions in the supply industry, the Municipal Employees Association and the Enginemen and Firemens' Union. Agreements for mutual support were signed in August 1922. The employers, however, were far from happy at these developments and in the autumn of 1922 the storm broke at the NJB.

On 18 November Alderman Walker told the EPEA representatives at the NJB meeting that he had to make a 'serious statement'. The employers had unanimously decided, he said, not to continue as a Board if it were true that after they had made agreements which were satisfactory to the EPEA, members of the Association were to be compelled to act against the employers by other organisations not represented on the Board or parties to its agreement.

> The employers noted with great regret the altered relationship between themselves and their staff which would be caused inevitably if the EPEA adhered to the policy they had just adopted. It was felt that the effect of the entanglements which they had made or proposed to make with certain of the workers' organisations would have a most disastrous effect on discipline.[13]

Relations at the NJB were already strained by the failure to agree a revised Schedule (see next Section) and when the employers' demand that the Association should withdraw from the agreements was refused, lengthy meetings of the NJB Negotiating Committee failed to produce a solution. The employers' side carried out their threat and withdrew on 8 December from the Joint Board. EPEA members were united in their approval of the Association's adherence to the agreements. Indeed it is difficult to see why, other than through prejudice, the

employers objected so much. The agreements were
intended, as the EPEA claimed, to rule out lightning
strikes or the threat of them, to prevent the supply
industry from being used to settle disputes originating in
other industries and to advance the cause of Whitleyism.

There was support for the Association in the technical
press. Typical of the comment was that in the *Electrical
Review*:

> Had the Association agreed to comply with the employers'
> terms, it would have ceased to command the respect of
> honourable men; and that would have been its ruin.
> Regardless of the terms of the agreements we are of the
> opinion that to have denounced them at the bidding of the
> other party on the Joint Board would have been equivalent to
> walking under the yoke in Roman times. The employers' side
> were ill-advised in putting forward so impossible a proposal; it
> did not place the Association on the horns of a dilemma – it
> left the representatives of the latter no option. Much as we
> regret the occurrence, we are bound to express our approval
> of the decision that they made.[14]

For three months there was no National Joint Board
machinery; it was, as all concerned recognised, a crisis.
Serious disputes over the Schedule occurred in the period,
particularly at Halifax, which were exacerbated in the
absence of a forum in which to settle them. But any hope
on the side of the employers that the Association might
weaken evaporated when a ballot of EPEA members gave
an overwhelming majority in favour of giving the NEC full
authority to take whatever steps were necessary, including
'national drastic action' to secure 'the continued operation
of the National Joint Board Salary Schedule and
conditions and the provision of adequate machinery for
giving effect to the decisions of the National Joint Board'.
Armed with this, the Association wrote to the Ministry of
Labour to ask for a Court of Inquiry, and under the threat
of a national strike Sir David Shackleton of the Ministry
brought the parties together at a conference at the end of
March.

It was, J W Thomas recalled, a memorable and crucial
meeting resulting in an agreement which preserved

Whitleyism in the electricity supply industry and added to
the NJB agreement a clause providing for arbitration by the
Industrial Court in the event of failure to agree. Most
importantly for the Association their action was vindicated
in an admission from the employers that they 'did not object
to an agreement between the EPEA and any other trade
union which provided for joint action or mutual assistance
against an authority which was not carrying out or refused
to carry out agreements arrived at by the Joint Board'.[15] It
had been a 'particularly strenuous and trying time' as
Arthur Jones wrote to the sections of the Association at the
beginning of June 1923, but one from which the Association had emerged stronger and 'high in regard' in the
industry and the profession.[16] With the crisis over, the NJB
was able to turn to the outstanding problems of unsettled
disputes and the revision of the schedule.

Revising the Schedule

It had become clear in the course of 1921-22 that some
revision of the Schedule would have to be made. The
Association itself wanted to improve on what had been
very much a first attempt; as the *Electrical Power Engineer*
noted in May 1922,

> To adopt the attitude, as some members do, that the
> Schedule must be considered as inviolate and sacrosanct, and
> that no one must approach the ark of the covenant except
> under penalty, would be tantamount to an admission that the
> Schedule is perfect, which no one in his senses would dream
> of admitting.

The employers, however, most of whom had not been
happy with some of the provisions, were also using the
economic situation to press for greater reductions in
salaries. But the first proposals offered by the employers
in July 1922 were wholly unacceptable to the EPEA. They
contained very little

> evidence of an attempt to remove or redress anomalies. On
> the contrary, the object sought seems to be the reduction in
> the salaries paid, the elimination of the standardization which

has been obtained in the Schedule and the introduction of methods which, in operation, will lead to endless disputes.[17]

The Association put forward counter proposals which proved equally unacceptable to the employers. At the end of October the subject was discussed again at a full meeting of the NJB, a discussion which 'at times became quite acrimonious on the employers' side'. The Association's representatives were warned that their refusal to accept the modifications to the Schedule put forward by the employers could have serious consequences: 'the probable result would be the breaking away from the Joint Board of numbers of Undertakings and the dissolution of the National Joint Board was not at all unlikely'.[18] No progress on the revision had been made when, a month later, the employers walked out of the NJB, ostensibly because of the agreements the EPEA had made with the manual workers' unions. It is however impossible to avoid the conclusion that the difficult negotiations over the Schedule, and what the employers saw as the intransigence of the Association, also played a part in creating the breakdown of communications and the crisis the NJB faced at the end of 1922.

Some undertakings, anxious to make economies, were only too eager to withdraw from the Whitley machinery and what they had come to see as its onerous obligations. Pontypridd Council withdrew from both the NJB and the NJIC early in 1922 but it continued to pay by the Schedule until October of that year, when it arbitrarily announced that reduced salaries and wages would be paid to all employees. George Essex successfully orchestrated the trade union response to the announcement. Following EPEA policy he persuaded the manual workers' unions (the ETU, AEU, General Workers' Union, Municipal Employees' Association and the Transport and General Workers' Union) not to strike immediately, as intended, but after all attempts at negotiation had failed, to threaten strike action, giving due notice. The action was organised by a joint committee of representatives of all the unions concerned, with George Essex as Secretary. Pontypridd drew some of its electricity by bulk supply from the South

Wales Power Company, and when the strike threat was
extended to employees of the company, Pontypridd Council agreed to reconsider. On the 2 January 1923, the day
before the strike notice expired, Pontypridd Council
agreed to rejoin the Whitley machinery.[19]

The Halifax dispute

A more serious problem arose at Halifax where in
February 1923 the Corporation gave one month's notice to
the 13 technical staff, offering at the same time to
re-employ them at salaries some 25% less than they were
then being paid. The Association's attempt to negotiate
with Halifax came to nothing and it became even clearer
that the Corporation was intent on implementing
reductions when, in what seemed an unnecessarily
provocative step, before the month's notice had expired it
summarily dismissed the members of the technical staff.
The ultimate indignity was that the chief engineer and
Chairman of the Electricity Committee were accompanied
by members of the police force when handing out the
dismissal notices. The justification for the reduction in
salaries was that the technical staff were being paid more
highly than other officials employed by the Corporation.
This was not a new argument. The Association had been
encountering it in other municipal undertakings for some
time and had always argued that such a comparison was
invidious; the technical staff were better educated and
qualified and thereby entitled to higher remuneration.
For the Association it was imperative to fight the case in
Halifax. As Arthur Jones pointed out to members,

> Another significant feature in connection with this dispute is
> the number of Undertakings in different parts of the country
> who have similar intentions, e.g. Hammersmith, Chesterfield,
> Dewsbury, Barnsley, Huddersfield, etc., and it is quite evident
> that we cannot afford to treat the Halifax dispute as a local
> disturbance, but rather must we look at the broad issues
> involved and be prepared to take national action if necessary
> to support and maintain the National Schedule.[20]

With the NJB out of action, all the Association could do

in Halifax was to try to prevent members from taking the jobs of those dismissed and give as much support as possible to the Halifax men. Their salaries were paid by the Association and, when they found other jobs, if they were at a lower rate the Association made up the difference. The Association was successful in finding jobs for all except five of the Halifax men as D Halliday, who was switchboard attendant remembers. He went to Woolwich power station, a move he never regretted.[21] Although an attempt by Halifax Corporation to recruit new technical staff from the British Thomson-Houston Company was successfully stalled by EPEA action, the corporation was able to attract and appoint a full complement of new technical staff, not of course members of the Association.

The settlement of NJB affairs and its resumption in March 1923 came too late to help in the dispute at Halifax. No pressure from the NJB employers' side had any effect on Halifax (who were entrenched in their decisions) and the dispute dragged on. Some of the lessons to be learned from this dispute were pointed out in the *Electrical Power Engineer* in March 1923;

> Hitherto the EPEA in its dealings with recalcitrant Corporations has made a point of giving reasonable notices, and adhering to them honourably. It has even gone so far as to insist upon other Unions doing the same. The Halifax dispute has, however, demonstrated that such scrupulous procedure is not necessarily the best from the point of view of ultimate success, and the Association cannot be blamed if it alters its tactics accordingly.

While noting that such a change would be 'highly detrimental' to the industry, the journal went on,

> The employers, however, cannot have it both ways, and unless they are prepared to condemn unequivocally the action of Halifax Corporation and take steps to have the wrong put right, they can hardly criticise the EPEA for following an example which one of their own number has set. ...the employers will have to make up their minds whether the EPEA is to be allowed to develop along the true lines of a professional organisation or whether it is to be forced into

degenerating into a mere fighting machine, with its aims concentrated upon wrestling from reluctant employers the best possible terms for its members.

Following from that the writer warned:

> If the Association is to be exposed to a repetition of Halifax, whilst employers look on helplessly or even covertly applaud, we shall not merely have to maintain our present agreement, but take steps to make them more extensive in their scope and more intensive in their application.[22]

In April 1923 the *Electrical Power Engineer* issued a list of those who had accepted jobs at Halifax, regarded as 'blacklegs' and the Association continued to insert advertisements in the technical press advising all members not to apply for jobs at Halifax. But with no immediate solution in sight, attention turned to the revision of the Schedule and agreement was reached on that by the NJB in May 1923.

Agreement on the revised Schedule

The new Schedule was intended to be clearer and more precise in its wording in order to reduce the possibilities of doubt over interpretation which had plagued the application of the 1920 Schedule. Over holidays and sick leave the Association fought a battle, for the employers were determined to see a reduction of the provisions made in 1920, which they regarded as over-generous. In practice they had given the technical staff better conditions than other municipal employees and this had been a running grievance for three years. Some reduction, although not as much as the employers first suggested, was negotiated.

The most contentious and difficult part of the revision of the Schedule concerned the classification of under-takings, which of course decided salaries. The Association had accepted and agreed with the employers' argument that the use of plant capacity as the measure of size bore unfairly on undertakings whose output, particularly in the conditions of economic recession, did not reflect that

capacity. The 1920 Schedule had been drafted in the
conditions of post-war boom.

Maximum load, it was agreed, was a better and fairer
determinant, but the problem lay in deciding how to
measure it. After protracted negotiations agreement was
reached on a method of calculating the average maximum
load acceptable to both sides. A percentage margin of
variation of 75% was agreed, the figure a considerable
achievement for the Association's negotiators for the
employers' original proposal was a figure of 25%. In the
revised Schedule undertakings could choose whether to
take plant capacity or average maximum load, whichever
was the lesser, as the measure for classification.

The sliding-scale which provided for reductions (or
increases) related to the cost of living, which had been in
the first Schedule, remained. The implications of the new
Schedule were set out by the Association for members:

> Generally speaking, its effect in the downward direction will
> be comparatively small. It will approximately mean a
> reduction all round from 1 per cent to 2 per cent in
> consequence of the modifications in the cost of living scale.
> Probably 10 or 15 per cent of the membership will also suffer
> an additional reduction by reason of the altered method of
> classification which has been introduced. ...As a set-off to this,
> however, a few undertakings will even go up in salaries on
> account of the alteration to the steps in the classification
> table.[23]

The Association had, as it admitted, been largely
successful in maintaining salaries, which in the circumstances of the industrial depression and the reductions in
wages and salaries being experienced in other industries,
and by the manual workers in electricity supply, was the
more remarkable. As the *Electrical Power Engineer* noted

> during the negotiations [the Negotiating Committee]... were
> acting on the defensive and that they have succeeded in
> conserving the position won in 1920 almost intact is a tribute
> to their skill in negotiating.[24]

By and large the new Schedule was accepted, although in February 1924 the Association noted an increasing tendency for undertakings to advertise positions 'under box numbers, and to ask applicants to state salary required'. Regarding this as an attempt to undermine the Schedule, and in some cases to attack EPEA solidarity by appealing to individual greed, there was little that the EPEA could do. The NEC brought it to the attention of the NJB and the Association advised members not to apply for such jobs; the advertisement remained a constant although minor characteristic of the years between the wars.

The Halifax settlement

Throughout 1923 Halifax continued to be a problem. 'From Hull, Hell and Halifax, Good Lord deliver us' members reiterated as the Corporation refused to consider the reinstatement of the technical staff it had dismissed. Considerable negotiations behind the scenes went on but it was not until April 1924 that Halifax rejoined the NJB and it took until July 1925 to reach agreement about reinstatement. All but five of the 13 original staff had found other jobs by then and the settlement agreed allowed for the reinstatement of three of the five. The other two, Priestley and Love, formerly station superintendent and chief assistant respectively, continued to be supported for the rest of their lives by the Association. In the 1930s Love was appointed as Assistant Secretary (Southern) for the Association because he was unable to get another job in the industry. If every society needs its heroes and martyrs, Priestley and Love supplied them to the Association. They and the Halifax dispute became legends in the Association, in their lifetime and afterwards. But few, if any, trade union commitments to members have been on as generous a scale as was that of the EPEA to Priestley and Love. It was a long and costly struggle for both parties – Halifax Corporation had ended up employing more technical staff, which cost them a larger salaries bill than that which they had been trying to reduce.

Moreover the technical competence of the 'blacklegs' was questionable: throughout the two and a half years of the dispute Halifax suffered from interruptions to the power supply, causing considerable inconvenience to the town. In money terms alone the dispute cost the Association nearly £7,000 between February 1923 and July 1925 and it was to continue to cost them for many years to come in supporting Priestley and Love.[25] But as the *Electrical Power Engineer* noted in July 1925,

> If the Association cannot claim a complete victory, neither can the Corporation; in fact the principal moral of the dispute is that it is unwise for either employers or employees to violate agreed awards. Both sides have had to pay a heavy price for this quarrel. For ourselves we have no regrets, as no price is too heavy to pay for principle.

It has been said that it was the Halifax dispute that turned the EPEA from an Association of gentlemen into a trade union. As part of the protracted struggles of the early 1920s, the dispute undoubtedly played a part in hardening attitudes within the EPEA. But the conflict between the ideas of a professional association and of a trade union was never far below the surface in the EPEA in these years. It emerged again in the discussions which went on between 1922 and 1926 as to whether the Association should affiliate to the Trades Union Congress.

A bona fide trade union?

One of the grounds on which the ETU based its contention that the EPEA was not a 'proper' or 'genuine' trade union was the Association's non-affiliation to the TUC. Although the Association was a member of the National Federation of Professional, Technical, Administrative and Supervisory Workers (NFPTASW) – a body in whose formation the EPEA had been instrumental just after the war – the permanent officials, and some members, became increasingly aware in the early 1920s of the Association's lack of 'clout' particularly in public affairs and parliamentary representation.

These at least were some of the reasons put forward for

joining the TUC, but the *rapprochement* with the manual
workers' unions also influenced EPEA thinking and when
the NEC considered the question in July 1922 they
decided that it should be referred to general meetings of
all sections. The then President, W J Jeffery, (who had
been involved in Association affairs since 1913) put one of
the arguments to members in a letter in August 1922:

> One aspect of the case must be borne in mind and that is
> our success or non-success depends on the sympathy or
> antagonism of the manual trade unions and their pioneer
> work has made it possible for us to exist. We must live as a
> Trade union, side by side with them and provided that we can
> conscientiously do so must conform to similar rules. As far as
> can be judged membership of the Trade Union Congress
> comes within this category and should be agreed to by us.[26]

But the membership was divided in their views, with
those in the North generally unfavourable and those in the
South, particularly in London, much more favourably
disposed. The NEC itself was not unanimous on the issue
but was broadly speaking in favour because it claimed the
TUC could give valuable support in parliamentary affairs
– 'Contrasted with many manual workers' unions the
EPEA is politically ineffective' it lamented – and because
affiliation would establish once and for all the Association's status as a *bona-fide* trade union. Typical of the
opposition to affiliation was a letter to the *Electrical Power
Engineer* from one member, A B Johnstone:

> I cannot see any benefit to be derived from the proposed
> affiliation except the questionable advantage of performing
> another acquiescent 'salaam' before the Manual Workers'
> Unions, a proceeding which might easily result in being
> kicked or trodden on sooner or later.[27]

Through 1923 the arguments went on and many
protests were sent to Head Office when pledge cards for
the *Daily Herald* were distributed with the journal in July
that year. In reply the editor stated that distribution of the
cards was not advocacy of the cause, but an 'act of courtesy'
(which must have seemed a specious argument to those

who had seen 'red' at the distribution!). He urged members to note that the *Daily Herald*,

> quite apart from its politics is the only daily paper which can be looked upon as the organ of the Trade Union movement and it was the only paper that consistently and accurately reported the statements issued by the Association to the Press in connection with the recent NJB crisis and the Halifax dispute.[28]

By September 1923 opinions for and against affiliation within the Association were vehemently held and expressed and when the NFPTASW established a joint committee with the TUC to look at working more closely together the matter was left to them for the time being. The divergence of views within the Association reflected the wide span of its membership, a problem discussed in 1924 by the Panel of Past Presidents. That body, recently established as a way of using the talents and experience of the past presidents who were no longer members of the NEC, met at least twice a year to discuss the activities of the Association. In November 1924 the meeting covered, among other subjects, the question of how to satisfy the senior men of the industry and keep them as members while at the same time having a policy to appeal to junior workers in the industry. It was admitted that the emphasis on protective activities and the *rapprochement* with the manual workers' unions appealed to the juniors but made a good many of the senior men 'doubtful in their allegiance to the EPEA'.[29]

In 1924 EPEA membership fell below 4,000 for the first time since 1921, and although there is no detailed evidence about the 283 members who left in that year, some undoubtedly were in London. The withdrawal of the London supply companies from the NJB reduced the incentive for their technical staff to belong to the Association. Many of them paid the scheduled rates or above in any case; The London Power Company, for example, paid its technical staff one grade higher than the NJB schedule. The columns of the *Electrical Power Engineer* suggest that company men in general were better paid than municipal and consequently more apathetic about joining. There was also a tendency, as the journal rather sourly noted, for some members, 'having received the Schedule, consider there is nothing more to be got from the EPEA so they are gradually dropping out as quietly as they can'.[30] The loss of membership was not serious, compared with the effect that the depression had on trade union membership generally; between 1921 and 1923 trade union membership overall declined by a third.[31] The TUC was anxious to rebuild its membership and in July 1925 the Association received an invitation from its Assistant Secretary, Walter Citrine, to join it. In his reply Arthur Jones was cordial, although he refused the invitation for the time-being. He promised a reconsideration in a year's time.

> My National Executive Council have on two occasions agreed by a bare majority as to the desirability of affiliation to the TUC, the decision however being opposed by a minority whose acquiescence it is desirable to secure before such an important decision is put into operation. A good deal of this opposition is as you will appreciate psychological but it is real enough to make the step which you suggest inadvisable at the present time.[32]

But when the time came to consider affiliation again a year later, circumstances had changed, as we shall see in the next chapter.

APPENDIX
JULY 1920

THE POLICY OF THE ASSOCIATION
IN INDUSTRIAL DISPUTES

1. The EPEA wishes to refute emphatically the allegation that it is an Employer's Association and that it has been organised in the interests of the Employers.
2. It repudiates emphatically the suggestion that it exists for the purpose of defeating the legitimate claims of other Trade Unions in the Electricity Supply Industry.
3. It has in fact every sympathy with those claims when advanced in a constitutional manner.

4. Its endeavour will be to maintain as far as possible a neutral attitude when disputes in furtherance of such claims are embarked upon in a constitutional manner by other Trade Unions.

5. At the same time it is of the opinion that though the application of the strike is on occasion necessary and proper, it should not be applied indiscriminately or on trivial pretexts and only after negotiations have failed.

6 It is of the opinion that most disputes can be settled and ought to be settled by negotiation and that the strike weapon should only be used as a last resource.

7. For this reason it heartily supports the principle of Joint Industrial Councils or Joint Boards and believes that they can be made effective in the settlement of industrial questions.

8. It therefore strongly advocates that matters of dispute should be referred to such Councils or Boards and that a strike should not be embarked upon until the question at issue has been considered and an effort made to arrive at a decision. It is of the opinion that agreements arrived at by these Councils or Boards should be upheld and put into operation.

9. If the Council is unable to arrive at a decision, or will not negotiate, a strike may be necessary and justifiable, and if the members of the EPEA are affected, such members will endeavour as far as possible to maintain a neutral attitude.

10. If an agreement in the Electricity Supply Industry is not honoured by an Employer, the EPEA will extend its support to the Trade Union affected by taking such action as it considered necessary.

11. On the other hand, it is of the opinion that Trade Unions should also honour the agreements arrived at by such Councils and the EPEA cannot support a strike on an issue which contravenes such agreements.

12. In all strikes arising out of trade disputes in the Electricity Supply Industry, the issues of which do not come within the purview of such Councils or Boards, if the EPEA is satisfied that an honest endeavour has been made to settle the dispute by negotiation without success, the EPEA will not permit of its members carrying out the operative duties normally performed by the men on strike, nor will it permit of an interchange of duties on the part of its members.

13. In all cases of trade disputes outside of Statutory Under-takings to which the EPEA is not a party but by which its members are affected, provided that the EPEA is satisfied

that an honest endeavour has been made to settle such disputes by negotiation, such members will not do the work of the men on strike nor will they supervise blackleg labour.

14. The EPEA is of the opinion that in the Electricity Supply Industry (being a public utility service) hasty and ill considered action is strongly to be deprecated.

15. It is of the opinion that no strike in the Electricity Supply Industry is justified which does not allow of ample time for the EPEA to be notified that a strike has been decided upon, and further, the Section of the EPEA affected should be put in possession at an early stage of the salient features of the dispute.

16. Further, no strike in the Electricity Supply Industry is justified which is called before a period of 24 hours has elapsed after notification to the Employer that a strike is to take place, and the EPEA will reserve to itself the right for its members to take such action as they may think necessary to maintain supply during that period in the interests of public safety.

17. Further, the EPEA dissociates itself from the practice of employing blackleg labour, and its members in the Electricity Supply Industry will not supervise such labour under any circumstances where constitutional negotiations between the parties immediately concerned as indicated in this policy have been tried and have failed, except in such cases where the public safety is involved.

18. The EPEA suggests that in the interests of harmonious working in the Electricity Supply Industry, it is desirable that in all areas where the EPEA members are likely to be affected by the strikes embarked upon by other Unions, Joint Committees should be set up for the consideration of issues which are likely to eventuate in a strike. In cases where such Committees are set up with adequate representation of the EPEA, the Association will be guided in its actions by the decisions arrived at provided that the provisos above indicated are safeguarded.

Notes

1. The *ETU Journal*, quoted in the *EPE*, March 1920, p 143.
2. Information from S G Hodges.
3. *EPE*, May 1920, p 178-9.
4. *Ibid*.
5. *Ibid*.
6. EPEA General Reports, Vol I.

7. *Ibid.*
8. *Ibid.*
9. *Ibid.*
10. *EPEA*, June 1920, p 205, July 1920, p 4.
11. NEC minutes, May 1921.
12. *Ibid.*
13. NJB Minutes, November 1922.
14. *The Electrical Review*, 15 December 1922.
15. J H Thomas in *EPE* December 1963; also minutes of meeting 24 March 1923, EPEA Reports, Vol 3.
16. Letter in EPEA General Reports, Vol 3.
17. *EPE*, August 1922, p 148.
18. EPEA, General Reports, 1922.
19. EPEA, General Reports, 1922; *EPE*, January 1923.
20. EPEA General Reports, 1923, Letter to TRs.
21. Letter from D Halliday to the author, 14.11.86.
22. *EPE*, March 1923.
23. *EPE*, June and July 1923.
24. *Ibid.*
25. Finance Committee Minutes, 1923-25.
26. EPEA General Reports, 1922.
27. *EPE*, October 1922.
28. *EPE*, August 1923.
29. EPEA General Reports, 1924.
30. *EPE*, July 1921.
31. Clegg, *op cit*, p 345.
32. EPEA General Reports, 1925.

Chapter 5

1926 – The General Strike and the Grid

'It is no rash claim to make that in no other industry are the relations between employers and employed so harmonious or the staff so contented, as in the Electricity Supply Industry.'
Electrical Power Engineer, January 1927.

In February 1926 the new President of the Association, A J Ostler, wrote the open letter to members which was now customary upon taking presidential office; in it he noted that there were 'at the present time no outstanding questions under consideration'.[1] Perhaps it may then have seemed so, particularly in contrast to previous years but the Association was not yet sailing into calmer waters; events over which it had no control were to make 1926 yet another difficult year.

There were still problems associated with the acceptance of the Schedule, although long-standing differences with the undertakings at Northampton and Peterborough were finally settled satisfactorily in the early months of the new year. Of great significance for the long-term future of the electricity supply industry and the Association was the Government's clearly signalled intention to legislate in 1926 for the re-organisation of the industry; the Bill was introduced into Parliament in March. And there was the unresolved issue of how the Association would respond to the invitation made in 1925 to affiliate to the TUC. But in April and May 1926 all these matters gave way to the crisis in the coal-mining industry.

Coal-mining problems lead to the General Strike

Britain's old-established and staple industries, iron and steel, shipping, textiles and coal-mining, had all been badly affected by the slump. For the many mine-owners – and the fragmented structure of the industry was itself a contributory cause of some of the industry's problems – there was surplus capacity in the 1920s, as export markets were lost to more efficient competitors, particularly the USA and Germany. To sell coal competitively meant reducing production costs and the most obvious way of doing that for the employers was to cut wages. On this issue there had been intermittent warfare between the two sides in the industry since 1919, when the industry was returned to private ownership. Increasingly the miners looked to the Government to provide remedies for the ailing industry and to fellow-members of the TUC for support if they were driven to strike action. From October 1924 until June 1925 there was for the whole of industry, including coal-mining, an extended period of industrial peace, but in July the miners refused to accept a wage cut and threatened strike action.[2] They were backed by the TUC which proposed to place an embargo on coal, in the first instance, to support the miners. Reluctant as it was to intervene, the Government agreed to appoint a Royal Commission to investigate the industry and in the meantime to give a subsidy for nine months to the mining industry.

'Red Friday' – 31 July 1925 (as opposed to 'Black Friday' in 1921 when the miners were forced to give in because they were not supported by fellow-members of the Triple Alliance, the transport workers and the railwaymen) was widely regarded as a victory for the trade unions. But many of the Government's supporters both in and outside Parliament saw the subsidy and the inquiry as capitulation. They considered that a further confrontation would come and that the Government must win. Preparations therefore began for a 'national emergency'.

It was as part of those preparations that in December 1925 a circular was issued by the Institution of Electrical Engineers to its charge engineer members in the London area, asking them whether, in the event of an emergency, they would volunteer to maintain supplies of electricity. To many members of the EPEA this approach seemed inappropriate and Arthur Jones raised the matter at the NJB meeting: his Association, he said took the view that the NJB and the NJIC should have been consulted and Alderman Walker, Chairman of the NJB, was asked to write an official protest letter about the circular.[3]

The Royal Commission submitted its report on the mining industry in March 1926. In April talks between the mine-owners and the miners over its recommendations were deadlocked and the Government, anticipating strike action not only by the miners, at the end of the month when the subsidy ran out, continued to make arrangements to combat it. In the electricity supply industry, the Government was determined to keep essential services going but realised that power stations were vulnerable to militant ETU action, particularly in London. There may also have been doubts in the official mind about what action EPEA members would take, given the Association's *rapprochement* with the manual workers' unions in recent years.

It was therefore at the Government's instigation that the IEE issued a further circular to its members in London, which again came under discussion at the NJB meeting held in April. Members of both sides of the Board were this time 'emphatic' in their opinion that the Government's action was ill-advised: 'it was put on record that the position of the electricity supply industry had been jeopardised by the line of action taken.'[4] It is indicative of the importance of the issue to the Government that representatives of the Ministry of Labour and the Home Office hastened to apologise to the NJB and assure them that no slight on the NJB or the EPEA had been intended.[5]

In the last days of April and the first of May both Government and TUC prepared for battle and, as the strike was imminent, members of the EPEA's General Purposes Committee were called to an emergency meeting on 2 May to discuss the crisis. The meeting passed the resolutions which were to determine the Association's stance during the strike, viz:

1. That the essential public services in connection with the supply of electrical energy should be maintained.
2. The Association deprecates the introduction of volunteer workers in the Electricity Supply Industry, but in the present emergency this Executive Committee agrees that to maintain the essential public services it hereby instructs its members to co-operate in the Government scheme for the maintenance of such services.
3. That to prevent a situation arising which may operate to the detriment of the foregoing resolutions, it is advisable for instructions to be given by His Majesty's Government to all Electricity Supply Undertakers that to maintain the supply of energy for such essential public services care shall be exercised that a supply of power shall not be given to an industrial works engaged in work of a non-essential character.

The resolutions, the meetings decided, were to be communicated officially to the Government, the NJB and the DJBs.[6]

Association members maintain essential supplies during the strike

The general strike, as it became known – at the time the TUC preferred to call it a national strike – began at midnight on 3 May 1926. It has been estimated that between one and a half and two million workers were on strike on 4 May, that number not including the million miners who were locked out. The strikers were in key industries – transport, printing, iron and steel, heavy chemicals, building and some electricity and gas workers. The plan for the strike, hastily drawn up by the General Council of the TUC, was for a selective strike on a national basis which, if not successful in the first instance would be extended by stages.

The TUC's instructions to electricity workers were to work out a scheme to cut off power supplies to industry, but not to homes and hospitals. Shortly before the strike began Arthur Jones met a delegation from the newly constituted Electricity Supply sub-committee of the TUC and reported back to the Association's GPC that their views on the maintenance of essential supplies were similar.[7] In practice, however, it was neither easy nor simple to work out such schemes for not only was the term 'essential services' capable of many interpretations, but also discriminatory supply services as suggested required the co-operation of the undertakings. It was anticipated, rightly as it turned out, that only a few Labour controlled municipal undertakings would willingly implement such schemes; after some days of negotiation the TUC Public Services Committee came to an arrangement with ten of the Greater London area generating stations to restrict power supplies. Few of those co-operating were prepared to go as far as Clement Attlee, then Chairman of Stepney borough electricity committee, who told industrial consumers that they 'would have their fuses pulled and would be without light also' if they used power.[8]

Over the country as a whole serious interruptions to essential services were few. The report made after the strike by the Ministry of Labour's Chief Conciliation officer for the North East on the area illustrates this:

> This area was only affected seriously in the case of Hull, Leeds and Bradford and three or four men at Rotherham and there was no suspension of the operations owing to the loyalty of the members of the EPEA ... The trade union officials on the whole were not in favour of the extension of the general strike to the electricity workers and if only for one solid fact that the technical staffs of the EPEA were carrying out their duties and, short of a serious breakdown could continue to supply current.

> It was not however only the technical staff who did not strike in all cases. At Portsmouth ETU members employed by the municipal undertaking told the chief engineer that they were satisfied with their employment and would not join the strike.[9]
> In York

> the local power workers were as confused and divided by the instructions issued by the TUC as they were elsewhere. Though they were unable to persuade ...the Electricity Committee Chairman to cease supplying power to industrial users they did manage to stop the municipal trams from

running by threatening to strike.[10]

By contrast, in Glasgow where the strike was in general more solid than elsewhere, the Central Strike Co-ordinating Committee was unable to stop the trams running because it failed to close down Pinkston Power Station which supplied the power.[11] It has been estimated that in all some 15,000 manual workers came out on strike, probably about half of those employed in the supply industry; although the ETU continued to claim total support and loyalty from its members.[12]

According to the Association, 'the conduct of affairs on most undertakings was such that supplies were maintained without any abnormal incidents'. One of the few exceptions to this was the municipal undertaking at St Helens, where the Labour Council decided by resolution to place

> the machinery of the Electricity Department in the hands of the ETU and that the ETU be requested to find the labour necessary to work these machines on the understanding that the members of the EPEA continue to do the supervising only and that vital services be maintained.[13]

The significance of this lay in the fact that there were no ETU members at the St Helens' undertaking – the manual workers were members of one of the small unions, the National Union of Electricity Supply employees. Seeing the resolution as the ETU's way of using the national emergency to get itself installed at St Helens, the EPEA took its objections to the District Joint Board and following further representations, the Civil Commissioner for the area, appointed by the Government under the Emergency Regulations, took control of the undertaking. Shortly afterwards he handed over the responsibility for the control and running to the District Joint Board for the duration of the strike. It was, it seems, a unique incident.[14]

As the strike wore on and the Government showed no sign of giving way there was greater tension in some areas. It was reported that in Sheffield

> The position ...at the end of the first week of the stoppage was... decidedly electrical ...both a section of the workers and

also of the authorities seemed to be working up to the point of a contest. Strong efforts were made on the workers side to call out the Sheffield electricity workers but it was decided first of all to approach the EPEA and ...the technical staffs [EPEA members] used their influence in regard to the non-starting of the Sheffield Tramways until the calling off of the general strike.[15]

At Pontypridd in Wales, where after initial dis-agreements about TUC instructions between the ETU and the Strike Committee the Council had agreed the Committee's terms about supplying only essential services a further threat of complete withdrawal on 11 May was made to bring the chief electrical engineer into line.[16]

The most militant branches of the ETU were in London and there, except in the ten stations which had come to terms with the TUC, all the manual workers ceased work on 7 May. They were replaced by naval ratings sent in by the Government: at Gravesend the naval authorities took control of the undertaking.[17]

From the 8 May onwards the TUC was considering whether to call out all the workers in electricity, but at the same time they were also searching for a compromise solution which would enable them to end the strike. By 12 May, although the miners still refused any of the proposed compromises, there were, it seemed to the TUC leaders, cogent reasons for calling off the strike: the government's determination not to give in had been enhanced by the success of its emergency transport system, while for the TUC the shortage of funds and the risk of a drift back to work became more serious everyday.[18] On 12 May the TUC met the Cabinet and, with no conditions and no settlement for the miners, they agreed to send out instructions to return to work. The dispute in the coalmining industry remained deadlocked, with the miners locked out for another seven months.

The Association after the strike

The Association felt that it had emerged from the General Strike not only 'without a blot on its escutcheon', but also 'with added prestige and even greater solidarity than it possessed before'.[19] In the *Electrical Power Engineer* published shortly after the end of the strike two letters of thanks were published. The first, dated 11 May came from the Minister of Transport and asked the General Secretary to inform members of the Association

> that their action in remaining at their several posts in generation stations and in maintaining the supply of electricity has been of the greatest possible value in the present national emergency, and the Government trust that the Association will continue their splendid work in the interests of the community.

More fulsome words came from the Mayor of Hackney on 25 May:

> Now that comparative peace reigns in our midst it is my duty and privilege to offer my deep and sincere gratitude of both the Council and myself to you and your excellent organisation for the magnificent spirit you revealed during the National Crisis. It was an inspiring thought to know that you were standing by us. Your work in connection with the 'Loyalties' will not easily be forgotten. We owe you all a sense of gratitude. The old country will go as from strength to strength assisted by such men as you are able to command.

In the EPEA, the inquest which followed the emergency was short, for the only criticism voiced came from a few members who would have preferred, they claimed, the instruction sent out on the eve of the strike to have been simply and unequivocally to carry on and maintain normal supply. At the time Baldwin's successful presentation to the public of the strike as 'political' and 'unconstitutional' carried conviction; the Prime Minister had written on 6 May in the Government newspaper, the *British Gazette*,

> Constitutional government is being attacked. Stand behind the Government, who are doing their part, confident that you will co-operate in the measures they have undertaken to preserve the liberties and privileges of the people of these islands .... The General Strike is a challenge to Parliament and is the road to anarchy and ruin.

In retrospect it is clear that Baldwin knew perfectly well that for most of the strike leaders and trade union members involved the strike was a trade dispute and they had no wish to overthrow the Government. But at the time the issue of the political strike was unresolved and therefore to designate the strike as 'unconstitutional' would not only establish a precedent but also gain support for the Government.[20]

In the prevailing atmosphere of 1926 then it is hardly surprising that the strike put an end to EPEA indecision about whether to affiliate to the TUC. At its first post-strike meeting, held at the end of May, the NEC decided briskly that a ballot of members was unnecessary, that affiliation was not in the interests of the Association and that was the end of the matter. As the *Electrical Power Engineer* editorial noted:

> It has always been one of the firm principles of the Association that the Electricity Supply Industry must not be made the battleground whereon the contests of other industries are waged, and so long as the TUC has it within its power to extend its disputes in the way it has just exhibited, the EPEA must decline to be associated with it.[21]

Jointly with that determination that the electricity supply industry should not be a battleground, went the belief in the Association in the value and importance of the Whitley machinery. It was therefore an added source of satisfaction to the EPEA that the NJB and the DJBs had played an important role during the strike, and had gained recognition for this particularly in the case of the St Helens undertaking. It was not so for the manual workers; the NJIC suspended operations in May and did not resume its meetings until October 1926. There is some evidence that fears that this would be the case had contributed to ETU reluctance to strike outside London: the Ministry of Labour's Chief Conciliation Officer for the North East reported that the ETU's representative in the area had confirmed to him that the trade union side 'were loath to part from the Whitley Council'.[22]

ETU accusations of black-legging

The EPEA however could hardly have hoped to escape from the trade union inquest on the General Strike without the accusations of blacklegging which were made in the ETU journal. The militant London District Secretary of the ETU, W J Webb, with whom the EPEA had already clashed swords on a number of occasions (see pages 16 and 72) went further. It was his wish, apparently, to clear the EPEA out of the supply industry 'bag and baggage' at least in the London area! In an attempt to secure that, Webb had written to several London borough councils asserting that the EPEA had

> on the eve of the General Strike issued a statement through the Press instructing their members to blackleg and also assuring everyone through the agency of the British Broadcasting Co that they supported the Government in their attack on the miners.

This was something of a distortion of the EPEA statement.

Webb went on to ask the Councils to receive a deputation from his committee with a view to

(a) In future not recognising the EPEA as an organisation to which any of your employees, staff or operative grade can belong.
(b) Fixing a date for those employees who are members of the EPEA to join the ETU.[23]

The Association did not mince its words in response to what it saw as ETU skulduggery. It notified the Ministry of Labour of what was afoot and, noting with relief that the London Borough Councils thus approached – Poplar, West Ham, Stepney and Shoreditch – had not been moved by Webb's plea, the *Electrical Power Engineer* commented that the strike had revealed conclusively

> the weak and chaotic organisation of the ETU ...[which] is reaching the end of its tether in the supply industry and is becoming a discredited and bankrupt organisation.[24]

This view is supported by evidence from the Ministry of Labour's Chief Conciliation Officer for London, who reported after the strike of the ETU:

> This union is not nearly so strong numerically as before the general strike and has lost members in many of the power houses where they were fairly strong in London. The old time threat of holding up the London power and light by the London District Committee has lost its potency.[25]

It was not, however, only the ETU who misunderstood the Association's action during the General Strike. At the opposite end of the spectrum many employers and chief engineers rapidly changed their perception of the Association. Instead of being viewed as 'an organisation of questionable character and of doubtful utility', the EPEA became 'stamped with the hallmark of a highly respectable organisation' and 'a model of what a Trade Union ought to be both in regard to its loyalty to the Industry and its sanity of outlook'. The view that the EPEA had ended its 'days of coquetting with the manual workers' unions' and by so doing 'had saved its soul and had proved its worth' was put forward at a DJB lunch held in the autumn of 1926, by Blackmore, chief engineer at Stalybridge and formerly one of the Association's fiercest critics. Coming from such a source, the appreciation was, as the *Electrical Power Engineer* noted, particularly gratifying for the Association, which had from the outset wished only for respectability, recognition and acceptance. But the journal continued

> we would not like it to be forgotten that in behaving as it did ...the EPEA did not shape its course to catch a passing wind of popularity or to please either the Government or Employers.[26]

It was not an easy course to steer.

The General Strike wounded the trade union movement as a whole, and left it with a legacy of betrayal, bitterness and defeat.[27] While the miners' dispute dragged on, the Government introduced in June a new Coal Miners Bill which extended the permitted hours of work underground from seven to eight hours. The *Electrical Power Engineer* which had not until then commented on the dispute which had generated the strike, expressed in an editorial its regret at such legislation:

> Not only is it likely to embitter the contest and make a settlement still more difficult of accomplishment ...in our opinion [it] will not provide a solution of the problem.[28]

In the following year the Government introduced the legislation which had been expected ever since the strike, the Trade Disputes Bill, intended *inter alia* to make illegal the sympathetic strike. It was condemned at the time and until its repeal in 1946, as a piece of vindictive revenge for the General Strike; but it seems unlikely that the Conservative Party would have settled for less.[29] Trade union opposition was muted because of demoralisation. The EPEA resolved to fight the proposals which it described as 'a point blank attack upon the reasonable and legitimate activities of trade unions', which was likely to 'engender ... an atmosphere of friction and hostility'.[30] There was, however, little they or anyone else could do and the Trade Disputes and Trade Unions Act became law in 1927.

The extent to which the General Strike marked a watershed in British industrial relations continues to be a matter of dispute. In recent years it has been suggested that factors other than the Strike were responsible for the decline in industrial disputes which followed 1926.[31] But in 1975 Lord Feather (formerly General Secretary of the TUC) wrote

> It is one of the half-dozen events in our recent history to have left a permanent mark on the psychology of the nation. It is, in a sense, still true that the nation divides itself into those whose sympathies lie with miners determined to insist 'Not a penny off the pay, not a minute on the day', and those for whom the memory of undergraduates driving buses is a symbol of the national will to resist revolution. [32]

For the EPEA, which determinedly refused to be recruited into either of the two camps, the General Strike

did mark a turning point. On the one hand the National
Joint Board machinery and the Association's status
emerged unscathed and enhanced; on the other, the
Association turned away from the TUC and the wider trade
union movement and, for the next 16 years ploughed a
lonely furrow. The failure of joint action in any case led to a
wider loss of trust in the TUC and its General Council; in
the late 1920s trade union membership fell, although
unemployment, rather than the effect of the strike, was
responsible for most of the loss. By contrast EPEA membership rose steadily throughout the inter-war years (see Table
3) the rise being fuelled both by the increasing respectability of the Association and the changes in the supply
industry.

Table 3 EPEA membership 1919 – 1929

Year	Members at beginning	New Members	Numbers leaving	Members at year end
1919	2297	1130	12	3415
1920	3415	914	173	4156
1921	4156	147	154	4159
1922	4149	244	322	4071
1923	4071	178	297	3952
1924	3952	191	283	3860
1925	3860	250	144	3966
1926	3966	317	165	4118
1927	4118	289	151	4256
1928	4256	280	247	4289
1929	4289	350	220	4419

Source: Annual Returns to the Registrar.

Reorganisation of the supply industry – the Grid

In a memorandum drawn up in January 1926 the
Association noted that 'there has been an undoubted
parochial attitude of mind adopted towards the generation and supply of electricity in past years'.[33] No doubt
those members of the EPEA who drafted the memorandum had in mind the hostility between, and the fierce
independence of, the company and municipal undertakings in the British supply industry, which had vitiated
almost every attempt by the Electricity Commissioners to

rationalise and integrate the system. The solution to Britain's fragmented supply industry laid down by the Act of 1919 – voluntary interconnection supervised by Joint Electricity Authorities – had made little headway. As the Association's memorandum went on to note, 42 of the UK's 584 public generating stations were responsible in 1925 for more than half the output (56%) but the other 542 stations were needed to produce the remaining 44% of total output and that at a much higher cost of production. There were also 17 different frequencies still in use over the country as a whole. The demand for a plentiful and cheap supply of electricity from industrial consumers had grown and, at a time when British industry was meeting increased competition from Germany and the USA, both of whom had the advantage of more efficient, more technically advanced and cheaper electricity supplies, industrialists were pressing for improvements.

The need for change was recognised by the first Labour Government but its term of office was too short for anything to be done; in the autumn of 1924 however, when Baldwin took office, he turned to Lord Weir, a Scottish engineering industrialist with considerable experience of Government committee work, 'to review the national problem of electrical energy'.[34]

Mindful of how the lack of a plentiful and cheap supply of electricity was handicapping Britain's industrial revival, Weir's small committee (himself and two others) started work in January 1925 and handed its report to the Government four months later. Its recommendations represented, as Weir had promised, 'a new electrical energy policy involving in its application courage and ... a considerable financial investment'.[35] Weir suggested the creation of a Central Electricity Board, financed by the state, whose major responsibility was to be the planning and building of a 'grid iron' – the grid as it became known – of high voltage transmission lines covering the country. The grid would provide a system of interconnection, taking its electricity from 'selected' power stations, some of which would be the larger and most efficient of the present stations, some would be new ones planned by the CEB. Power stations would still be owned and run by the existing municipal and company undertakings, who would also distribute electricity as before but the Electricity Commissioners would have the authority to close down, compulsorily if necessary, small and inefficient stations not 'selected' to supply the national network. Standardisation on 50Hz would also be implemented as part of the scheme. The Weir Committee envisaged that the total investment in electricity supply would be £250m over the next 15 years, with the grid itself costing £25m, and the committee recommended that about half of the total should be raised by the CEB, probably backed by some form of government guarantee.

The Weir report was not published at that stage, but the Government appointed a Cabinet Committee in May 1925 to draft the legislation which was introduced in Bill form in March 1926, embodying most of the Weir proposals. As might well have been expected, opposition from the supply industry, both from the IMEA representing the municipal undertakings and from the company side, was fierce and delayed the passage of the Bill; but this time it failed and in December 1926 the Electricity Supply Act,substantially in the form in which it had been introduced, received the Royal Assent.[36]

Throughout the Bill's passage through Parliament the EPEA had kept a close watch on the debates and proceedings, reporting and analysing them in the columns of the *Electrical Power Engineer*. Of the most immediate concern to the Association in its protective role were the clauses which dealt with compensation for those working at power stations which were closed down, either permanently or temporarily. With the other trade unions concerned, NALGO and AMEE (but not with the ETU) the Association successfully promoted a number of amendments which improved and added to the occasions on which those working in the industry would be entitled to compensation. The effect of the amendments was that not only when a station was closed or acquired but also if there was an alteration in the working or use of a generating station, or if a part or whole of a transmission line was acquired, the employees who were affected would be entitled to compensation.[37]

There was, it seems, no publicly stated Association view of the desirability or otherwise of the new legislation. No comment was made at least until January 1927 when the *Electrical Power Engineer*'s editorial was unenthusiastic, restrained and cautious.

> It is hardly likely to bring a new heaven or a new earth ... It may be, however, and in fact will be, if technical engineers can make it, a step in the right direction ... But no-one with any knowledge of the supply industry can have studied its contents with any care without realising that it has many defects, that some of the changes it proposes may prove in practice to be unworkable, or that much has been omitted which ought to have been included ... The advisability of embarking on drastic schemes of standardisation of frequency has been very gravely questioned by many of our members more especially by those in the non-standard areas. They have visualised not only the enormous expense which will be incurred and also the grave inconvenience but the practical difficulties which will have to be faced both in the generating station, on the mains and in the consumers' premises ... [but] the Industry must take it as it is and make the best of it.[38]

Time and experience, the journal said, would show the defects, but on balance the reverse has been true. As Dr Reader has pointed out the Act was one of the most important pieces of legislation between the two wars. Not only did it rescue the electricity supply industry from the consequences of its 19th century origins (the kind of operation from which several other basic British industries could have benefited, given the chance), but it also brought technical progress to the forefront of the industry. As a nationalised corporation in fact if not in name, the CEB did much both to establish and make respectable a business form still as yet largely unacceptable.[39]

It is difficult to resist drawing the conclusion, from the stance taken by the Association on the two major issues of 1926, that conservatism had triumphed and any swing to the 'left' discerned in previous years (see page 76) had been reversed. In that sense the year had marked a turning point in the inter-war period.

Notes

1. *EPE*, February 1926, p 57.
2. H A Clegg, *op cit*, Vol 2, p 383. For problems in the coalmining industry see N K Buxton in N K Buxton and D J Aldcroft (eds), *British Industry Between the Wars*, Scolar Press, London 1979. For the General Strike see R Page Arnot, *The General Strike. 1926*, repub. EP Publishing 1975; M Morris, *The General Strike*, Penguin Books 1976; G A Phillips, *The General Strike: the Politics of Industrial Conflict*, Weidenfeld and Nicholson 1976 and L Hannah, *op cit*, pp 271–3.
3. NJB Minutes, 18 December 1925.
4. NJB Minutes, 23 April 1926.
5. *Ibid.*
6. EPEA, NEC/GPC Minutes, 2 May 1926.
7. *Ibid.*
8. R Jenkins, *Mr. Attlee: an interim biography*, Heinemann 1948, p 113; Clegg, *op cit*, p 404; Morris, *op cit*, pp 240-41.
9. Public Record Office (PRO) LAB 10/881 Memo, 9 June 1926; *The Electrical Times*, 20 May 1926, pp 595–6.
10. R I Hills, *The General Strike in York*, Borthwick Papers 57, 1980, p 12.
11. Morris, *op cit*, pp 395–6.
12. Phillips, *op cit*, pp 218–9.
13. *EPE*, May 1926.
14. *Ibid.*
15. PRO LAB 10/881.
16. Morris, *op cit*, pp 418–9.
17. *Ibid*, pp 38, 241; *EPE*, May 1926.
18. Clegg, *op cit*, p 409.
19. *EPE*, June 1926.
20. A Fox, *History and Heritage*, Allen & Unwin 1985, p 330.
21. *EPE*, June 1926.
22. PRO LAB 10/881.
23. *EPE*, July 1926.
24. *Ibid.*
25. PRO LAB 10/5.
26. *EPE*, November 1926.
27. Morris, *op cit*, pp 276–7.
28. *EPE*, July 1926.
29. Fox, *op cit*, p 335.
30. *EPE*, 1927.
31. Fox, *op cit*, p 334; Clegg, *op cit*, pp 419–26.
32. Introduction to R. Page Arnot, *op cit*, p vi.
33. NEC Minutes 1926.
34. W J Reader, *Architect of Air Power*, Collins 1968, p 130.

35. *Ibid*, p 131.
36. For a detailed account of the opposition and passage of the Bill see Hannah, *op cit*, pp 96–9.
38. *EPE*, January 1927.
39. Reader, *op cit*, p 135.

Chapter 6
The Grid, and the Depression

'The Association has been fortunate in operating in an industry which has not experienced the depression which has lain so heavily upon others.'

Electrical Power Engineer, January 1930.

The modest upswing in economic activity which took place between 1925 and 1929 gave way, after the Wall Street crash of 1929, to the depression which lasted until the mid-1930s. From then until the outbreak of war, rearmament provided a stimulus to industrial recovery. For British industry in the inter-war years the failure and decline of the basic industries – coal, steel and cotton – went hand in hand with the success and the expansion of new industries such as motor cars and electronics.[1] Industrial consumption of electricity rose in the period, as also did the amount of electricity used by the transport network (rail and trams) and by shops and offices. In the home electrical appliances became more common, at least in the homes of those in work and in urban areas; although lip service was paid to the idea of extending electricity supplies to all rural areas, the progress made in the 1930s was slow. Undertakings were reluctant to enter into the expense of connection when it was uncertain whether consumers would be able to afford to pay for either the installation or use of electricity; agriculture was particularly badly hit by the depression.

For the EPEA the 1930s represented a decade of consolidation. Membership rose steadily as the table shows, reaching the 5,000 mark in the year in which the

Association celebrated its 21st birthday. Between 1933 and 1939 membership rose by 27%, not as large a figure as the 43% increase in membership enjoyed over the same period by the trade unions as a whole, but then the Association had not suffered the haemorrhage of members endured in the previous decade by the major unions.[2]

EPEA membership 1930-39

Year	Membership at the start	New Members	Numbers Leaving	Members a year end
1930	4419	353	182	4590
1931	4590	334	171	4753
1932	4753	246	218	4781
1933	4781	254	154	4881
1934	4881	407	160	5218
1935	5128	399	162	5365
1936	5365	409	127	5647
1937	5647	423	219	5851
1938	5851	491	220	6122
1939	6122	329	247	6204

Source:Annual Returns to the Registrar.

In the 1930s, therefore, the Association, strengthened by an expanding membership and in a growing industry, was able not only to defend its members' interests successfully, but also to extend its activities in various directions.

The effect of the grid on jobs

Following the legislation of 1926, planning the grid started in 1927 and, by what Professor Hannah has called a 'happy accident', the construction of the 132kV lines took place mainly in the years 1929 to 1933; happy because in the depth of the slump there was surplus labour and no shortages of materials or machinery to cause delays. By 1934 the grid was in business over most of the country and the CEB itself was employing more than 1200 workers, over half of them technical staff, some of them EPEA members attracted away from the company and municipal undertakings to the new organisation.[3] At the same time many of those working in generation found, as the Association had rightly anticipated when pushing its amendments to the 1926 Act, that their jobs changed.

In the early 1930s therefore the Association represented many members in making claims for compensation. While some arose clearly and directly out of the CEB's generation activities, in other cases the reasons for the change were less obviously attributable to the CEB.

At Rochdale the municipally-owned generating station closed down in 1931. The Corporation had started to take a bulk supply from the Lancashire Electric Power Company in 1920, extending it by a series of agreements over the following years. As demand fell in Rochdale, the Corporation was able to negotiate an agreement for bulk supply on such favourable terms as to make it uneconomic for it to continue generating electricity itself. On behalf of its member, Kelsey Lee, who had been employed by the Rochdale undertaking for 15 years, the Association claimed compensation under the 1926 Act. The Corporation however contested the claim on the grounds that the generating station had been closed down, not by the CEB, but by the severity of the industrial depression in Rochdale.

The difficulty was, as the *Electrical Power Engineer* pointed out, that for an employee engaged in a generating station to claim compensation

> it is not sufficient to prove that he suffered loss of employment or diminution in salary, he must, in fact, forge a chain of evidence, not one link of which must be missing. First he must prove that the loss of employment was definitely the result of a scheme, agreement or arrangement having come into operation or been entered into by authorised undertakers or of the closing of a generating station or restrictions imposed on the working or use of a generating station. Next he must prove that the agreement, scheme or arrangement or the closing or restrictions were under or in consequence of the Electricity Supply Acts.[4]

The case took almost a year to settle, hindered in the first instance by Rochdale Corporation's refusal to allow the Association access to the necessary documents. The

Corporation was determined to fight the claim, if necessary in the courts, and, dissatisfied with the decision of the Referee appointed by the Ministry of Labour and of the Electricity Commissioners, it went to appeal. But before the case finally came to court, the Corporation negotiated a settlement and Mr Lee got his compensation. The EPEA felt vindicated: not only had it won Kelsey Lee compensation of £1,500, but controversial issues had been 'thrashed out' and an important precedent had been established. As the journal pointed out, where such complex issues were involved a costly fight was necessary and that was one that few individuals on their own were likely to be able to afford. The Association had 'shown the extent to which it is prepared to go in order to safeguard the interests of the members', and the lesson of Rochdale was a 'valuable propaganda asset' to be 'rammed home' to the membership at section meetings.[5]

In the following year complications of a different kind arose at Wakefield, where the municipal generating station was a CEB 'selected' station. It was however designated for standby purposes only during the winter months and it was to be closed down for the rest of the year. The four charge engineers at Wakefield had to make sure that while the plant was closed it was kept in working order to be ready for its three months of standby. Because of the adjustments to the grading of the four engineers following the changes, each of them had a net reduction of salary of £34 a year, a not inconsiderable sum since it represented a loss of almost 10% and carried implications for superannuation benefits. The Association successfully claimed compensation for the Wakefield members.[6]

In the industry as a whole the 1930s was a decade of change and reconstruction. Some of the smaller under-takings merged with larger ones and that too could lead to compensation claims. The Banbury Electricity Company was taken over by the Shropshire, Staffordshire and Worcester Company who closed down the Banbury station in 1936. Charge engineer C M Young found his average annual salary of £243 arbitrarily reduced to £190 and, with the help of the EPEA, gained compensation for the loss of salary and status.[7] The Association's success in obtaining compensation for many more of its members not only secured for it their gratitude and loyalty, but also built up a body of expert knowledge in the area. J W Thomas, now practising at the Bar, was closely involved and his rare if not unique combination of legal expertise with technical knowledge of electricity supply was of great benefit to the Association.

At the same time new and larger power stations were built and commissioned, some of which were already on the drawing board before the Electricity Act of 1926 and some which were planned as part of the grid system. Birmingham Corporation, whose chief engineer R A Chattock was noted for his technical innovation, commissioned in 1929, the year of his retirement, the Hams Hall A station which had sets of 30MW and 50MW. Deptford West, commissioned in the same year by the London Power Company, had sets of 35MW and 50MW. The same company's jewel in its crown, Battersea, commissioned in 1933, had a set of 105MW, the largest in Europe when it was installed and for some years after. Barking B and Dunston B were commissioned in the same year as Battersea and in 1936 Fulham, with its five sets of 60MW and one ancillary 'house' set, came into operation, around the same time as Tir John, Swansea Corporation's showpiece, was commissioned.[8]

Although the basic technology was not new, the electricity supply industry benefitted in the 1930s both from the economies of scale offered by the new, larger generating stations and from the improvements in operating efficiency that were achieved in the decade.[9] As a corollary of those developments, however, some parts of the supply industry required technical staff of a higher calibre than previously.

An expanding education role

In the early days the Association had proclaimed its intention to concern itself with the education and training of electrical engineers. While this served in some instances as a useful camouflage for more controversial activities, there were some among the pioneers, particularly J W

Midland Divisional Council, 1927.

Chairman : J. N. WAITE, M.I.E.E.
Vice-Chairman : P. J. BURGESS, A.M.I.E.E.

National Executive Council Delegates :
P. J. BURGESS, J. N. WAITE.

District Joint Board Representatives :
(No. 5 Area)
T. A. G. MARGARY, P. J. BURGESS, J. KITSON,
J. N. WAITE, H. W. MASON, G. W. ESSEX.

Hon. Secretary :
P. M. PINDER, A.M.I.E.E.,
169, Newhampton Road,
Wolverhampton.

Hon. Treasurer :
D. J. DUFFY, A.M.I.E.E.,
166, Waterloo Road, Wolverhampton.

North West Midland Section Committee. 1927.

Chairman : D. J. DUFFY, A.M.I.E.E.
Vice-Chairman : P. M. PINDER, A.M.I.E.E.
J. N. WAITE, T. A. G. MARGARY, P. WARDLE,
A. T. GILBRIDE, G. O. EDWARDS,
H. GRIFFIN, A. W. POWELL.

Divisional Council Delegates :
J. N. WAITE, P. M. PINDER.

Hon. Treasurer :
J. N. WAITE, 2, Salisbury Avenue,
Shelton, Stoke-on-Trent.

Hon. Secretary :
A. W. POWELL,
5, Lysways Street, Walsall.

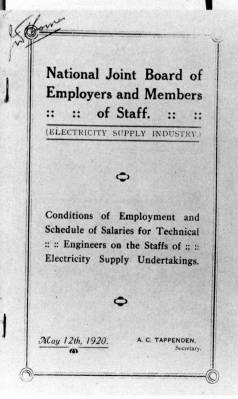

National Joint Board of Employers and Members :: :: of Staff. :: ::
(ELECTRICITY SUPPLY INDUSTRY.)

Conditions of Employment and Schedule of Salaries for Technical :: :: Engineers on the Staffs of :: :: Electricity Supply Undertakings.

May 12th, 1920.
A. C. TAPPENDEN,
Secretary.

Vol. I.]   15th May 1915   [No. 5

AESE

Progress

Official Organ of the Association of Electrical Station :: Engineers ::

Issued monthly for gratuitous circulation among the members of the Association

8

Published at the
HEAD OFFICE OF THE ASSOCIATION
OF ELECTRICAL STATION ENGINEERS
41 WARREN ROAD, LEYTON
LONDON, N.E.
Telephone—STRATFORD 205.

Fragments from the early days of the AESE and the EPEA

At Dover in July 1921 the Association employed 15 sandwich men to publicise their case against the employers

Employees of the Wyecombe Electric Light Company photographed during the interwar years

Association recruitment propaganda in 1929

This photograph taken in 1923 shows (back row) H. Bowden, J.F. Heslop (President 1921–22), J.H. Parker (President 1920–21); (front row) J.W. Thomas, Assistant Secretary, W.J. Jeffery (President 1922–23) and W.A. Jones, General Secretary

Penny wise - Power foolish

The Power Engineers' Protest
Published by the Electrical Power Engineers' Association
102 St. George's Square, London, S.W.1

In 1957 the Association issued thousands of copies of the pamphlet *Penny wise – Power foolish* setting out their case and the dispute stimulated the production of the cartoon

Frustration erupted in May 1971 when a demonstration of 300 members took place outside the Bonnington Hotel where the NEC was meeting

The balloon goes up! The FUSE (Federation of Unions Supplying Electricity) campaign against electricity privatisation was launched in March 1987. All the major unions in the industry took part. From left to right: Fred Franks (National Officer EEPTU), John Edmonds (General Secretary GMB), John Lyons (General Secretary EPA), Alan Jinkinson (Deputy General Secretary NALGO)

Thomas, who always intended to develop the EPEA's educational role; from the mid-1920s the Association's technical and educational activities expanded.

There were a number of routes to the achievement of professional qualifications in electrical engineering. University education remained, until after the second world war, very much the preserve of the rich; in the interwar years only four out of every thousand children at elementary school reached university.[10] Most of the technical staff in the electricity supply industry followed a course of part-time study while working an apprenticeship. The terms and conditions for articled pupils had changed little since the previous century, as the recollections of a retired EPEA member who joined the Northampton Electric Light and Power Compant in 1924 show.

> The Company undertook to train me in the duties of a 'central station engineer' for a period of three years and I undertook to 'perform all their lawful and reasonable commands and requirements and keep their secrets'. I received no remuneration over this period. My father had to undertake to supply me with 'sufficient board, lodging, clothing, pocket money, medical attention, books and drawing instruments, etc'. In effect technical education was left entirely to the pupil.[11]

Another retired member recalls that when, at the age of 18, he left the local grammar school and was taken on as an articled pupil by the Borough Electrical Engineer at Tunbridge Wells, his father paid 100 guineas for the privilege and he worked for nothing.

> The first 18 months was spent with the fitters and the second doing a regular shift on the switchboard so upon looking back it appears to have been less a training scheme than a way of getting well educated labour cheap.[12]

Aware of the shortcomings and the variety of training and education, the Institution of Electrical Engineers turned its attention in the 1920s to creating what it rightly regarded as an indispensable requirement for professional standing, a common standard of education for electrical engineers. Under the aegis of the Institution and the Board of Education, part-time courses of instruction leading to the award of Ordinary National Certificate (ONC) and Higher National Certificate (HNC) and full-time courses leading to Ordinary National Diploma (OND) and Higher National Diploma (HND) were instituted in 1923-4. ONC and OND exempted their holders from Part I of the IEE examination – the graduateship as it was known from 1929 – which, with 'responsible experience in electrical engineering' gave access to corporate membership, at Associate level, of the Institution.

HND was considered the equivalent of a university degree (it took three years' full-time studying and longer on a part-time basis) and the numbers taking it in the interwar period were small. HNC and its existing equivalent, the City and Guilds Certificate in Electrical Engineering, exempted their holders from Part II of the IEE examination.[13]

As the Association was well aware, it required a sustained effort over a period of years to acquire these professional qualifications.[14] For some young engineers, however, attendance at evening classes was made difficult if not impossible by the nature of their employment and geographical location. It was particularly for them that the Association's Correspondence Tuition Scheme (the CTS) was launched in October 1931, with the Panel of Past Presidents administering and guiding the scheme. It seems, from those who wrote in to the journal, that it served the purpose successfully. In 1939 the Association decided to offer a Diploma of its own, to students of the CTS who had completed certain courses and passed an examination set by the Association. The EPEA diploma was not intended to compete with the existing diplomas and certificates, but to be 'confined to those special subjects for which there is at present no recognised certificate'. The diploma therefore was limited to courses on electrical technology, electricity supply (generating) and salesmanship and economics.[15]

In the 1930s there was an increasing awareness of the

importance of the commercial side of the industry. The development of the grid placed as great an emphasis on distribution as on generating and reluctantly some, although by no means all, in the supply industry came to recognise the truth of the dictum of the IEE President in 1922:

> that question of economics is the fundamental problem of the engineer; let him neglect it and, even though brilliant, he becomes something else, a physicist perhaps, a mechanician or a constructor, but not an engineer.[16]

The IEE introduced an optional paper into Part III of its examination in 1934, on engineering economics, and the EPEA's Correspondence Tuition Scheme courses on salesmanship and economics (the latter was introduced in 1933) reflected this changing emphasis.

In the 1930s the Association publicised its ability and willingness to cater for sales engineers and worked to establish grades for them in the NJB Schedule. These activities met with a mixed reception. Among those in generation there lingered on contempt for sales engineers frequently expressed in the columns of the *Electrical Power Engineer*; there was also resentment that the Association should be spending its time on improving their status and remuneration. Thus an anonymous AMIEE wrote to the journal:

> Of these sales members, or potential members, it is open to question whether the greater percentage are entitled, either by qualification, training or experience, to class themselves as engineers, and I would suggest that until they are so qualified the 'Shop Assistants Union' would be the more appropriate body to cater for them.[17]

From the start the *Electrical Power Engineer* had regularly included articles on technical matters and from 1927 onwards, in order that they should be readily available and reach a wider audience, they were republished as technical pamphlets, offered to members at 8d (3.3p) and non-members at 1s.2d (5.8p) including postage. Nineteen pamphlets had been published by 1939. The continuing

interest of members in technical matters was also catered
for at the local level. Section meetings often had a speaker
who was sometimes an official on pressing matters (usually
pay) and sometimes a specialist lecturing on a technical
aspect of the industry. Sections also arranged visits to the
new power stations and to the electrical engineering
manufacturers and suppliers, many of whom advertised
regularly in the journal.

In the 1930s the Technical Groups, established by the
Association in the previous decade, developed further.
The groups, working in cooperation with representatives
of manufacturers in the industry, were intended to keep
members informed of progress in design and methods.
The driving force behind the establishment of the groups
was J W Thomas and some who had been EPEA members
since 1918 were instrumental in the formation of the
groups in London, Manchester, Midlands and Glasgow.
J R Cowie, formerly a member of the Glasgow section,
was by 1928 working for A Reyrolle & Co Ltd and he was
able to do 'yeoman service' in getting the London group
off the ground.[18] Oliver Howarth, who became sales
manager and technical engineer of the Lancashire Electric
Power Company was the first secretary of the Manchester
Technical Group.[19] Over the winter each group ran a
programme of lectures, with one or two each month
covering a variety of topics. The London Technical
Group, for example had a lecture in November 1938 on
'Commissioning of a large modern power station'
(Fulham) which was afterwards published in the *Electrical
Power Engineer*; in February 1939 the group was offered a
taste of the future with a lecture on 'Television'.

A call for reorganisation

By the early 1930s the work of the Association was being
carried on by an administrative structure laid down almost
15 years before and some members had come to feel that
the time was ripe for a change. At the NEC meeting which
took place over the last weekend in September, 1933, H A
Gray, who had represented the Manchester section on the
NEC for some years (he became President of the

Association in 1941), moved that 'the constitution and
organisation be reviewed with a view to eliminating
redundant committees and councils, simplifying procedure, increasing efficiency and reducing expenditure'.
Gray had apparently had reorganisation in mind for some
time and had made similar proposals in the past. Four
years before he had suggested at an NEC meeting that the
Association should hold an annual national conference;
but the majority of the then members of the NEC had
been opposed to the idea, not least on grounds of expense
and Gray's proposal had been roundly defeated.[20] This
time the abolition of Divisional Councils was, it became
clear in the discussion that followed, Gray's particular
target, an objective shared by the Northern Division. As W
H Simpson, reporting the NEC meeting for the *Electrical
Power Engineer*, noted,

> Divisional Councils in recent years have had their thunder
> stolen by the Area Investigation Committees and they have
> become wan and bloodless organisms ... when matters have
> reached this pass the question arises whether it is not more
> the merciful course to make use of a lethal chamber.[21]

But Divisional Councils had their staunch supporters too,
not least W J Oswald, a keen member since the earliest
days and now National Treasurer.

The NEC decided therefore

> that an investigation of the EPEA would do no harm and
> might possibly have good results. To appoint a committee to
> go into the matter was a nice comfortable non-committal sort
> of action.[22]

The five members of the NEC appointed to the committee
took two years to consider the reorganisation question. It
was not until the autumn of 1935 that the committee's
report came up for consideration at a special meeting of
the NEC.

By that time the enthusiasm for wholesale changes of
the organisation had clearly dissipated, nor apparently was
the need for economy any longer uppermost in the minds
of the members of the NEC. Indeed one of the few

changes which was agreed added to the Association's
running costs: another permanent official, a third assistant
secretary, was to be appointed it was decided, making the
Association's permanent officials number five in all. The
committee's recommendation that Divisional Councils
should be replaced by Area Committees was firmly
rejected in favour of the *status quo*. According to their
advocates the Councils

> had been the bulwark of the Association almost since its
> inception. They added dignity and prestige to it, and were a
> valuable medium for the exchange of information. They
> acted as intermediaries between the sections and the National
> Executive Council and as clearing houses of the recommen-
> dations of Sections on their way to the supreme governing
> body. Instead of their powers being curtailed, they ought, in
> fact, to be enlarged by the restoration to the Councils of those
> functions which had been filched from them.[23]

Some area changes to the Councils were agreed, both to
equalise divisional strength and to bring the divisional
areas 'into closer approximation' with the CEB areas. The
Sheffield and West Yorkshire sections were added to the
North Eastern Division for example, a change made
mainly to reduce the size of the unwieldy Northern
Division, but one which would coincidentally, it was noted,
strengthen the municipal representation in the North
Eastern which was dominated by NESCo. Change,
however, was not popular and the North Eastern Division
was initially opposed to it on the grounds that it would add
to their members' travelling and expenses. With only five
divisions covering the whole of England and Wales,
travelling was a common problem. The South Western
Division, for example, stretched from Cornwall to north of
Birmingham, taking in West Wales. And within the
divisions the sections also took in vast areas. The Barrow
and North West section noted in 1936, in mitigation of the
poor attendances at its meetings, that its area extended
over 2,000 square miles.

The reorganisation committee had also considered the
powers and position of the technical representatives. No
changes were made and, in line with the discernible but

not articulated policy of the Association at the time, the discussion centred on limiting the powers of the technical representatives to conduct negotiations with undertakings. The NEC noted that while 'friendly discussions' between technical representatives and managers sometimes brought about a settlement, 'there should be a clear understanding that where a difference arose it was time for the permanent officials to be brought in.'[24] Overall in the 1930s the Association centralised authority at Head Office, a trend which did not always go unremarked in the sections. In 1934 the Newcastle section noted without enthusiasm a change in the procedure for paying subscriptions: it appeared 'to deprive the section of some of the authority and vest[ed]Head Office with still more autocracy'.[25]

That change was made because the collection of subscriptions presented a permanent problem for the Association. In the hope of fostering a competition between the divisions to achieve fully paid up status early in the year, the *Electrical Power Engineer* published regularly a ranking list, a 'financial ladder', showing how successful – or otherwise – each division had been in getting the subscriptions paid. It was anticipated that by this means those who were publicly revealed to be at the bottom of the ladder would be shamed into making a greater effort! Typical was the list published in June 1933 showing that 77.2% of the Association's revenue for that year had been received at Head Office by the end of May. Divisional contributions to this were as follows:

Division	*% paid*
Scottish	89.8
Midland	81.8
Northern	79.9
Southern	77.4
Western	74.6
North East	67.3
Irish	58.1

Throughout these years the Irish Division was usually bottom of the league. The EPEA's main strength lay in Belfast, for after the establishment of the Free State many

of the technical staff in the South joined the Engineers'
Association. Recognising that 'Ireland is not only
separated from this country by a strip of water but by
national sentiment'[26], the EPEA sought friendly relations
with the Engineers' Association so that the two organisations could work together.[27]

There were then no major changes made in the way the
Association ran its affairs, in the wake of the lengthy
deliberations of the reorganisation sub-committee. The
system as a whole worked and although members were
aware of the failings there was it seems a consensus that
change might not necessarily lead to improvement. As the
Teesside section noted in the journal:

> The Association's system of layers of Committees through
> which things rise like bubbles in treacle maintains the ideal of
> representation, but also has its drawbacks, such as people
> dealing with issues of which they have only indirect
> knowledge and on which they have no convictions.[28]

And later the same year the North West Midlands section's
grouse was muted: 'We feel the wheels of the EPEA grind
exceedingly slowly, but perhaps we are an impatient little
section.'[29] On the issue of pay, however, impatience was
not to be found, only in the North West Midlands Section.
Once again negotiations on the linked questions of
remuneration and revision of the Schedule were
prolonged and as the years went by the patience of many
Association members was tried to the limit.

Pay and the demand for a revised Schedule

Two dominant features can be seen in the Association's
policy on pay in the 1930s: in the first place, a
determination to defend the existing standard of living as
far as possible and, secondly, to achieve a restructuring of
the Schedule which would recognise the increased
responsibilities that Association members, particularly in
larger power stations, were carrying.

Although the electricity supply industry was less badly
hit by the depression than other industries, employers

nevertheless were still eager to cut costs. Less responsibility for the technical staff equalled a smaller salary in the employer's book but at the same time few employers recognised the logic of the counterpart to that – more responsibility equalling a higher salary.

When the Association submitted a revised Schedule in 1928, it suggested adding eight more classes of undertaking, station or area, and proposed salaries, at the top of the scale in the largest units, of just over £1,000 a year.[30] There were other reasons too for the Association's urgent demands for revision of the Schedule, chiefly the need to clarify the language of the clauses which consistently led to difficulties in interpreting.

In 1931 when an arbitration which had taken two years, with the Clyde Valley Electrical Power Company, was eventually settled, the *Electrical Power Engineer* had drawn attention to an 'important moral' to be drawn. The editorial noted 'the necessity for clearly defining the terms which are used when the new Schedule is being drawn up' and went on to say:

> It is not a very creditable reflection either upon the employers' or the employees' side of the NJB that a term was inserted in a document seven or eight years ago and that the two parties should have been still in doubt as to its exact meaning. The arbitration will have served its purpose if it emphasises the need for making the language in the new document clear and unambiguous.[31]

But the employers prevaricated for four years and the economic crisis which came to a head in August 1931, destroying the Labour Government and creating the so-called National Government, led to an 'atmosphere in industry generally ... not very favourable for negotiations'.[32] As a result of the crisis wage and salary cuts were the order of the day in industry; all those paid by the state had 10% cuts imposed in the autumn of 1931 (except the police who had 5% and teachers who had to take 15%) and negotiations to revise the Schedule had to be abandoned. Indeed in the national economy campaign which was waged in the autumn of 1931 the Association had to resist the imposition of arbitrary salary reductions, particularly

in the municipal undertakings. Some of these asked
employees to take cuts voluntarily, in the name of patriotism; regarding such attempts at persuasion as 'insidious
propaganda' the Association pointed out that not only had
its members already taken reductions in salary because of
the sliding-scale but that such 'arbitrary encroachments'
would destroy the NJB machinery. The NJB issued a letter
pointing out the cuts already accepted by the technical staff
of the industry, and it seems that most undertakings gave
up the attempt to impose or demand further cuts.

By July 1931, because of the steady fall of the cost of
living index, the operation of the sliding-scale had reduced
scheduled salaries of Grade 1 staff at the top of the scale by
12%. Those at the bottom of the scale had fared even worse
with reductions amounting to 20%. The *Electrical Power
Engineer* countered criticisms from members thus:

> it should not be forgotten also that on theoretical grounds a
> sliding scale is a just and equitable arrangement, because it
> ensures that real wages are kept constant and that employees
> do not suffer in their total purchasing power as a result of the
> fluctuations of price levels. The sliding scale of the EPEA
> Schedule has worked fairly satisfactorily in the past, and we
> would do well to hesitate before asking for its suspension
> merely because at the moment it is operating against us.[33]

The index continued to fall steadily; in June 1928 it had
been 65 and by June 1933 it was down to 36, triggering
further salary adjustments downwards in July of that year.
By then the total of 17 points reduction which had been
made had resulted in cuts of £92.9s (£92.45) per annum
on the highest salary, £79.5s (£79.25) on the mean salary
of £499 per annum and £57.2s (£57.10) on the lowest
salary of £252.

In June 1933 the EPEA representatives raised the
question of revision at the NJB but a battery of reasons for
not proceeding came from the employers' side:

> ... there was still a feeling prevalent amongst members of
> some Municipal Councils that the salaries of the technical
> staffs were too high and there was a danger that they might
> seize upon the opportunity afforded by the launching of a

new schedule to free themselves from the imposition of any schedule at all or to put into operation reductions .... The employers did not think that the anomalies in the existing schedule were so numerous or so substantial as to justify the launching of a new one which might throw the whole question of salaries of the technical staffs into the melting pot. [34]

There was also, and this was the argument that weighed most with the Association, the possibility of new legislation which would impose more change on the supply industry and in such circumstances 'it would be unwise to formulate a schedule'.[35] The matter was therefore left for the time being but the pay of the technical staff was seriously eroded over the course of the next two years. After a further reduction in January 1934 negotiations on a new Schedule started, but they were protracted and by early in 1935 Association members were 'feeling keenly the incidence of the cost of living deductions and the failure to provide increased remuneration for their growing responsibilities'.[36]

In March 1935 the NJB discussed the possibility of stabilising salaries, but the offer made by the employers was, in the Association's view, too low; furthermore it was accompanied by an unwelcome stipulation that any further revision of the Schedule should be suspended for a period of two or three years.

The Association found these proposals, particularly the condition of no further revision, 'most objectionable' and rejected them briskly. In its leader on the subject the *Electrical Power Engineer* did not mince its words:

under the employers' proposals ... the salary of a charge engineer in a station between 150,000kW and 200,000kW would be £443.5s [£443.25]. Can anyone say that this is an adequate salary for an engineer in charge of such a large station containing so much plant, representing such heavy capital expenditure and requiring such a large staff? Even a bank manager in a small country town or a teacher in a school receives this amount. Similar remarks apply to switchboard attendants and control room attendants. The present pay to these men is not commensurate with their responsibilities particularly in these days when so much depends upon prompt action and initiative as well as knowledge of large and intricate systems. [37]

The editor blamed both the employers and the Association for the unsatisfactory situation:

> It is really time that the Employers examined a little more critically the responsibilities of the staff under their control. The Association, however, cannot exempt itself from blame; it has perhaps been too quiescent and too amenable when it should have been more persistent.... Something clearly must be done and speedily otherwise the seething discontent is likely to have serious repercussions up and down the country.

As 'a powerful tide of dissatisfaction swelled', it was noted in the journal that 'the temper of the majority of the membership is back to where it was in 1921'. [38]

Perhaps mindful that the Association had not used such terms lightly in the past, the negotiations made better progress between March and June when a settlement was reached. It did not represent the complete overhaul of the Schedule originally anticipated by the Association but there were three main alterations which were embodied in a Supplementary Schedule. Firstly it was agreed that salaries should be stabilised at three points above the existing figure and there should be no more cost of living adjustments for three years. Secondly, the table of salaries was to be extended to cover the creation of new classes up to a capacity of 250,000kW, for both generation and distribution technical staff (the employers had tried to exclude distribution staff). The third alteration was a novel and permanent feature, the introduction of merit increments between classes, based on years of service. The increments were small, but the Association considered them to be a step in the right direction, designed to prevent stagnation for staff in undertakings whose size did not change.

As the Association recognised, some members would be disappointed – even profoundly so – and some would be resigned on the basis that half a loaf was better than no bread, but it was hoped that most would be relieved that the uncertainty of the past four years was ended and with some improvements.[39]

In retrospect, it is clear that had the Association chosen and obtained stabilisation for a three-year period in 1931 or 1932, its members would have fared better. As it was the cost of living index started to rise slowly in 1936 and, by June 1938 when the three-year period ended it stood 15 points higher. It was not until the autumn of 1939, after the outbreak of war, that it started to rise sharply. But retrospective judgements are often unfair; in 1931 it was unclear how far the index would fall and, equally in 1935 the prospects of recovery seemed still to be a long way off. On balance over the decade Association members, like others in work during the depression, found themselves better off than before because of falling prices. At its lowest the cost of living was 60% less than in 1914 and Schedule salaries were higher than in 1914, if not yet as high as members had hoped. Some members did better than others, mainly those employed in the company undertakings, many of whom paid at rates over the Schedule. The larger enterprises too could afford to pay for technical excellence and expertise. For all the technical staff in the supply industry some improvements had been secured, if not as much as might have been if the Association had been less 'quiescent' and 'amenable'.

The remuneration of the technical staff was of course influenced by the salaries paid at the top, to the chief engineers. In the 1930s these proved to be a source of irritation and dissatisfaction.

'A distressing episode'

Although the Association had intended to cater for all levels of technical staff in the supply industry, the position of chief engineers was and remained difficult. In 1931 the *Electrical Power Engineer* noted 'it is encouraging to know that the number of Chief Engineers in our ranks is growing and we trust that it will be further augmented as time goes on'. But many chief engineers belonged to AMEE, the Association of Municipal Electrical Engineers, which originated in London as a local group, meeting to discuss technical and commercial problems. In 1919 AMEE extended itself nationally and started to make representations about the remuneration of its members. Its President, R A Chattock (chief engineer of Birmingham, see p 116), was able to persuade the IMEA that a committee should be formed (chaired by the ubiquitous Alderman Walker) to consider pay and conditions. A scale of salaries, the 'Walker-scale', which related remuneration to the sales (in GWh) of the undertaking, came into operation in 1921. It was never, however, accepted and applied by all the members of IMEA and, particularly in the 1930s, as many undertakings increased their sales but were trying to reduce costs, it became even more difficult to enforce the Walker-scale.[40]

In the spring of 1931 Nelson Corporation advertised for a Borough Electrical Engineer. The salary offered was inadequate, less than the Walker-scale and subject to a sliding scale related to the cost of living; but even more 'objectionable' to both the EPEA and AMEE were the conditions attached to the appointment. It was stipulated that the successful applicant would be expected to act as Tramway Manager, and to supervise the training of pupils without further remuneration. Both Associations therefore advised members not to apply but in May the *Electrical Power Engineer* was obliged to report

> a humiliating situation ... in connection with the filling of the post at Nelson. The person selected was no less than a past President of the EPEA, and to our dismay and disappointment he has accepted it.[41]

Many members expressed their anger, shame and outrage in letters to the journal. It was not until the September NEC meeting that T D Martin (who had been President in 1929) appeared to explain his action in accepting the position at Nelson, 'contrary to the instructions of the Association'. But the past President was unable to offer any convincing defence of his action and the NEC

> by a large majority ... resolved that his conduct was open to severe censure, and that it had been against the best interests of the Association. There was no other course open to them

therefore but ... with very great reluctance ... to expel him from membership.

It was, by all accounts 'one of the most distressing episodes in the history of the Association'.[42]

From then on AMEE and the EPEA continued to work together in banning appointments advertised at inadequate salaries. By 1936 some EPEA members were less than enthusiastic about the ban and a motion put forward by the North West Midlands section that the banning was ineffective and the whole position should be reviewed. The motion was circularised to other sections – a manoeuvre regarded with suspicion by the NEC as a 'subtle means of undermining its authority', but it gained a good deal of support. At Bedford the attitude of half the members present at the meeting was probably not untypical – '[they] failed to see why it should be necessary for the Association to take in Chief Engineers' dirty linen'.[43]

In 1937 the heat was taken out of the debate, at least for a short time, when a National Joint Committee was formed, as Whitley machinery for chief engineers. But some local authorities refused to participate and, as with the NJB schedule, refused to pay. The difficulties were unresolved when war broke out in 1939.

The EPEA – Every Possible Evening Away

The Association's stand with AMEE was a reflection of the longer view: if chief engineers' salaries were depressed, levels of pay further down the scale would be correspondingly reduced. It may also have reflected the influence of increasing numbers of EPEA stalwarts who became chief engineers in the late 1920s and the 1930s. A number of past presidents, including J H Parker, and T A Margary, who became respectively Borough Electrical Engineer at West Hartlepool in 1926 and Wolverhampton in 1930 were among these friends in high places. Other active members achieved promotion before high office in the Association. In 1935 Edward Jones, then senior Vice-President, was appointed City Electrical Engineer and Manager of the Cardiff undertaking, and

although he gave up active work and the Presidency he
would have held in 1936, he continued to be an EPEA
member. J N Waite, a founder member, became City
Electrical Engineer in Hull in 1929 (his later post-
nationalisation career was also distinguished). At Hull an
already active sub-section was delighted to welcome him
and the extensions to the distribution network and
generating plant that he organised meant an increase in
staff and EPEA membership there.[44]

Chief engineers who were sympathetic to the Association were an asset. In some undertakings working
conditions remained exceptionally harsh in the 1930s. R J
Rennie, now a retired member, joined Glasgow Corporation's undertaking in 1926, after graduating as an
engineer at the university there and serving his
apprenticeship with Metropolitan-Vickers in Manchester.
In 1928 he joined the Clyde Valley Electric Power
Company as an assistant district engineer.

> We had one evening from 5 p.m. to 11 p.m. off duty and one
> day from midnight to midnight off-duty each week. This was
> worked on a six weeks cycle.

Apart from annual holidays (two weeks at first, later three)
the stand-by rota meant that there were only eight
weekends a year when Saturday night was free. Clyde
Valley was considered particularly harsh; only the
Yorkshire Electric Power Company 'operated the same
degree of tyranny'.[45]

But there can be no doubt that stand-by duties and shift
working mitigated against regular attendance at section
meetings. In every section therefore the burden fell on a
small group of activists, and this was mirrored at all levels
in the Association. Those who were most involved in
activities came to know each other well, enjoying the
rhythm of the EPEA year – meetings, outings, the
traditional 'smoking concerts' in the North and the
dinners – sectional, divisional and Technical Group. The
dinners and sometimes dinner-dances, often graced with
the presence of chief engineers and supply industry
notables, were formal and, it seems, expensive. In the

account of the Teesside Section annual dinner dance held at the Grand Hotel, Middlesborough in 1936 the writer noted,

> we thought it rather tactless of the President to remark on the almost entire absence of young members ... the plain truth ... is that our younger members cannot afford it. A glance at the Supplemental Schedule, including increments (if any) is proof enough that functions of this sort are out of the question for many of us.[46]

For the active members who took on the burden of running the Association's many committees – a new one was added in 1934, the National Propaganda Sub-committee, to recruit more members – it was, as Mrs Duffy, wife of the 1933–34 President, suggested, 'Every Possible Evening Away'. This impression of a cosy Association world is conveyed in the articles written for the *Electrical Power Engineer* by Hugh Roberts. A member of the Bedford section, his literary reports of section activities written in the style of Pepys and others attracted attention. He graduated to reporting on NEC meetings and his erudite, amusing and often irreverent accounts suggest that by the mid-1930s the Association's secure position could allow it to permit itself to be taken not too seriously sometimes. In 1934 he wrote of Jim Wallace, then Scottish and Northern area assistant secretary, later to be General Secretary:

> Following a speech by Mr Wallace is an exhausting and nerve-racking business. He reminds us of an ancient car engine with badly sooted plugs. He starts off like a rocket, quite unexpectedly, and, after a few minutes hard going splutters himself into silence. Then, when he has given us the impression that he has conked out, he explodes violently into top gear with a spate of spluttering detonations and takes us completely by surprise. We spend another five minutes galloping madly after him in a vain attempt to overtake him until eventually his inlet valve again sticks and he conks once more into silence.[47]

Hugh Roberts became assistant editor of the *Electrical Power Engineer* and in January 1938, assistant secretary of

the Association. Sadly the promise he showed, 'the pen of
a ready writer [and] a very capable speaker and organiser ...
a keen brain and an alert mind ... in fact ... those rare
qualities which are so necessary for a successful permanent
official' was lost to the Association in 1939, by his sudden
and tragic death at the age of 36.[48]

The failure to reorganise the industry

Throughout the 1930s there was growing dissatisfaction
with the structure of the electricity supply industry.
Criticism centred on the division of responsibility for
generation between the CEB and the undertakings. At the
same time it was widely recognised that although technical
change had made economies of scale both possible and
desirable, rationalisation and integration of local distribution systems were blocked by the entrenched interests of
companies and municipalities. Professor Hannah has
called the failure to come to grips with the problem, by
successive governments, the 'drift into stalemate'.[49] The
Labour government of 1929 had intended to legislate for
reorganisation but failed to do so before it was swamped in
the crisis of 1931; in 1933 legislation was again intended
but it became bogged down in political differences and the
Government took refuge in appointing yet another
enquiry into the industry. The outcome of that enquiry,
the McGowan Report, advocated greater integration of
distribution and a reduction of the number of undertakings; McGowan was published in 1936 and followed by
a Government White Paper in 1937. But by May 1938 the
difficulties in getting agreement to reorganisation from
the divided parties in the industry led to a government
retreat. Under the excuse of the worsening international
situation, reorganisation was shelved yet again.[50] The
electricity supply industry therefore entered the war years
with the responsibility for generation split between the
CEB and more than 500 undertakings; in the hands of the
latter, some municipally and some privately owned,
remained the responsibility for distribution, as it had now
been for half a century.

Notes

1. N Buxton and D Aldcroft (eds), *British Industry between the Wars*, Scolar 1979, p 13.
2. C J Wrigley (ed), *A History of British Industrial Relations 1914–39*, Weidenfeld and Nicholson 1987, p 116.
3. L Hannah, *Electricity Before Nationalisation*, *op cit*, p 119.
4. *EPE*, August 1933.
5. *Ibid*.
6. *EPE*, October 1934.
7. Information from C.M. Young.
8. Hannah, *op cit*, p 132; *Electricity Supply in Great Britain. A Chronology*, The Electricity Council 1977.
9. Hannah, *op cit*, p 133–6.
10. A J P Taylor, *op cit*, p 308.
11. B Tyler in a letter to the author, 10.12.87.
12. W E Leshley in a letter to the author, 26.11.87.
13. W J Reader, *A History of the IEE*, *op cit*, pp 132–6.
14. *Ibid*.
15. *EPE*, May 1939.
16. Quoted in Reader, *op cit*.
17. *EPE*, June 1939.
18. *EPE*, October 1948.
19. *EPE*, March 1948.
20. *EPE*, June 1929.
21. *EPE*, November 1933.
22. *Ibid*.
23. *EPE*, October 1935.
24. *Ibid*.
25. *EPE*, January 1934.
26. *EPE*, July 1929.
27. *Ibid*.
28. *EPE*, July 1936.
29. *EPE*, September 1936.
30. EPEA Archives, Draft revision of Schedule, July 1928.
31. *EPE*, March 1931.
32. NEC Minutes, January 1932.
33. *EPE*, August 1931.
34. *EPE*, July 1933.
35. *Ibid*.
36. *EPE*, January 1936.
37. *EPE*, July 1935.
38. *EPE*, June & July 1935.
39. *EPE*, June 1935.
40. Hannah, *op cit*, pp 286–7.
41. *EPE*, May 1931.
42. *EPE*, October 1931.
43. *EPE*, June 1936.

44. W F Chappell, letter to *EPE*, March 1976. W F Chappell, letter to author, 1.12.87
45. R J Rennie to author, 14.12.87.
46. *EPE*, January 1936.
47. *EPE*, 1934.
48. *EPE*, September 1939.
49. Hannah, *op cit*, pp 137, 289.
50. *Ibid*.

Chapter 7

From War to Nationalisation

'Everywhere the view is expressed that with the still upward trend of wages and prices the position and prospects of electricity supply as a profession have not improved a great deal'.

Electrical Power Engineer, January 1947.

It is a truism that for many industries war is a stimulus to change and proves to be a turning point in one way or another. So it was for electricity supply; after more than a decade of governmental shilly-shallying it became clear from 1943 onwards that there would have to be reorganisation of the supply industry.[1] The Labour Party's return to power, with an overwhelming majority, in 1945 made it certain that the industry would be nationalised. The EPEA's own suggestions for post-war reconstruction set out in 1943 were mirrored in the structure established by statute in 1947.

For Association members who carried the burden of running the industry in wartime it was a period of intense strain. The changing climate of opinion in wartime Britain which contributed to the Labour victory in 1945, a growing conviction that there must be change and that after the war things would not be the same, may also have played a part in the Association's decision, made in 1942, to affiliate to the TUC.

The war also brought rising prices and as the cost of living soared the Association's officials were pressured to negotiate salaries which would keep pace with inflation. After the war the struggle to maintain the position so hardly won for the technical staff in the years before the war, and to improve it, did not come to an end with nationalisation.

The strain of war on the industry and EPEA members

At the start of the war there was considerable uncertainty about what the demand for electricity would be and, during the period of the 'phoney war', the CEB made cuts in its plans to expand generating capacity. Load forecasting, never an accurate science even at the best of times, suggested that the effect of the blackout combined with industrial and commercial disruption and an anticipated fall in domestic consumption would reduce sales of electricity drastically. Looking even further ahead the experience of the years following 1914-18 suggested a slump at the end of the war, so that fears of excess capacity in the future also played a part in the CEB's decision to shelve 862MW of the planned expansion.[2] But as the phoney war ended, munitions production expanded; in addition, many of those evacuated from London in the autumn of 1939 returned – electricity sales in London had fallen particularly dramatically at the beginning of the war – and demand picked up. The CEB revised its load forecasts and in 1941 the plant commissioning programme for the following year was restored to 75% of the original plan.[3] During the rest of the war years the capacity of the supply industry expanded steadily although not by as much as the CEB planned. Shortages of materials, money and labour led the Government to refuse to sanction some extensions and increased demand was met as well as it could be by extending the grid.

As well as extending existing power stations by the addition of new sets, some new stations were brought on stream during the war. The Midlands was an important centre of munitions manufacturing and, at Hams Hall, Birmingham Corporation's B station (321MW) was commissioned in 1942; with the A station (249MW) already on site, Hams Hall, with 570MW, then represented the greatest concentration of generating plant in Europe. In the same year two 'war emergency' power stations were commissioned; the one at Early, near

Reading, had the unique distinction of being owned by the CEB and it was built in the record time of 22 months. The other, Castle Meads, belonged to Gloucester Corporation. It was not until later in the war, in 1944, that the first section of Battersea B, with its 100MW cross-compound set, was commissioned.[4]

But even so the increase in generating capacity proved inadequate as the demand for electricity grew and maximum output had to be extracted from existing plant. Load factors were increased, from 36% in 1938 to 50% by 1942, and the intensive use of all existing generating capacity meant that sometimes sets were run on overload and with inadequate safety margins.[5] The burden of supplying electricity in such circumstances fell heavily on the technical staff of the industry. So too did the fact that, through conscription, transfer to munitions manufacturing, death and retirement the supply industry lost more than half its workforce in the war years. Not all of them were replaced by the older workers and the women who were recruited to make up some of the loss. In 1944 a labour force of 30,000 fewer people than in pre-war days was working to provide 40% more electricity.[6]

These difficulties were enhanced by problems of fuel supply which became worse during the war. Generating stations were often unable to get adequate supplies of coal and, even if supplies were available, they were often of poor quality and likely not only to reduce the efficiency of generation, but also, on occasion, to damage machinery. In other areas of civilian life, such as food and clothing supply, the government war machine imposed rationing to provide a fair distribution of scarce resources. But a rationing scheme for electricity was thought to be impracticable and the government therefore relied upon exhortations to economise on its use. There were remarkably few power cuts, mainly because the grid lines suffered less damage than had been envisaged in the pre-war planning for the emergency. In fact the President of the IEE claimed, in 1945, that 'far more damage had been done to transmission lines by trailing cables of drifting barrage balloons than by enemy action'.[7]

The loss of generating capacity by enemy action also, in

the event, proved to be less than anticipated, particularly in the later years of the war. The worst damage in London was sustained during the Battle of Britain; in September and October 1940 six sub-stations and 26 power stations were put out of action – although briefly in most cases – by the bombing. At Battersea the worst damage was to the control room, which was a jungle of wires and machinery after the raid. By working through from Sunday to Wednesday morning, *day and night*, the technical staff were able to have the station running again on the Wednesday morning.[8] A direct hit on Fulham power station put 190MW of plant out, but the grid was able to restore supplies within a few hours. It took, however, nearly six months to restore Fulham completely although a good deal of the plant was back in operation within three months. Power stations in areas such as Plymouth and Coventry, which suffered heavy bombing in the Blitz in 1941, were also damaged.[9]

For the technical staff this was a period of strain not only when there was damage to be repaired quickly, as at Battersea, but also over the longer term. Not untypical was the experience of R J Rennie who, as district engineer for Westminster and Chelsea from September 1940, for twelve months spent every third night sleeping on a camp bed in one of the cable tunnels under the sub-station. After that a shelter was built under the yard at Eccleston Place where the accommodation was 'much less spartan' than the tunnel.[10]

Association activities in war-time

Unlike 1914, there was at the start of the war in 1939 no suggestion that it would be 'business as usual'. The government war machine, the fruit both of the experience of 1914-18 and the planning carried on since 1936, rolled into action with a spate of legislation and controls. As the *Electrical Power Engineer* noted at the time, as much legislation was enacted in the early days of September 1939 as in the whole of the year 1914. In the Association many members and officials, not least the General Secretary, Arthur Jones, had clear recollections and first hand experience of the body blows that war had dealt to the young AESE between 1914 and 1916. While the EPEA, numbering over 5,000, was not to be so lightly blown away, it is hardly surprising that the Association hastened to remind members that 'the need for an organisation to safeguard the interests of supply engineers will [not] be any the less in wartime than in peace'.[11]

Uncertainty about what would happen – most people expected immediate air raids in September 1939 and were puzzled when they did not materialise – led the Association to cancel all its social events and many of its meetings. The ban, however, was not accepted by all its members.

> True to form, the Manchester Section set the ball rolling by holding the first General Meeting since the war began. Unperturbed by the vetoes of the NEC and the mild panic created at Headquarters when news of the impending meeting filtered through, the Section only paused to obtain the necessary sanction from the local Police ... before gathering at the Engineers' Club [on October 12] for a most successful meeting.[12]

The meeting was addressed by J W Thomas who assured members that

> there was every intention on the part of the EPEA to keep going as usual as far as this was possible. The Association had built up an efficient democratic machine and it would be little short of a disaster if its normal operations were interfered with to any serious extent.

The Manchester members – 48 of them attended – regarded the immediate actions of the NEC as showing a degree of panic, and were anxious to hold regular meetings to keep in touch.[13]

As Thomas rightly predicted to the Manchester meeting, it was not long before the various Association committees were functioning again, if not on the same scale as in pre-war days. The NEC delegated much of its work to a small Emergency Committee at first, and the General Purposes Committee met less frequently, but the columns of section reports in the *Electrical Power Engineer* in 1941 and 1942 suggest that meetings were held fairly regularly.

Despite the difficulties of travel, which were considerable, and ARP, Home Guard and firewatching duties, many members managed to attend meetings, and the General Secretary and assistant secretaries also visited sections round the country as frequently as possible; in March 1942, for example, Arthur Jones attended the Manchester section's general meeting.[14]

The programmes of the National Technical Groups, however, were suspended for the entire duration of the war and, from the summer of 1941, responding to the national shortage of paper, the *Electrical Power Engineer* adopted a format of much smaller pages. It was to be more than a decade before paper was again available for the more familiar large pages and print. Even in war-time however the heavy advertising by the electrical machinery and supplies manufacturers, which since the 1920s had financed much of the journal's production cost, continued.

By January 1942 there was a growing conviction that 'though the struggle may be prolonged for some time yet the final outcome is no longer in doubt'.[15] The *Electrical Power Engineer* noted that 'as far as the Association itself is concerned, although its activities have not returned to normal, it has in many senses almost returned to a pre-war state of affairs'. Most importantly, 'the National Joint Board and its Negotiating Committee continued to function and almost as many meetings were held as in pre-war days'.[16]

The National Joint Board in war-time

Even before the war broke out the NJB, in anticipation, had established a committee to consider the question of reserved occupations. From October 1939 and through the early months of 1940, the NJB's National Service Committee was involved in lengthy negotiations with the Minister of Labour to settle a schedule of reserved occupations and ages for the electricity supply industry. The agreement reached listed most of the NJB scheduled jobs as reserved occupations at the age of 25 which meant that few qualified technical men holding positions of responsibility were called up. In fact some of those who had volunteered in the early days of the war were recalled from active service because their skills were needed in the supply industry.

There were other important matters too for the NJB in the war years, not least the perennial problem of pay. The cost of living rose rapidly; by 1942 it was 43% higher than in 1938 and by 1944 it was 50%. Salaries of Association members had returned – after the three year stabilisation period negotiated in 1935 (see p 128) – to the sliding scale related to the cost of living in 1938. But although they therefore rose in war-time, they did not give the technical staff incomes to match average earnings which, by 1944, had risen by more than 80%, outstripping the rise in the index.[17] Moreover taxation rose sharply to pay for the war: the budget of April 1941 raised income tax to 10s (50p) in the pound, and at the same time lowered the allowances, thereby bringing most industrial workers above the tax threshold. Thus many of the technical staff found themselves paying more income tax and, as salary increases were always behind price rises, they were worse off in real terms as the war progressed.

An EPEA suggestion that war taxation should be taken into account in the Schedule increases was not pressed in the circumstances of 1940.[18]

In the same spirit in 1940 it was agreed that holidays would be restricted, but in 1942 the employers strongly resisted the Association's request to return to the holiday allowances in the Schedule and the claim had to go to the Industrial Court for arbitration. The Court's award, made in March 1942, gave the technical staff more than the employers had intended although not all that was asked. Depending on years of service, most would get a fortnight's holiday, plus bank holidays, which was regarded as a satisfactory outcome by the Association. The *Electrical Power Engineer* noted:

> In one respect it may prove beneficial that holidays have been made the subject of an Award, as it will provide less excuse for

those undertakings who have tried in the past to limit annual holidays to seven days, and it will put into the hands of the Association a weapon with which to ensure that the staff secure fair treatment.[19]

So too did a claim for grade 7 status for shift charge engineers which had, by 1942, been outstanding for almost nine years; the award, made in May 1942, limited the grading to the larger power stations.[20] Most of the disputes which arose in the war years however were settled within either the District or National Joint Boards. Indeed Alderman William Walker claimed at the No 3 District Joint Board annual luncheon held in January 1942, when despite rationing, 'the fare provided was all that one could reasonably expect – and better', that in his view 'the machinery had never functioned so harmoniously and efficiently as it was doing today, and that was saying a great deal'.[21] The strength of the NJB was enhanced during the war as several company undertakings which had previously refused to be a party to it decided to join, although the London companies remained obstinately outside.

The Association was involved in manpower planning through the NJB, but it was excluded from the closer councils of the government and organised labour which took place through the medium of the TUC. It was a matter of increasing concern to the permanent officials and to some members that the Association played no part, and had no representation, in the consultations that preceded legislation and Orders in Council which affected them.

Members vote for TUC affiliation

In May 1941 at the NEC meeting held at the Royal Station Hotel in York, R Telford, a long-time member of the NEC and a past President (1925), moved a motion that the NEC should recommend to members that the Association should seek affiliation to the TUC and that a postal ballot of members should be held to seek their views. W H Simpson, reporting in his own inimitable style on the meeting, made clear where he stood:

Does this sound startling? Does it cause a flutter in the dovecot? Does the average member experience a sensation of prickly heat when he meditates upon so radical a change in the outlook of the EPEA? Indeed there is nothing revolutionary about the business: rather it ought to be regarded as evolutionary.[22]

The opposition was led, as Telford expected, by W J Oswald, a founder member, who had served as President in 1923 and had been National Treasurer for many years. Oswald clung to the belief that there were three parties in industry, and that the Association represented the middle: the TUC had done 'immense good' he conceded, but it was not the right place for the EPEA. The case against affiliation which he presented was very much the same as he had put forward in 1925-6 (see p 88). There was a long discussion at the meeting. Not all the older members of the NEC shared Oswald's stance. J W Thomas did not agree with 'the notion of the third party' and, as a lawyer, stressed the role the TUC had played in securing important legislation. Arthur Jones argued that although

the prospect of an EPEA delegate obtaining election to the TUC General Council might be remote [it was in fact to be 40 years before John Lyons, as General Secretary, was elected to the Council] ... the actual business of the TUC was carried out by Group Committees and it was on these that the Association would be more likely to be in a position to exercise an influence.

J F Wallace, the assistant secretary for the Northern and Scottish areas, claimed that the EPEA was 'too modest': he had no doubts, he said, that 'we should be leaders in the TUC if we became associated with it, and we should give the benefit of our superlative qualities for the good of others'.[23] In the end Telford's motion was carried by 21 votes to 5. Five members of the Council had been unable to attend the meeting but the decision at what was then the Association's supreme policy-making body was clear enough.

Within the Association the debate continued until October, fuelled by the Memorandum proposed by Telford and agreed by the NEC, which set out the

arguments pro and con, and was sent out with the ballot
papers. It was discussed too in the columns of the technical
press, the *Electrical Times* and the *Electrical Review*. The
result of the ballot was revealed in January 1942. Of the
3578 votes cast, representing 68% of the membership, 2374
were in favour of affiliation and 1144 against. Taking the
votes *en bloc*, every division voted in favour and, of the 32
sections, only two returned a vote against, and those by a
very small margin. The West Yorkshire section voted 131
for and 132 against, while the Edinburgh section had 22 in
favour and 27 against. At the NEC meeting in January
there was a last-ditch attempt to block the, by then, almost
inevitable decision: it was proposed that the NEC should
only seek affiliation if 75% of the ballot was in favour, and if
not less than 70% of the membership had voted. But the
proposal was rejected.[24] The Association affiliated to the
TUC and ended almost 30 years of isolation.

The event did not appear to lead to the resignations
which opponents of affiliation had feared, even from the
more senior technical staff. Membership continued to rise
during the war, passing the 6,000 mark. There was a new
phenomenon too, as women were employed in the
industry for the first time in jobs which made them eligible
for EPEA membership, they were admitted to the
Association for the first time in 1942. The Bedford section
claimed the distinction in April of being the first 'to enrol a
lady member', she being a Miss Wallis, chief chemist at a
power station in the area.[25]

The EPEA plan for restructuring the supply industry

In 1942 many organisations, not least the Government,
started to think about what shape British industry and
society should take when the war was over. Indeed some
began even earlier; at the IEE, post-war planning was
mentioned in March 1941.[26] At government level
Beveridge's plan for universal social security was
completed by the beginning of 1943, and in the November
of that year Lord Woolton, who as Minister of Food had
presided over the successful scheme of rationing, was
appointed Minister of Reconstruction, with a seat in the

war cabinet. The EPEA was no exception to the rule and, towards the end of 1942, its Post-War Planning Sub-Committee started work. At its first meeting it was decided that the Sub-committee's terms of reference should not be narrowly limited to planning for its own future as a protective organisation, but should be extended to embrace the supply industry as a whole.

The Association was not alone in looking at the reorganisation of electricity supply, which the Government had so thankfully shelved in 1939. From 1942 onwards the subject was on the government agenda again and a variety of reports and committees examined the problem. The solutions suggested were equally varied, ranging from greater coordination of the existing undertakings at one end of the spectrum, to the nationalisation advocated by most although not all in the Labour Party at the other.

Arthur Palmer, then a young engineer in London, wrote in his report for the Fabian Society in 1943, *The Future of Electricity Supply*, that 'complete nationalisation in the near future is impracticable'. He advocated instead the creation of a National Planning Authority for the industry, extension of the CEB's ownership of generating stations and amalgamation of the existing undertakings to form larger units, the latter, if necessary, to be carried out by compulsory powers given to the Electricity Commissioners.[27]

The Association's own recommendations, embodied in the report of the Post-War Planning Sub-Committee in the summer of 1943, were more far-reaching. The report argued that a National Electricity Board should be set up, to acquire all the undertakings and the CEB. Distribution would be controlled through regional boards. Public ownership would enable the industry to be coordinated and planned so as 'to obtain increased technical efficiency and give improved service to the public'.[28] Such radical proposals for reorganisation did not meet with the approval of all the Association's membership, but a majority of the NEC agreed them and they became Association policy, reiterated in a Memorandum published in June 1946.[29] In fact when reorganisation came in 1947-8, in the shape of nationalisation, the structure of the industry was very much as delineated by the Association in 1943. The only significant difference was that the Area Boards were larger than the regional boards suggested by the Association.

By then the uncertainty over the future shape of the supply industry had been resolved. In the summer of 1945, after Victory in Europe, the war-time coalition was dissolved and a general election was held. The Labour Party was returned to power with a large majority, with nationalisation of the energy industries as part of its manifesto. It was clear that after coal, which had the highest priority on its legislative programme, nationalisation of electricity supply would follow.

The need for pay increases

As the war drew to an end the hopes of a better social order and the determination that there would be no return to the miseries of the 1930s which had produced the Labour victory, were reflected in the Association. Apart from the industry's organisation there were many other pressing problems, chief among them pay, for the increases awarded to the technical staff during the war fell far short of those gained by the manual workers. To redress the balance was a matter of urgency, the NEC realised in June 1945, as discontent became vociferous. It was decided that a percentage increase on all salaries offered the simplest solution and accordingly a claim for a 20% increase went forward in the autumn of 1945.

There was also the problem of chief engineers' pay. The working arrangements, dating from before the war, between the EPEA and AMEE had continued. Although a new salary scale was agreed in 1941 for chief engineers, a number of undertakings tried to avoid paying it as they had done in the previous decade. The Association therefore worked with AMEE in advising members not to apply for appointments advertised at salaries below the scale and in some cases were successful. In June 1942 the *Electrical Power Engineer* was able to report that the municipal undertaking at St Helens, which had been banned when it advertised for an electrical engineer and manager at £1,200 a year, had subsequently advertised at an amended salary of £1,450, a figure which was satisfactory, and that the embargo on applications had therefore been lifted.[30]

Near the end of the war, a dispute arose at Wimbledon involving W J Oswald, chief assistant engineer there. Wimbledon's chief retired before his successor was free to take up his duties and Oswald was asked to fill the gap, being offered by the Corporation a salary of £1,200, which represented just over a half of the figure to be paid for the new appointment. Oswald refused to accept the post on those terms but, as a 'man of the utmost integrity', he 'undertook, under protest, and in the interest of the maintenance of supply, the responsibility of the control of the undertaking' while the Association took his case to the Ministry of Labour and the DJB. With the help of the Ministry, a satisfactory settlement was reached.[31]

There was again criticism of the Association for its efforts on behalf of AMEE and the chief engineers, some of it voiced more publicly than before in the columns of the *Electrical Review*. The *Electrical Power Engineer* classed its critics as shallow and shortsighted, noting in October 1945:

> The job of chief engineer to a Corporation supply undertaking is a key position, much in the public eye, by which the standing of those that serve the industry is largely judged. When we look after the interests of the chiefs we defend at the same time the salaries and conditions of everybody; 'unity of all grades' should be the slogan for the battles ahead.[32]

And again two months later the Association applauded the loyalty of those who had refused appointments and rejected promotion when offered on 'black', underpaid terms:

> the chief engineers' positions are the proper ambition of the technical staffs; the salaries attached to them are the ceiling of our standards. If too low, they depress every salary on the staff tree. Legitimate self-interest calls on us to look to the

future; self-respect demands that we live up to the principle of collective action.[33]

The 'Old Warrior' goes

In December 1945 the Association's General Secretary, W Arthur Jones, retired. The NEC paid 'a tribute of regard and affection to the man who more than any other has been responsible for the successful initiation and build-up of the EPEA and its present-day prestige'.[34]

Instrumental in founding the Association, Jones had presided over a growth in membership taking it to almost seven times the size it had been when he took on the post of General Secretary. He had headed the battles to secure the acceptance of the Schedule and seen the NJB develop an established position in an industry which had changed almost beyond recognition from the one in which he had started his own career. As General Secretary since 1918 Jones' name was synonymous with the EPEA; W H Simpson, a member almost as long as Jones, no doubt voiced the thoughts of many:

> Can we visualise an official document emanating from Head Office with a new name subscribed in place of the familiar "W. Arthur Jones"? Is it possible to imagine a session of the NEC minus that calm, imperturbable personality on the President's left, whose wise counsel, the fruit of long and unrivalled experience of the Association, has always been available and has functioned as a beacon light, burning clear and steady in fair and foul weather?[35]

The NEC recommended that J F Wallace, Scottish Divisional Secretary 1921-29, Assistant Secretary 1929-1945 and more recently Assistant General Secretary, should succeed Arthur Jones. The recommendation was accepted by the membership: 'his intimate knowledge of Association affairs, his many years experience of negotiations, his familiarity with details of EPEA history ... and his proved ability' made his succession inevitable, even if, as Simpson noted, he was 'getting a wee bit long in the tooth in the opinion of some'.[36] It was therefore to Wallace that the difficulty of pressing the claim for 20% and £100 fell, a claim which, as Arthur Jones remarked, bore an uncanny resemblance to the claim for 20% and £90 which the Association was pressing when he became General Secretary![37]

Discontent on all fronts

The 'high hopes' with which the Association entered 1946 were to be disappointed in many ways in the two years which elapsed before nationalisation. For the country as a whole it was an unhappy period. The Labour government was faced with an economy distorted for war purposes, a vastly enlarged national debt, lost export markets and huge international debts.[38] Reconstruction was made more difficult by shortages of materials and money, and industry was exhorted to export rather than supply the home market. Rationing remained in force and austerity was enhanced by the severe shortage of fuel which in the severe winter of 1946-47 forced more power cuts than ever before.

In the spring of 1946 the Association's negotiators settled their claim for a 20% increase, made the previous year, on a basis which gave members between 11% and 14%. The new agreement retained a cost of living clause and although the claim was not met in full, it was felt by the negotiators that there was no more to be gained by going to arbitration. The settlement was not however well received. At many section meetings the view was expressed that the NEC was out of touch with the membership and even the presence of NEC members giving their personal explanations of the acceptance of the employers' offer failed to mollify those who were most vociferous in their discontent, such as South Wales.[39]

On 1 June 1946 the West Yorkshire section held a special meeting at the request of members in Huddersfield, Hull and Halifax. Over 100 members passed unanimously a motion severely censuring the NEC 'for its failure to further adequately the members' interests and for its apparent ignorance and lack of understanding of the members' wishes particularly in relation to the recent salaries claim'.[40] The meeting went on to discuss reform of

the Association, for in the wake of the specific
dissatisfaction with the new NJB agreement, a rising tide
of criticism of the way the Association ran its affairs was
appearing. Many members suggested that there should be
an annual conference, the case for which was forcibly
argued in the *Electrical Power Engineer* by Arthur Palmer,
the journal's new editor who was also now a Member of
Parliament, elected against his own expectations in the
1945 surge of pro-Labour enthusiasm.

The NEC's response to the demand for reform was, as
usual, to appoint a committee to consider the constitution
of the Association, including section boundaries and the
role of divisional councils as well as the question of an
annual conference. In the event the Revision of the
Constitution Committee's recommendations, some of
which were made in the autumn of 1948 and others to the
NEC in May 1950, were limited to minor changes to the
Association's rules and an adjustment of sectional and
divisional boundaries designed to regroup membership to
conform to the geographical areas of the Area Electricity
Boards and Generating divisions established by nationalisation. The changes left untouched the position of the
National Executive Council as the chief policy-making
body of the Association. The idea of an annual conference
was rejected at this time and at intervals over the next 30
years, But the growth of the Association meant that
adequate representation at the NEC made that body
increasingly unwieldy. In 1948 W H Simpson pointed out
the problem, which dogged the Association over three
decades:

> If the disadvantage and excessive size in the case of a
> legislative body which aims at getting things done with the
> greatest possible avoidance of waste of time had not
> previously been fully realised, it was amply demonstrated at
> the January meeting of the National Council. Resulting from
> a continuous growth of membership of the Association,
> representation has automatically increased, and the NEC has
> become bloated and, consequently unwieldy, by reason of the
> excess of numbers composing it where you have an
> assemblage of upwards of fifty representatives [by the 1960s it
> became nearly 70], each having an indisputable right to air his

views, the rate of progress is bound to be impeded, however strictly standing orders are applied by the presiding chairman.[41]

1946 also saw a wave of unofficial strikes among the manual workers in the supply industry and Association members were advised by the NEC to carry on with 'normal duties' but not to undertake work which did not come under that definition. The years between the end of the war and vesting day were particularly difficult. Expectations had been aroused which the existing undertakings were not prepared to meet and there was considerable uncertainty in the industry.

The interim period

The Government's intention to legislate for the nationalisation of electricity supply was announced in 1946 and the following year was therefore to a large extent dominated by the passage of the Bill through Parliament. In March 1946 representatives of the EPEA and the manual workers' unions of the NJIC met to establish the Electricity Employees' National Committee. Acting co-operatively for the first time, the committee's role was to ensure the preservation intact of the existing national bargaining machinery, as well as to act in the interests of the NJB and NJIC employees on matters such as training and compensation. In 1947 the committee was extended and strengthened by the addition of representatives from AMEE (for the chief engineers) and of the unions which were to be members of the new NJC for clerical and administrative workers in the industry (see p 156). The committee's chairman was Frank Foulkes of the ETU; Jim Wallace was Secretary and Treasurer.

In the austere conditions of the immediate post war-years the added uncertainty about the industry created an unfavourable climate for the negotiation of improvements in pay and conditions. In these circumstances the Association found the employers at the NJB in an intransigent mood. Some concessions were made on pay for standby duty, on hours of work, holidays and shift work although the full extent of the EPEA claim was not met. The difficulties in this interim period are illustrated by the course of the negotiations over the EPEA's claim, made in November 1947, for a £100 increase on all scheduled salaries. It was rejected by the employers early in 1948 on the grounds that there had already been many improvements since 1939 for the technical staff and that any further salary adjustments should wait until after nationalisation, given that a complete review of the classification and grading scheme would be necessary then. Aware that their responsibilities were ending soon, the employers were reluctant to commit themselves in the short term and their successors in the longer term to large pay increases, particularly given the constant exhortations by the Government to restraint. The Association, however, 'conscious of the exasperation of our members at the suggestion made to suspend any action on the claim until the BEA took over the industry',[42] refused to accept a complete moratorium and pressed the claim. Reluctantly, after long and hard negotiations, the Association accepted a lower offer at the end of February 1948. Salaries were to be increased by 10% on the first £300 and 5% on the remainder. The increase took effect on vesting day, 1 April 1948.[43]

Nationalisation brings changes to the Association

The Act of 1947 laid down that on vesting day the British Electricity Authority (the BEA) should take over the responsibility for the generation and transmission of electricity in England, Wales and Scotland with one exception; that was the North of Scotland Hydro-Electric Board, established in 1943, on the model of the CEB, to exploit Scotland's water resources. The Hydro Board, which did not start to generate until 1950, remained independent of the BEA, to which, on 1 April 1948, the assets of the CEB network and of the 200 private and 369 municipal undertakings were transferred. Distribution was decentralised in the hands of 14 Area Boards – each of them larger than the regional units proposed by the Association itself in its 1943 and 1946 proposals.

Appointments to the Area Boards were made by the Minister of Fuel and Power, Hugh Gaitskell (he replaced Emmanuel Shinwell in the autumn of 1947). Not surprisingly many of the appointments both to the BEA and the Area Boards were of those who had distinguished themselves in the supply industry and included some Association stalwarts. The retired General Secretary, W Arthur Jones, was appointed to the London Area Board and W J Oswald to the South Eastern Board.

The BEA itself also recruited among Association members for its new jobs: J W Thomas became the Authority's chief education and training officer and two of the labour relations officers appointed in June 1948 were active EPEA members – V R O Hutchinson was the President-elect and G O James had just completed his term serving as President. A serious loss to the Association was that of some of its permanent officials to the Authority. Chief among these was George Essex, who had been with the Association since 1920. He accepted the appointment of deputy labour relations officer to the Authority, a post he held until he retired in 1956. The only surviving member of the original National Joint Board of 1920, he now became secretary for the employers on the new NJB. Two other permanent EPEA officials also became labour relations officers for the BEA: H S Smith, who had joined the Association as an assistant secretary in 1936 and was, at the time of his appointment Assistant General Secretary; and C G Hancock, who was the EPEA's assistant secretary in the North West area. Pleasure and pride no doubt were mingled with regret at these appointments, for at such a time the Association could ill afford to lose the expertise and experience of its permanent officials.

In July 1948, Harry Norton, National Negotiations Secretary since October 1947, was appointed as the EPEA's new Deputy General Secretary. Norton had joined the Association in 1944 as assistant secretary in Scotland, the first non-engineer to be appointed as a permanent official. Educated in Sheffield, Norton worked for some years in the Transport Department of Sheffield City Council, where he was an active member of NALGO and became chairman of the Sheffield branch. When he was recruited by the EPEA he was the youngest member of NALGO's Executive Committee and had already developed a reputation as a skilful negotiator.[44]

The 1947 Act gave statutory force to the Whitley machinery in the supply industry. As well as the NJIC for the manual workers and the NJB for the technical staff two new sets of machinery were to be established, the NJC for clerical and administrative workers and, of greater interest to the EPEA, a body to settle the salaries and conditions for managerial staff in the industry (see Chapter 8). Labour relations at the Authority were officially the province of Ernest Bussey, formerly the General Secretary of the ETU, but its real director, from whom the impetus for the extension of the collective bargaining machinery came, was Lord Citrine himself. Appointed as chairman-designate of the BEA in May 1947, Citrine had started life as an apprentice electrician and had risen through the ranks of the ETU to become General Secretary of the TUC (see p 90). An ardent advocate of the nationalisation of the supply industry since the 1930s, Citrine, even as chairman of the BEA, devoted so much of his time and energy to labour relations in the early days that he evoked criticism from some of his colleagues, particularly Harry Randall, London Area Board chairman.[45]

There was, however, general agreement on vesting day that the arrangements for such a major change in the industry had gone remarkably smoothly. Nevertheless much remained to be done.

Notes

1. L Hannah, *Electricity Before Nationalisation, op cit*, pp 137, 289
2. *Ibid*.
3. *Ibid*, p 292–3.
4. *Electricity Supply in Britain, A Chronology, op cit*, Electricity Council.
5. Hannah, *op cit*, p 298–9.
6. *Ibid*, p 300.
7. W J Reader, *A History of the IEE, op cit*, p 153.
8. Information from Arthur Palmer.
9. Hannah, *op cit*, p 293–4.
10. Letter to author, 14.12.87.
11. *EPE*, October 1939.

12. *EPE*, December 1939.
13. *Ibid*.
14. *EPE*, May 1942.
15. *EPE*, January 1942.
16. *Ibid*.
17. A J P Taylor, *English History, op cit*, p 550.
18. *EPE*, December 1940.
19. Industrial Court Award, March 1942, *EPE*, April 1942.
20. Industrial Court Award, May 1942, *EPE*, June 1942.
21. *EPE*, February 1942.
22. NEC Minutes, May 1941, *EPE*, June 1941.
23. *Ibid*.
24. *EPE*, February 1942.
25. *EPE*, May 1942.
26. Reader, *op cit*, p 150.
27. A M F Palmer, *The Future of Electricity Supply*, Fabian Publications, Research Series No 69, 1943.
28. EPEA Post-War Planning Sub-Committee Report, 1943.
29. Memorandum to nationalisation of the Electricity Supply Industry, June 1946, EPEA Archives.
30. *EPE*, June 1942.
31. *EPE*, August 1945. Information from Arthur Palmer.
32. *EPE*, October 1945.
33. *EPE*, December 1945.
34. NEC, September 29–30, 1945.
35. *EPE*, October 1945.
36. *Ibid*.
37. *EPE*, February 1946.
38. Taylor, *op cit*, p 509. A Sked and C Cook, *Post-war Britain*,Penguin 1979, pp27–9.
39. *EPE*, April, May and June 1946.
40. *EPE*, July 1946.
41. *EPE*, March and November 1948, August 1950. NEC, May 1950.
42. *EPE*, April, May 1948.
43. *Ibid*.
44. *EPE*, January 1953.
45. L Hannah, *Engineers, Managers and Politicians*, Macmillan 1982, p 126.

Chapter 8
The Years of Expansion

'We do not challenge necessarily either the right or the desirability of the State regulating incomes in the general public interest but it is undoubtedly true that such regulation is likely to have maximum and sometimes unfair effect in those fields where the Government has the direct opportunity and power to intervene openly or more probably covertly, ie in the public services and the nationalised industries.'

EPEA evidence to the Donovan Royal Commission
on Trade Unions, 1965.

From nationalisation until the late 1960s the electricity supply industry enjoyed what Professor Hannah has called a spirit of buoyant expansion, as its share in the final energy market rose from 14% in 1948 to 29% by 1963.[1] Over the same period the British economy was plagued by recurring balance of payments crises and by inflation which, creeping in the 1950s, accelerated to a gallop in the 1960s. Successive governments, both Conservative and Labour, sought therefore to reconcile the apparently incompatible objectives of maintaining stable prices and full employment (accepted by all political parties as a major government obligation as laid down in the 1944 White Paper) at the same time as balancing the books.

Through the two decades covered in this chapter government attempts to regulate the economy therefore combined price and pay restraint with incentives to encourage greater productivity; when voluntary restraint failed, statutory prices and incomes policies were tried. Inevitably government pressure to keep wages and salaries down was applied where there was most chance of it succeeding, particularly in the nationalised industries.

Over the same period there were significant changes in the supply industry. The most obvious was its growth, but there were also technological improvements and the introduction of new fuel sources, oil first and then, most importantly, nuclear fuel. All these changes had to be absorbed by the Association in framing its policies and restructuring its organisation. The first priority after nationalisation, however, was the negotiation with the BEA of a new salary Schedule.

Lengthy negotiations over the new NJB Agreement

The new National Joint Board was inaugurated with a luncheon organised by the BEA and held at the Café Royal in London at the end of April 1948. Also guests of the Authority at the function were members of the two other national negotiating bodies, the NJIC and the newly created NJC as well as the Ministers of Fuel and Power and of Labour, Hugh Gaitskell and George Isaacs respectively, while Citrine himself took the chair.[2] At the NJB meeting which followed the lunch the new Board adopted, for the time being, the 1947 Agreement, although both sides were aware that the reorganisation which was taking place in the industry would require a complete overhaul of the Schedule. The *Electrical Power Engineer* noted:

> Nationalisation severed generation from distribution, changed the geographical areas of operational units, created undertakings greater than any to which the old Agreement could apply and reshuffled the duties and responsibilities of the technical staff to a degree which made it almost irrelevant.[3]

In the autumn of 1948, the EPEA appointed an Agreement Revision Committee whose deliberations resulted in the presentation of a proposed new Agreement and Salary Schedule to the NJB in March 1949. As Deputy General Secretary, Harry Norton, explained to members:

The salient features of the [proposed] new Salary Schedule are a minimum salary of £400; 8% increases per grade and per class; the consolidation of old Classes A to E into the new Class A and its extension by four new classes to embrace large units like Areas, Divisions and Grid Control Areas. All scheduled salaries would increase by five biennial increments of 3%.[4]

Holiday and sickness allowances had already been agreed, on a more generous scale than pre-war and the Association also proposed a redefinition of standby duty.

The negotiations over the new Schedule proved to be a lengthy affair, however, and it was not until February 1950 that agreement was reached at the NJB. As discontent mounted again among the technical staff, Harry Norton argued that the delay was caused not only by substantial disagreements, but also by the complexity of the matter, which led to changes in negotiating practice:

When negotiations began with the Electricity Board's representatives, it soon became evident that on certain major issues agreement was impossible unless both sides had before them the same information, impartially collected and factually displayed. Repeatedly the Joint Secretaries were called upon to obtain, coordinate and submit to the Negotiating Committee as a Negotiating Committee and not as separate sides all the necessary detailed information upon which an eventual joint decision could be made. Perhaps no other single factor helped more to sustain through complex argument, which often became heated but never rancorous, an underlying unity of purpose and a belief that both sides had all their cards on the table. I regard this abandonment of the old system of each side bluffing on an undisclosed hand as a major step forward in negotiating practice.[5]

Major step forward or not, the Association did not gain all it had hoped for in the negotiations. The levels of salaries in the new Schedules were considerably lower than the EPEA had suggested. In Schedule A, for example, which covered 75% of members' jobs, the Association had proposed for a Grade 7 engineer in a station with between 200 and 250MW plant capacity an annual salary of £864. In fact the 1950 Agreement gave him between £736 and

£770 a year. Other levels in differently sized power stations or distribution areas (where the classification was based on units sold) were also correspondingly lower. In the years after the war inflation and higher taxation eroded the real value of salaries; it was calculated that, to offset the effects of tax to provide a net personal income of £500 in 1948-49, a salary of £640 was needed; even then, because of inflation, the £500 would only buy half as much as it had in 1931.[6]

As early as February 1948 the *Electrical Power Engineer* had criticised the BEA's levels of senior salaries.

> The salary for the Chief Engineer to the Authority is fixed at £4,750 while his deputy is to obtain £3,000 per annum. Judging by salaries already paid in the industry it would not have been, in our view, unreasonable for the man who holds the biggest technical job ever created in British electricity supply to receive at least £7,000 a year.

The journal's leader went on to suggest that the two possible explanations for such 'meanness' were both wrong. In the first place it was wrong in principle to take the salaries of the Chairman (£8,500 pa) and of the Deputy Chairman (£5,000 pa) as the starting point:

> Appointments to public authorities of the type of the British Electricity Authority and the Area Boards are of some considerable honour. It should be possible to obtain sufficient men and women both disinterested and capable to serve the country and the principles in which many of them believe without the carrot of a salary well above that of their chief executive officers. In other words, there is no real anomaly in the Chief Engineer, for instance, of the Central Authority or of an Area Board, being paid nearly as much or even more than his Chairman.

In the second place, if the Minister had 'deliberately discouraged the payment of salaries that will outshine the scales laid down for the high Civil Service' then the 'idea that the Civil Service yardstick should be used to measure salaries in what is a trading and industrial undertaking, even if publicly owned, should not be tolerated for a moment.'[7]

There can be no doubt however that the Area Board

Chairmen's salary level – £4,000 a year – did impose a ceiling which constrained all those below into a tight pyramid. The 1950 Agreement set the highest salary for Grade 1 in the largest power stations at £1,627, rather than at the £2,177 proposed by the EPEA. The framework imposed on the industry as a whole from the top was reflected in that Agreement and played a part in the narrowing of differentials which created so much discontent among the technical staff from the mid-1950s (see p 175-7).

It was not only the negotiations leading up to the 1950 Agreement that were protracted however; there were long delays too in implementing the Agreement. In August 1950 Harry Norton wrote in the *Electrical Power Engineer* that the fact that an agreement signed in February was still a promise rather than a performance required an explanation.

> Negotiators and negotiating machinery must always steer an uncomfortable course between the Scylla of careless haste and the Charybdis of over-pernickety delay. ...the National Joint Board is so near Charybdis that only a sharp swing towards Scylla can avert shipwreck.

Creating a common structure was bound to be a lengthy task and one not to be skimped, he averred and in the course of so doing anomalies were bound to arise. But his explanation highlighted some of the problems in the new nationalised undertaking:

> I confess that if I were told of some other industry that nearly six months had elapsed since the signing of an agreement yet many of those affected by it did not seem to be within measurable distance of learning its practical effect on them, I would not accept as reasonable any explanation tendered. I decline to believe that all Area Boards and Divisions have treated the task of applying the Agreement with the degree of urgency it merited. Time has been wasted; sometimes merely because a proper degree of administrative priority was not given; sometimes because somebody did not like the decisions of the negotiating machinery and therefore exaggerated the admitted difficulties of application; sometimes because sight of the new Agreement stirred an impulse to 'reorganise' the

staffing before applying it: sometimes because those charged with drafting an Electricity Board's proposals were too timorous to rely upon their own interpretations; sometimes because an Electricity Board considered literal application unfair to its staff; and more often than for any other reason, because as each problem arose which could have a national application, every Electricity Board was reluctant to make a decision and so "create a precedent".[8]

Commenting on the new situation created by nationalisation, Norton noted that previously many, if not most, problems would have been solved by direct local negotiations, partly because what went on in one undertaking did not always affect another. But he went on,

> under the new conditions two facts must be faced: that our own members are not prepared to accept inequality of treatment between man and man in the same Area or Division, as between Area and Area or, where like conditions apply, between Areas and Divisions. Thus both sides – Electricity Boards and Association – shrink from concessions in relation even to one individual whenever the same set of circumstances exists elsewhere. Both are conscious of the difficulty of refusing to apply in every other similar case a decision made in relation to the first such case considered. Inevitably this leads to continual reference to the centre, to appeals for 'guidance' on matters which pre-vesting might have been settled in forty different ways in forty different undertakings without any one of the forty knowing or caring what the other thirty-nine did. Inevitably such an appeal to the centre results in a general standstill until a central decision goes out.[9]

The implementation of the new Schedules went ahead in the autumn of 1950 although the appeals against, and approvals of, individual gradings continued well into the following year. There were, for example, 155 appeals against gradings in the East Midlands Board alone, and the President, W Ingledew, suggested pessimistically to a meeting of the Devon Section in October 1950 that it could take two years for the full implementation of the Schedule.[10]

The new Schedule was not the only matter which involved the EPEA's officials in lengthy negotiations: so too did the discussions about establishing new collective bargaining machinery (called the fourth leg, or estate) for the more senior managerial employees in the industry.

The establishment of the 'Fourth Leg'

Citrine's belief in collective bargaining machinery was reflected in a determination to see it extended to cover as many jobs as possible in the supply industry. Although he had to allow that some appointments would have to be excluded, and would be the subject of individual bargaining, he was anxious to restrict their number and eager to establish machinery on the same lines as the NJIC, NJB and NJC for the senior posts in the industry. Discussions therefore started in 1948 between the Authority, the EPEA and the AMEE, the latter retaining the same initials while renaming itself the Association of Managerial Electrical Executives. Despite the cooperation between the two Associations in the 1930s and during the war (see pp 130, 150) there was an old rivalry between them and, during the course of the discussions, the *Electrical Power Engineer* regularly assured members that it was representing them and that there was a 'firm mutual understanding' that the AMEE would not enrol EPEA members. By the summer of 1949, however, the discussions were deadlocked by disagreement between the AMEE and the EPEA over the borderline grades, and deciding which grades should be at the top of the NJB scale and which should come within the province of the new managerial machinery.[11]

The discussions resumed in 1950, with NALGO joining them, since by then it was clear that it too had members among the senior administrators who should be represented in the machinery. Early that year it was agreed that jobs then carrying salaries of £1,250 and over should come within the scope of the National Joint Managerial and Higher Executive Grades Committee, and those earning £1,500 and over were to be represented by AMEE (an agreement which subsequently lapsed). Settling the detail still took longer than anticipated and it was not until August 1951 that the agreement was finally signed. Some 1300 managers were party to the agreement, leaving only 150 individuals, mainly those earning £2,000 and over, excluded from collective bargaining.[12] The EPEA had five representatives on the main negotiating committee of the managerial committee and Harry Norton was asked to represent the staff side, including AMEE and NALGO, as secretary; the Association's strength in the new body was reflected in its representation on the three sub-committees established to deal with different areas of responsibility – the EPEA had a majority on each, with five out of seven on the operational sub-committee, four out of seven on the district managers' and all four on the station superin-tendents' sub-committee.[13] Relations with AMEE, which continued to endeavour to recruit EPEA members when they were promoted, remained precarious.

As with the new NJB Schedule, the preparation of and agreement on salary scales was also a protracted business. It was not until December 1953 for most managerial staff, even September 1954 for some, that the new scales were agreed. One problem which was particularly acute among the senior staff in the industry was that while most former municipal employees found themselves better off after nationalisation, those who had worked for the privately owned undertakings had, pre-vesting, enjoyed higher rates of pay and other benefits. Salaries in the nationalised industry therefore offered little improvement, and for some of them even a reduction, in income. There were similar anomalies in other benefits such as pensions and car allowances and much the same reasons as those put forward by Harry Norton for the delay in negotiating NJB schedules prevailed in the negotiation of the managerial scales. Some senior men – although they were mainly in the posts outside the machinery, which came to be known as the non-negotiable appointments – were paid 'personal allowances' to compensate them for the differences and persuade them to stay in the industry.[14]

To meet the needs created by the formation of the managerial machinery – the NJMC as it became known – the Association created new managerial sections; by early

1952 there were 13 of them, two in each of the EPEA's
Divisions except the South East which had three. The
managerial sections participated in the EPEA Divisional
structure and through that were represented on the NEC.
But it was the Association's principle in negotiations – 'that
negotiators should be selected and directed by those for
whom they are to speak and whose salaries and conditions
are at stake' – which necessitated the establishment of the
separate sections so that they could elect the Managerial
National Investigation Committee. That in turn appointed
and controlled the EPEA representatives on the NJMC.[15]

Joint Consultation – a common purpose ?

The statutory authority given to the collective bargaining
machinery which covered all but a few of those working in
the supply industry was part of Citrine's grand design for
industrial democracy. He also wanted greater participation by employees in decision and policy making and the
establishment of the consultative advisory machinery was
intended as a step towards that goal.[16]

In January 1947 the Association had welcomed the
statutory recognition in the Electricity Bill of the
importance of the welfare, health and safety of employees
and of the means for advancing their skill and
education.[17] The EPEA had therefore participated,
through the Employees National Committee, (see p 153)
in the discussions which led to the setting up in January
1949 of the National Joint Advisory Council. Representatives of all the trade unions in the industry were matched
by an equal number from the Authority, and the national
council was to be replicated at district and local level.
Initially the Association was wary about the local
committees because it feared an attempt to use them to
short-circuit negotiations which were properly a matter
for the District Joint Boards, but by March 1949 the fears
had been allayed and the *Electrical Power Engineer*
welcomed the new venture whole-heartedly.

Joint consultation is one of those things often talked about in
a familiar or knowing fashion, but it becomes surprisingly

ethereal when actual definitions are demanded. Let this be said: joint consultation is possibly one antidote to bureaucracy, the inevitable malady of large-scale organisation, whether publicly or privately owned.[18]

For Citrine the consultative machinery represented more than an 'antidote' to the bureaucratic structure of committees which now ran the Authority's affairs. The NJAC was to be the vehicle through which consultation between managers and workers and joint participation in decision-making would make a reality of his vision of the supply industry – socialism working in practice. In his opening speech at the inauguration of the NJAC, Citrine told those attending, 'The whole basis of this machinery rests upon the assumption that there is a contribution which all of us can make to a common purpose'.[19]

Citrine's hopes for the NJAC were not fully shared at the time, or later, by all BEA and Area Board managers or by all the trade unions concerned, but if the NJAC did not realise all his hopes, a good deal was accomplished there, at least in the first 15 years.[20] By the early 1960s the development and achievements of the joint advisory system in the electricity supply industry had won admiration for its success in bridging the gap between management and workers.[21] In the period covered in this chapter the EPEA found in the NJAC and its district and local committees a forum not previously available for the discussion and resolution of issues concerning welfare, health, safety and training.It was not until the 1970s that, in the then changed climate and relationship between the Boards and its employees, the NJAC came to be seen as little more than a talking shop and the EPEA initiated positive steps to create greater participation (see Chapter 10).

The Association had consistently, from its inception, urged on the employers the importance to the industry of these issues, particularly safety and training. Much of the responsibility for the safety of lives and plant was borne, on a day to day basis, by Association members and was regarded by them as part of their professional duty. Safety involved not only extra care but also the application of technical ability and expertise, often in conditions now called 'abnormal', for which NJIC members could claim 'danger' money. The NEC of the EPEA always resisted any moves to claim extra remuneration, regarding such responsibility as the hall mark of professionalism which differentiated the technical staff from the manual workers. The Association's own Safety, Health and Welfare committee has made important contributions to the nationalised industry.[22]

The expansion of the collective bargaining machinery, however, combined with the establishment of the advisory machinery, made considerable demands on the time of Association members and officials.

Coping with change and a growing membership

Nationalisation proved a stimulus to the membership of the EPEA, and it grew rapidly. From 7,000 members in 1945 it increased to 10,000 in 1949 and by 1953 had risen to 13,000. The Association itself was perhaps a little equivocal about the influx of members. In January 1949 the *Electrical Power Engineer* noted:

> Many among the technical staff, previously cold towards trade unionism, are finding now that it has considerable everyday advantages when there are statutory negotiations over salaries and conditions. We welcome all those who enter our ranks, but would respectfully ask newcomers not to look upon the EPEA as a kind of automatic machine in which a subscription is inserted and an immediate material return awaited. The Association was founded and built up in the days of hardship and difficulty; the pioneers never counted the cost to themselves. They were prepared to sacrifice, not only their leisure, but often their chances of professional advancement in the cause of justice to their fellows. No such sacrifices are demanded today of EPEA members, but let us be on our guard to see that familiarity does not breed contempt for principle or quantity in membership be substituted for quality in leadership.[23]

At the end of 1952 Jim Wallace retired as General Secretary. He had presided over a period of unpreceden-

ted growth in the Association and change in the industry,
'years of a fresh confidence a spreading of the wings of the
EPEA – much of it flow[ing] from the zest for living of J F
Wallace.'[24] At the NEC meeting held in London over the
last weekend in November 1952, Harry Norton was
appointed General Secretary. His was the only nomination
received from all seven divisions. At the same meeting
farewell was said to Jim Wallace. Once again W H
Simpson's NEC Jottings provide a more colourful picture
of the proceedings than the more formal minutes:

> It must surely have warmed the cockles of Mr Wallace's heart
> to listen to the flowing tributes accorded to him by many
> members of the Council as well as by representatives of his
> staff.... From all accounts No 102 St George's Square under
> his regime housed a happy team who viewed his coming
> departure with profound regret. Many references were made
> to Mr Wallace's peculiar gift of oratory. I call it peculiar
> because it is indeed *sui generis*.... In recent years we have
> noticed a toning down and mellowing of his style of delivery
> but have been made aware from time to time that the old fiery
> eloquence was only dormant and still on tap and could be
> brought out when the occasion seemed to call for it... The
> proceedings ended with gusto though with possibly doubtful
> effect,

when, 'the whole Council stood up and burst into 'He's a
jolly good fellow', following with three hearty cheers.'[25]
   Harry Mayfield was appointed as the new Deputy
General Secretary. Trained as an engineer, Mayfield had
worked for Metropolitan Vickers before he joined the
Metropolitan Electric Supply Company. When he
accepted appointment as an EPEA official – Assistant
Secretary in London and the South – in 1948, the financial
sacrifice he made evidenced a commitment to the
Association which became plain to all in the years he
served as Deputy General Secretary.[26] A rearrangement
of responsibilities at Head Office followed Harry Norton's
appointment. Harry Mayfield worked with Norton on
NJB and salary matters as well as supervising the work of
the assistant secretaries over the country. There were now
five of them, each working in an area relating to one or

more EPEA divisions; J D Ewing looked after the South
and West and T W Lukehurst, London and the South
East. T G Allcock was responsible for the Midlands and R
P Stewart for the North West while G Millet looked after
the North which included both the North Eastern and
Scottish divisions. Only the small Irish division, which had
only two sections, one in the North and one in the East of
the country, had no permanent official.

Arthur Palmer not only edited the *Electrical Power
Engineer*, but also supervised the Technical Groups which
had resumed their activities shortly after the war, and
dealt with Advisory Council matters – education, research
and publicity. H W Hall, chief clerk to the Association
since the 1930s, was assistant editor of the journal and
responsible for the day to day administration including
membership and benefits. Last but by no means least Miss
E Smith was in charge of the Finance Department.[27]
Together it was not a large staff to service a growing
organisation in a changing industry; there were now,
following the post-nationalisation reorganisation, 46
sections, excluding the 13 managerial ones. New sections –
for example in East Yorkshire – had been formed to cater
for the expanding membership, and new generation and
distribution areas; probably the only section to disappear
totally was an overseas one. In the 1930s the Association
had a section in Shanghai, where there was a large (by the
standard of the time) expatriate British community some
of whom were involved in running electrical installations.
The latter were of course lost during the war, and
although jobs overseas were advertised regularly in the
Electrical Power Engineer in the post-war years – many of
them in what were still then British Colonies, in particular
in Malaya and Uganda – and there were overseas
members, the Association never had an overseas section
again.

A changing industry

Shortages of building materials and steel bedevilled the
early years of the BEA's power station construction
programme but gradually capacity was increased as new

stations were commissioned. The first new post-vesting station was Kingston B whose four 30MW sets were commissioned in 1948. The following year the UK's first hydrogen-cooled alternator was commissioned with a 60MW set at Littlebrook B. Continued extensions at Littlebrook provoked a crisis in 1953, when the EPEA found itself blacking jobs advertised for technical staff at Littlebrook. It had not been anticipated that such an 'unfortunate' situation would recur after nationalisation. Because of the extensions, Littlebrook had been reclassified according to NJB practice, but the management followed this with a list of vacancies for which engineers already working at Littlebrook were told they could apply. The *Electrical Power Engineer* reported,

> As justification for their extraordinary action the management argued that the extension of the station and the alteration of classification had in effect created a new station and made necessary a review of the staffing arrangements.

But, the editorial continued, 'The Association was not prepared to acquiesce for one moment in this bad business.' After the first blacking notice the Electricity Board initiated discussions which resulted in an agreement safeguarding existing jobs and advertising genuine vacancies. It was a small incident and speedily resolved but it left an unpleasant taste and could have damaged relationships more than it did. As the journal's editorial concluded:

> In common with the Association, responsible leaders of electricity supply are undoubtedly still anxious to maintain in spirit and practice the good relations that have hitherto existed between the technical staff and the Boards. But nobody had a right to expect EPEA collaboration under the circumstances so unfortunately created at Littlebrook.[28]

There were other pointers to the future in the changes which took place in the industry in the 1950s. The first of what was to be a range of new power stations in the Trent Valley was commissioned in 1950; Staythorpe A had the first standard 60MW set installed. Bankside power station

was commissioned in 1952, the first large public supply
station specially designed for oil-firing and was, apart
from Battersea, the only station with full-scale gas washing
plant. Reflecting the plentiful and cheap supplies of oil
then available, a programme for oil-firing at 17 power
stations was agreed in 1954.[29]

While it might have been thought that the industry had
enough to cope with – that certainly was the Association's
view (see below) – the return of a Conservative
Government in 1951 presaged a new look at the
nationalised industries. The reversal of the Labour
government's pyrrhic victory on steel was inevitable and,
although there was no question of denationalising
electricity supply, the Conservatives had promised to give
greater independence to Scotland and Wales within the
nationalised industries. It proved to be impracticable to do
so in Wales, but in 1954 legislation established the South of
Scotland Electricity Board which took over responsibility
for both generation and distribution in the parts of
Scotland not covered by the Hydro Board. As a
consequence the BEA was renamed the Central Electricity
Authority (CEA).[30] The change was made against the
wishes of Citrine, to whom the appointment of a
Committee of Enquiry (the Herbert Committee) into the
workings of the nationalised supply industry was equally
unwelcome. The Committee started work in July 1954 and
reported in January 1956.[31]

The Association's evidence to Herbert opened with an
uncompromising statement:

> the industry went through a major upheaval with the passing
> of the 1947 Act, and probably its greatest need now is for a
> period of 'peaceful' expansion in which new responsibilities
> and fresh loyalties can be consolidated.

The main suggestions for improvement made by the
EPEA were a simplification of Area Board organisation by
reducing a three-tier management structure to two tiers
and a move towards smaller rather than larger organisational units in generation. The CEA had tried as an
experiment an amalgamation of the North Western and
Merseyside generation divisions, which the Association

noted had 'caused much difficulty for the technical staff'. It concluded 'we deprecate such experiments suggested, apparently, by anonymous internal committees without consultation with those most affected.'[32] From the start the BEA had been criticised for its elaborate committee structure and although the Association itself was noted for its committees, its evidence to Herbert included a complaint on the matter:

> A growing habit in the industry which we deprecate is the creation of committees to decide each and every question. Engineers who should be running their jobs spend many hours sitting around tables drafting reports, often sadly enough of no direct value to the efficiency of the industry or to the public interest.

The Association gave considerable attention to education and training, stressing the role of the technically trained manager in the industry:

> the Association holds the view that the ideal manager for an electricity undertaking is a professionally trained engineer with administrative capacity. We dissent entirely from an opinion held in some quarters that the engineer should be confined to calculation, design and operation leaving general management in the hands of the professional administrator. It is only those with an engineering and scientific training who are able to appreciate the economies which can still be brought about in electricity supply working by continuing the search for improved techniques in generation, distribution and utilisation.

But, if the supply industry was to continue to recruit 'young men of quality and technical enthusiasm' it must be prepared to offer salaries comparable with manufacturing industry during training and the 'highest possible salaries' after training. The Association noted the contrast with pre-war days:

> In the 1930s many able young men from the universities were glad to enter electricity supply because of the relative security and good prospects offered. Today under full employment the man with high technological qualifications is

more likely to be attracted to the newer industries such as civil aviation, electronics and nuclear energy or to interesting developments in electrical manufacturing.[33]

The low level of graduate recruitment was worrying others in the industry – in 1955-6 the intake was only seven.[34]

The Association's plea for a period of 'peace' was not granted. The Government accepted the recommendations of the Herbert Committee for organisational change in the supply industry: the proposals were designed to remedy what the Committee saw as the most damaging effects of over-centralisation – a headquarters which was over-staffed and interfered too much – and to create an industry with a more forceful commercial outlook, paying greater attention to productivity.

The 1957 Electricity Act which followed therefore established two new statutory bodies in place of the CEA, the Electricity Council, which had few formal powers and a more or less advisory role for the whole of the supply industry in England and Wales, and the Central Electricity Generating Board (CEGB) which combined the duties of generation and transmission. At the same time the impulse to decentralisation gave the Area Boards greater financial responsibility.[35]

During the passage of the Bill through Parliament the Association, acting in concert with the other trade unions in the industry, was able to secure amendments to some clauses. The right of the Area Boards to generate was made conditional, and a suggestion that the strength of the Area Boards' representation on the Electricity Council should be counterbalanced was embodied in the Act, as were improvements to the compensation terms for employees adversely affected by the reorganisation. The Association remained however 'gravely disturbed by the increasingly detailed control of the industry by the Ministry', but it seemed that little could be done about that. The Association concluded that much would depend on who was appointed to head the two new bodies.[36]

It had been agreed that Citrine would retire and the Government appointed Sir Christopher Hinton, from the

UK Atomic Energy Authority, to head the CEGB, an appointment which reflected the importance attached to adherence to the nuclear power programme announced in 1955. At the Electricity Council, Sir Henry Self became a caretaker chairman while Ronald Edwards, Professor of Industrial Organisation at the London School of Economics, became his part-time deputy for a period to prepare him to succeed Self in the chair. The changes embodied in the 1957 Act were to take effect in January 1958 and it was therefore in the CEA's last year that a major confrontation between it and the EPEA took place.

The 1957 dispute speedily resolved

The course of pay negotiations since 1950 had not run particularly well for the Association. Not only did claims take a long time to negotiate but the Association usually ended up with less – sometimes considerably less – than the amount claimed. The events of 1952 were not untypical; in March of that year the EPEA asked for a 10% rise but the employers first prevaricated and then, in May, said they could not afford it. In July the EPEA again pressed the claim but when the employers side at the NJB proposed a 'breathing space' to help towards the national problem of spiralling wages and prices, the staff side agreed. In return they were thanked for their 'statesman-like behaviour'.[37] Eventually the claim was reiterated in November when increases were agreed. The Association's negotiators congratulated themselves but in fact the awards ranged from just under 3% to a maximum of 5%,: some members therefore got half of what had been demanded and many got less than a half. In 1954 a small cost of living increase was part of a package agreed which included some restructuring of the Schedules.

By 1955 the salaries of the technical staff were falling badly behind by any standard of comparison used. Differentials were being eroded as the manual workers secured larger rises and at the same time a constantly rising cost of living reduced the real value of incomes. One study suggests that differentials dropped from 26% to 22% between 1948 and 1956 and Professor Hannah has

indicated that over the same period top salaries in the
supply industry dropped by a third.[38] Aware not only of the
falling value of members' salaries but also of the increased
responsibilities of their jobs, with more to come in the
future, the Association submitted in 1955 a substantial
claim intended both to restore the technical staff to the
same percentage differential as existed in 1948 and to
provide for the upgrading of some designations whose
responsibilities had been increased by the application of
new technologies. The employers again prevaricated, but
after lengthy sessions in Negotiating Committee the
Association believed that it had persuaded most of the
members of the justice of its claim; but then the economic
situation worsened. In February 1957 Bank Rate was raised
to 5½% – then the highest since 1932 – and the Government pressed the nationalised industries to help to maintain a price plateau. The CEA responded with an
announcement of a freeze on electricity prices to last until
March 1957 and in the negotiations at the NJB offered only
small cost of living increases.

By January 1957 it seemed to the Association's negotiators pointless to attend any more meetings. On 9 February
therefore the General Purposes Committee decided on the
'strongest action' and on 11 February the Association sent
out copies of a statement setting out its case, *Penny wise –
Power foolish*. On 13 February work-to-rule instructions
were issued but by the evening of the following day frantic
activity on the part of Government and the CEA brought
the parties together at the Ministry of Labour. The work to
rule instructions were suspended and, after talks started at
the Ministry on 19 February it was quickly agreed that a
Board of Arbitration would be appointed and the work to
rule instructions were withdrawn.[39]

It was the first occasion on which the Association had
been driven to exercise its industrial muscle in the nationalised industry and there was considerable public support
for it. Many people felt, as the *Daily Telegraph* said, that the
engineers were responsible people: 'they must therefore
have been suffering under a great sense of grievance to
have taken so extreme a step.'[40] The *Daily Mail* put it more
picturesquely:

From the sash of complacent respectability an unsuspected
piratical cutlass was brandished aloft. And for twenty-four
hours it was delicately feathered against the nation's throat.[41]

It was a pattern that was to be repeated several times over
the next 15 years.

The Board of Arbitration hearings were held in April
and its findings – that salaries should be improved,
although the demand to return to the 1948 differentials
was not justified – were reflected in the new salary
Schedules agreed at a special meeting of the NJB at the
beginning of June. The new Schedules did to a large
extent restore the differential, at least for the time being.[42]
Apart from pay, which over the next few years moved to a
position at the centre of the stage and became an
increasingly contentious issue (see below), there were
many other matters with which the Association was
concerned.

Association membership grows with the industry

The years 1958 to 1962 have been labelled by Professor
Hannah as the boom years in the supply industry,
although to the outward eye the boom continued after
1962. In that year the first two Magnox nuclear power
stations were commissioned at Berkeley in Gloucestershire
and Bradwell in Essex. In 1964 the first Magnox station in
Scotland was commissioned at Hunterston and in the
following year Trawsfynydd, Hinkley Point and Dung-
eness were commissioned.[43] For the Association, nuclear
power and nuclear safety became issues of primary
concern, both in terms of servicing the interests of the
increasing number of members working in the nuclear
sector, and in terms of acquiring the expertise necessary
for dealing with this new sector of the industry. In 1964
the Government decided to change from the Magnox
stations to Advanced Gas Cooled Reactors (AGRs) for the
5,000MW of nuclear capacity it was planned to
commission between 1970 and 1975.[44] At Berkeley
Nuclear Research Laboratories were opened in 1961 and
the influx of technical staff there meant that a new EPEA

section was established. It was not only numbers that led to the establishment of new sections; at Leatherhead where the Central Electricity Research Laboratory (CERL) had been extended and upgraded in the wake of Herbert, the scientists felt their views were not adequately represented as part of a headquarters section and a separate CERL section was therefore set up.

In conventional power stations much larger units became common: in the late 1950s 14 power stations, including Kincardine in Scotland and Ballylumford in Northern Ireland, were equipped with standard 100/120MW sets before the CEGB started to instal the larger 275/300MW sets, for example at Blyth in Northumberland and West Thurrock, in Essex. In 1966 the first 500MW unit was commissioned at Ferrybridge. The significance of larger sets for the technical staff was considerable because a clause in the NJB Agreement provided for staff in stations 'of advanced design' to receive additional remuneration. As the industry grew so did the numbers of technical staff and Association membership increased commensurately.

In 1963 the Association celebrated its 50th birthday and reached the 20,000 membership mark, representing, it reckoned, almost 90% density. For many years the offices at St George's Square, occupied by the Association for more than 40 years, had been increasingly inadequate. A move had been contemplated immediately after the war but not implemented. In view of the escalating cost of office accommodation in London, in 1964 the EPEA moved out of London to new purpose built offices at Chertsey in Surrey. At that time reorganisation was on the agenda again; there was a growing number of members who argued that a structure established 50 years earlier, for a membership a quarter of its current size, operating in a simpler, smaller and more fragmented industry, was no longer either appropriate or democratic. The unwieldy nature of an NEC of more than 60 slowed down discussion. But once again conservatism prevailed and the changes made were minor.

There was one change which a decade later the Association came to regret. It was decided that the EPEA would no longer recruit industrial members. Although they had always been, in a sense, poor relations (and had paid a correspondingly lower subscription) there had been for many years a core of members working outside the supply industry for whom the Association had undertaken negotiations with individual employers and had won improved pay and conditions. The industrial members had a representative on the NEC and some of them, for example S Beeson, generation engineer at Boots in Nottingham, played an active role in their local sections. Before nationalisation, some industrial members had been represented on District Joint Boards but after 1948 that was no longer possible and, as the older members retired, there were other unions the younger electrical engineers in manufacturing industry could and did join. By 1964 the Association felt that it had not the time and resources to recruit more widely, especially as its membership in the supply industry appeared to be on an ever ascending curve.

There were innovations. In 1961 Arthur Palmer succeeded in introducing the first annual school, a scheme he had been nurturing for some time, which provided members with an opportunity to meet, learn about and discuss issues relevant to the industry and the Association. Much of the Association's educational work was now carried on through the advisory machinery, as the nationalised industry had, at Citrine's insistence, taken on responsibility for education and training to a greater extent than laid down in the 1947 Act. The EPEA's own educational initiative, the Correspondence Tuition Scheme (see p 118) had died quietly as changes in education and in the qualifying rules for IEE membership had made it inappropriate. The old conflict between professionalism and trade unionism was briefly resuscitated when the Association considered again whether a closed shop should be introduced. But after lengthy discussions it was decisively rejected in 1966; it was introduced for the manual workers in 1969.

But for a decade, while superficially the Association's life maintained an even tenor, and section and divisional meetings and social occasions such as dinner dances continued on an annual basis, one issue dominated all – pay negotiations.

The annual pay round and growing discontent

Pay negotiations from 1958 and through the 1960s took place against a background of national economic problems, particularly rising inflation, and in this situation governments of whatever hue increasingly turned to the industrial sectors where they had most influence to try to damp down salary and wage increases. In October 1957, the Prime Minister, Harold Macmillan, noted in a Cabinet memorandum to his colleagues that 'We should ... refuse to indicate in advance the attitude which we might adopt to hypothetical wage claims in industries over which we have some control, eg the nationalised industries'[45] and again in December that year he minuted: 'we have clearly reached the point where even a serious strike is more tolerable than a continuance of inflationary wage settlements ...arbitration can be a useful safety valve'.[46] Together these statements indicate the line of government thinking and policy which came to dominate as economic problems worsened in 1961 and 1962. As inflation increased the trade union response was to put in annual pay claims – hence the annual round as it became known. While the manual workers in the supply industry were among the front and successful runners in the round, the Association was less fortunate.

Although some progress was made in 1960 and 1961 towards a common salary scale instead of the four separate scales the actual increases gained were small. The same was true in 1962 when the Association claim was put in at the same time as the Government's pay pause was announced; the timing was unfortunate or inept. Thus although the salary ranges were widened the increase negotiated was only 3% and 'keen dissatisfaction' was voiced among members. It reached the NEC meeting, held in January 1963, by way of a motion from the South Western division, mild in tone but unusual, urging the NEC to explore all avenues as a matter of urgency which might lead to an improved salary award and 'greater satisfaction' among members.[47] In the debate that followed it was clear that it was primarily the younger members who were dissatisfied and that however useful in the long term the structural changes were, it had been expected and hoped that after lengthy negotiations the increases in the short-term would be more substantial. Nor had any link with productivity been achieved. The NEC was very evenly divided; the motion was carried with a margin of three votes, 33 to 30.[48]

In 1963 the award made in May was again small – 3½% – and at a section meeting in Glasgow the General Secretary gave his explanation of the 'low state to which national negotiations had been reduced'. The Association was faced, he said, 'with the challenge of continued outside interference in negotiations'.[49] And the attempt to link pay and productivity, which was being satisfactorily negotiated at the NJIC, had broken down at the NJB.

Between 1962 and 1965 negotiations at the NJIC resulted in the status agreement for the manual workers, a major development which involved changes in working and remuneration patterns. One of the major objectives of the employers was to reduce the amount of overtime and to that end earnings were consolidated into annual salaries. Improved holidays and pensions were part of the package which, in effect, gave to the manual workers all the benefits previously enjoyed only by white-collar workers. While the EPEA had no objection in principle to the extension of benefits, many members undoubtedly felt that they were owed some compensation, a feeling which contributed to the growing discontent.[50] In the course of introducing the status agreement, which was done in stages, there were considerable pay increases awarded to the manual workers. But when the EPEA put in its pay claim in 1964, intended in part to restore differentials, it was rejected. The Association therefore gave six months' notice of its intention to end the NJB agreement and warned that it would withdraw cooperation. Although the employers then made an offer, the Association considered it too little and too late and the claim went to arbitration.

At the same time the deterioration in relations between the technical staff and the employers was exacerbated by the latter's failure to make proposals on the issue of excess hours worked by EPEA members, an issue which had been raised 18 months previously and consistently deferred by the employers. Exasperated by the delays, in November 1964 the Association imposed a ban on overtime which was called off on 30 November when the employers reopened negotiations. In January 1965 the Association's pay claim was rejected by the Industrial Court which awarded the employers' smaller offer. The resumed NJB negotiations resulted in March 1965 in a settlement on the excess hours claim and revisions to the Agreement, which in return for allowing the Electricity Boards to instruct members to work abnormal hours involved a payment of £60. The notice to terminate the NJB Agreement was lifted by the Association.

The settlement was not well received among Association members and the correspondence columns of the *Electrical Power Engineer* were full of complaints that the EPEA had sold its members up and down the river.[51] There was among the technical staff, Harry Norton had noted in February 1965, 'a degree of unease varying from puzzled resentment to outright anger ... directed equally against the electricity boards and our own negotiators including myself.' He went on to say

> the ungenerous past policy of the electricity boards, the impression given to the technical staff that if they expect adequate rewards for increased cooperation and added burden they must fight for them; these are sufficient explanation for the growing militancy of the technical staff: but militancy of itself is not a policy.[52]

The negotiations had taken place against a background of national economic crisis. The Labour government which took office in the autumn of 1964 faced a balance of payments deficit and a sterling crisis; but although the National Board for Prices and Incomes was established in February 1965 and a $3\frac{1}{2}\%$ norm for pay rises suggested in March, pay restraint remained a voluntary matter and the $3\frac{1}{2}\%$ was largely ignored in 1965. The reluctance of the Association to implement militant action, despite the demand for it from many members, weakened its position in negotiations with the employers and created more discontent than ever before among members.

When in 1966 the Association produced and submitted to the NJB draft proposals for a new NJB agreement, many members were not pleased. 'Brutus' voiced their thoughts in a letter to the journal in October that year:

> I was angered not so much by the contents of this draft agreement but by the fact that it had been prepared and then submitted without first reference to the rank and file of the Association. I am only a member of a few years standing but have come to the conclusion that the Association is far from democratic and that the NEC does not represent the views of the members.[53]

It was the fusion of the resentment and anger at the Association's failure to achieve better pay increases with the growing conviction that the views of the rank and file members were not being represented by the NEC and the permanent officials that forced radical change on the Association.

Notes

1. Hannah, *op cit*, p 280.
2. *EPE*, June 1948.
3. *EPE*, March 1950.
4. *EPE*, April 1949.
5. *EPE*, August 1950.
6. D Seers, *The Levelling of Incomes since 1938,* Oxford University Press 1951; P Wilsher, *The Pound in Your Pocket 1870–1970,* Cassell & Co 1970.
7. *EPE*, February 1948.
8. *EPE*, August 1950.
9. *Ibid*.
10. *EPE*, October and December 1950.
11. Reported to the EPEA General Purposes Committee August 1949.
12. *EPE*, April 1950. Hannah, *op cit*, pp 124–5.
13. *EPE*, February 1952.
14. Hannah, *op cit*, p 124.
15. *EPE*, February 1952.
16. Hannah, *op cit*, p 125.
17. *EPE*, January 1947.
18. *EPE*, March 1949.
19. *Ibid*.

20. See *EPE*, 1952–68; Hannah, *op cit*, p 127.
21. M Shanks (ed), *The Lessons of Public Enterprise*, Jonathan Cape 1963, p 117.
22. I am grateful to H Page for his help here.
23. *EPE*, January 1949.
24. *EPE*, January 1953.
25. *Ibid*.
26. *EPE*, February 1953.
27. *EPE*, January 1953.
28. *EPE*, March 1953.
29. *Electricity. A Chronology*, *op cit*.
30. Hannah, *op cit*, p 161–3.
31. *Ibid*.
32. EPEA Evidence to the Herbert Committee.
33. *Ibid*.
34. Hannah, *op cit*, p 197.
35. *Ibid*.
36. *EPE*, April 1957.
37. *EPE*, August 1952.
38. Hannah, *op cit*, pp 185, 309.
39. *EPE*, March 1957.
40. *Ibid*.
41. *Ibid*.
42. Hannah, *op cit*, p 309; Proceedings of the Board of Arbitration, April 1957.
43. *Electricity. A Chronology*, *op cit*.
44. *Ibid*.
45. Public Records Office (PRO) Cabinet Minutes (CAB) 129/264.
46. PRO CAB 129/288.
47. NEC Minutes, January 1963.
48. *Ibid*.
49. *EPE*, May 1963.
50. Hannah, *op cit*; Sir R Edwards, *An Experiment in Industrial Relations*, Electricity Council, 1965.
51. *EPE*, 1965.
52. *EPE*, February 1965.
53. *EPE*, October 1966.

Chapter 9

From Reform Towards Recession

'Our strength must lie in a competent and determined leadership and solidarity among the members. The time has come to stand up and be counted and to demonstrate that the EPEA is no longer a paper tiger but is now a trade union that demands respect and justice for its members.'
Paul Thompson, *Electrical Power Engineer*, January 1974.

Dominated by accelerating inflation which was exacerbated by the massive rises in the price of oil imposed by OPEC, the 1970s saw the end of the long post-war boom. In the electricity supply industry the change was marked; whereas between 1960 and 1969 costs went up by 7% and prices by 28%, giving the industry a comfortable surplus, between 1969 and 1974 costs, in money terms, rose by 118% and prices by 57% taking the industry into deficit.[1] There was also mounting public criticism of the industry, of the CEGB for its monolithic structure and of the Electricity Council for its weakness; but after the Labour government's reorganisation Bill of 1970 lapsed when a General Election was called, successive governments were unable or unwilling to implement reorganisation. There was too, for the first time, discussion of 'hiving off' parts of the supply industry, in particular, Area Board showrooms, regarded in the industry as 'the thin end of a sinister wedge'.[2]

For the trade unions, too, the 1970s was a period of change: a decade characterised by exceptional growth of union membership started in 1969, the year in which Barbara Castle's proposals for legislation to reform trade union law were published as the White Paper, *In place of*

185

strife. But opposition from the TUC and the pressure it brought to bear on Labour MPs and Cabinet members forced the Government to abandon the attempt to legislate.

The General Election of June 1970 returned the Conservatives under Edward Heath, determined to legislate for trade union reform to reduce strikes. The Industrial Relations Act of 1971 established for the first time a state register of trade unions and the Industrial Relations Court. When the Labour Party was returned to power in 1974, the 1971 Act was repealed and replaced with the less draconian legislation of 1974 and 1975. Against this background the EPEA in the early 1970s was divided as it had never been before by the emergence and activities of a group of members demanding militant action on pay and reform of the Association's own organisation.

The Reform Movement

Over the 1960s the differentials in pay between the NJB and the NJIC rates were whittled away. In successive annual round negotiations the NJB settlement was made at something slightly under 1% less than the NJIC awards; while in each individual year the lower offer seemed unlikely to create a demand among EPEA members for militant action, compounded over eight or nine years the effect was substantial. Each year's negotiations were bedevilled by the increasingly complex nature of the Schedule to which, as power stations had grown larger in the years of expansion, new classes had simply been added. The effect had been to create a complicated classification system no longer appropriate to the structure of the industry. A situation rapidly becoming intolerable within the industry was made worse by rising inflation which, between 1968 and 1970, was running at nearly 6% a year. The discontent crystallised in 1970-71 during the lengthy negotiations to agree a new Schedule which the Association had initiated in 1966. An examination of the major stages in those negotiations indicates some of the problems of both sides.

The EPEA was unfortunate – and perhaps inept – in launching its proposals for a new Schedule in 1966 so that they coincided with the announcement by the Government of a 6-month wage freeze; in these circumstances the proposals were rejected outright by the employers. The freeze and the subsequent 6-month 'standstill' were followed by a period in which increases in wages and salaries were permitted but only if linked to productivity. The Electricity Boards with the co-operation of the EPEA brought in consultants Urwick Orr to 'evaluate' the jobs of the technical staff: the Association felt that the alternative to cooperation was exclusion – the Boards were in any case determined on the exercise.[3] But even while the job evaluation exercise was in progress the involvement of the technical staff in the NJIC productivity schemes was providing a fresh source of discontent. EPEA members found themselves obliged to supervise and be instrumental in the installation of schemes which, they could clearly see, resulted in a further whittling away of their differentials. Failure to agree any recompense for this with the employers led to a dispute: a work to rule by members significantly affected the operation of the supply system and the appointment of a Court of Enquiry under Professor A D Campbell quickly followed. In 1970, the Report of the Enquiry awarded some interim payments to those directly involved in productivity schemes and advised that ad hoc payments should be made, at the employers' discretion, to those involved in preparing productivity schemes. The Report recommended, however, that the only long term solution to the problem was a new salary Schedule.[4]

In the negotiations, which were resumed after Campbell reported, to work out a new Schedule based on the results of the job evaluation, the employers dragged their heels in fixing salaries to grades, delaying any settlement. Although the then Conservative government had initiated an undeclared policy of diminishing levels of pay settlements in the public sector, they were forced, when the EPEA threatened industrial action in the autumn, to urge the supply industry employers to come to a settlement. When the NEC met to consider the proposals

in London in May 1971 it found large crowds of angry
members outside the Bonnington Hotel, anxious to make
clear to their officials that they did not regard the new
Schedule proposals as satisfactory.

Coachloads of members from all over the country
assembled on both 15 May and 23 May when the NEC
met. Estimates vary widely – from 300 to 1500 – as to the
numbers at the second demonstration but, after making
their feelings plain outside the Bonnington Hotel, the
demonstrators 'marched with banners flying to Coram
Fields for a meeting'.[5] Unprecedented as such events were
in the Association, they were by no means unusual at a
time when trade union unrest was frequently demonstrated in the streets of London. When EPEA officials
apologised to the manager of the Bonnington for the
commotion, he replied that his American visitors were
delighted to be able to see a 'British type demo' from the
safety and comfort of their bedroom windows![6] Section
meetings held in the following months however showed
that those members who had travelled to London spoke
for many more.[7] The NEC itself was divided and, after a
long and heated debate, referred back the new Schedule
recommended by the staff side of the NJB as the best
obtainable at that time. After further negotiations which
produced no major changes, the new Schedule was agreed
in November 1971.

But the discontent which erupted into public demon-
strations in May 1971 was already being organised and
channelled into more constructive action. In October 1970
two members of the technical staff at Hinkley Point power
station, P Thompson and D Baker, suggested the
formation of a pressure group to their own West of
England section. There were, they noted, both short and
long term objectives for which such a pressure group
should work. The basic aims, to be achieved over the next
three years, were a 50% increase in all salary levels, a 35
hour working week with five weeks annual holiday, and
retirement at 60 with adequate financial arrangements. In
the longer term, the pressure group's objectives were to
replace the existing EPEA organisation with a simplified
structure in which a team of professional full-time officials

negotiated directly with the employers and there was much closer contact between the rank and file members and the full-time officials. They should also be working to obtain greater EPEA participation in management decisions.[8] Within a month the West of England section accepted the memorandum of proposals: the only change made was that instead of the specific 50% increase, there was a more general stipulation that there should be a substantial increase to achieve parity with other professions. Paul Thompson's own calculations showed that at least 45% was needed to bring power station engineers on a par with other professional earnings.[9] In the section committee elections in the autumn of 1970 the pressure group fielded five candidates in the West of England of whom four were successful.

It was soon clear to the organisers that their initiative was generating support further afield and a meeting held in Bristol in June 1971 agreed to form a national committee for the Reform Movement, as the pressure group was now called. Reflecting the Association's own organisation, divisional coordinators were appointed for five of the EPEA's eight divisions: those who held aloof were the Irish, the Scottish and the managerial divisions. As the Reform Movement issued its national manifesto in the autumn of 1971, it was able to point to the effect of the revised Schedule in creating 'a divided and disillusioned Association' as an example of the failure it intended to remedy.[10] No doubt the introduction of the Schedule played a part in the success of the Reform Movement candidates who stood in the section elections that month. Of the 113 known supporters and sympathisers who stood in 24 sections, 99 were elected – an 87% success rate described by the Reform Movement itself as a 'remarkable achievement'.[11]

A time for change

The rapid growth and success of the Reform Movement could not be ignored at Chertsey; this time it was clear the discontent was not going to dissipate and, as for the most part the members of the Reform Movement had carefully

acted constitutionally, no penalties could be imposed upon
them. It was an extremely difficult period as it became
increasingly clear that, along with the reorganisation of
the Association, the Reform Movement wanted a change
of General Secretary. Indeed a meeting was called at
Norwich in July 1971 specifically to debate the early
retirement of the General Secretary. At the Movement's
national meeting held at Lichfield on 5 March 1972 'the
Reform Movement activists combined with the existing
progressive members on the NEC to dominate the 1972
NEC'.[12] This alliance secured the election of the
Vice-President, R Blackburn, as President rather than the
President-elect as anticipated, and set the seal on the
Reform Movement's success.

As the *Electrical Power Engineer*'s editorial noted

> At the Spring meeting of the National Executive Council one
> EPEA era ended and another began. The results of the
> elections to leading honorary positions were amongst the
> most surprising in the history of our union.

Putting the event in perspective the editorial continued

> The fact is that Mr Kitteridge [the defeated Presidential
> candidate] and other excellent colleagues suffered the
> penalty of defeat mainly because they were associated with a
> salary settlement – whatever its justification – which active
> members with a capacity for organisation cordially disliked.
> Also there was a widespread opinion that long promised
> reforms in Association methods and procedures were taking
> much too long to bring about; even the EPEA cannot escape
> the restless spirit of the times.[13]

The new NEC's Presidential team were all sympathisers
of the Reform Movement (G Fisher, President-elect, had
been the Reform Movement's organiser in the North East;
M Greenbat and J Merriman, the Vice-Presidents, were
also members); it was clear to the Association that change
was imminent.

It was agreed in 1972 that Harry Norton would retire at
the end of the year as General Secretary. For the first time
ever the Association looked outside its own ranks for a
General Secretary, advertising the post publicly. The

appointment of John Lyons, then Deputy General Secretary of the Institution of Professional Civil Servants (IPCS), brought into the EPEA as General Secretary a man who, after completing his education at Cambridge, had started his trade union career as a research officer with the then Post Office Engineering Union. At the IPCS he had been involved for over 15 years in negotiating pay and conditions of service for its members, developing the skills and expertise which the Association so badly needed in the crisis it faced in the early 1970s.

John Lyons was to take up the appointment at the beginning of 1973, but illness forced Harry Norton's departure earlier than anticipated and for some months George Millett had to act administratively as General Secretary. Leadership of the Association during this interim period in practice fell on the President, R Blackburn who faced an extraordinarily difficult Presidential year in which he not only had to act as President and General Secretary but in that role try to secure unity between reformers and anti-reformers.

Harry Norton's illness proved to be terminal and he died in the autumn of 1976. In his early years with the Association he had been noted for his successful negotiating skills, and for many EPEA members it was a matter of regret that his last years as General Secretary were marked by division and discord. For those who had spent their formative years in the belief that a 'special relationship' existed in the supply industry between the Boards and the technical staff, it was not easy to see that the relationship had changed as too had the demands of members of the Association. In pre-war days EPEA members had been content with the promise of jam tomorrow, if they felt their skills and expertise were being recognised by status. But as Harry Norton himself had noted, pay *is* status, and the new generation of technical staff who joined the industry in the 1960s were no longer prepared to accept the promise of jam tomorrow, along with thanks for good behaviour and the exercise of restraint in the meantime.

In July 1972 a task group was formed to review the Association's structure and to consider what changes were needed but the immediate priority was to put in hand the demands for improved pay.

New militancy produces results

The urgent need for action on pay was highlighted early in 1972 when the NEC noted that restoration of the 1962 level of purchasing power alone now required an award approaching 39%; inflation rose to 8.6% a year between 1970 and 1973.[14] Nor was that the only problem. Reorganisation of the CEGB Headquarters, which had started the previous year, had created a need for the restructuring of the NJB Schedule for headquarters staff; and for all technical staff there was an outstanding claim for out of hours working. The leader in the *Electrical Power Engineer* in June 1972 noted:

> Let us hope that the new more resolute temper of the technical staff will be noted by the electricity boards. The feeling has been growing that some managements look on the EPEA as a 'paper tiger'; great in roar, small in deeds.[15]

It was therefore a sign of the times, when, as a result of the breakdown of negotiations on the Headquarters Schedule, the Association called a one day stoppage on 26 October 1972 of headquarters staff, not only at the CEGB but also at the Electricity Council and the Area Boards. The 94% turnout rate was considered a great success and although there had been fears of the effect on less militant members, in the event the Association had 500 applications from technical staff wishing to join to more than balance the 35 resignations.[16] Despite this however the grievances felt about the Headquarters Schedule were not fully redressed at that time and on its other claims the Association found itself caught up in the Heath government's attempts to control increases in wages and salaries. The introduction of the Programme for Controlling Inflation in November 1972 started with the by now familiar freeze, which was to last until March 1973. Stage II of the programme, from April to November 1973, allowed increases of £1 a week plus 4% and Stage III, introduced in November 1973, established the Pay Board to monitor the rises allowed of 7% basic plus threshhold agreements related to rises in the Retail Price Index.[17] In this context the increases the EPEA gained in the NJB and NJMC in annual round negotiations in 1973 extracted everything possible out of the formula of Stage II, including a restructuring of the salary tables which shortened the incremental scales and improved holiday allowances.

Association morale was boosted and, following a successful membership ballot, on 1 November 1973, after giving a month's notice, the Association started a ban on out-of-hours work in support of the claim for increased pay for out-of-hours work. The claim had been outstanding for a long time and a possible earlier settlement had been prevented by the introduction of the pay policy. With Stage III still in force the Association's action specifically challenged the Government's authority: it also coincided with a ban on overtime by the National Union of Mineworkers. For eight weeks the action was carefully orchestrated from Chertsey to secure maximum impact. Early in January, with escalation of the action threatened failing agreement, the battle was won. With the acquiescence of the Pay Board the Stage III pay code was interpreted generously to enable a settlement to be made. There was considerable public sympathy for the Association's members as their case became known; even the *Daily Telegraph* conceded that although the agreement stretched Stage III 'to its furthest limits, ... in this case a bit of stretching is not unjustified.'[18] A further result of the industrial action and the settlement was the ultimate resolution of the problem of out-of-hours working, a bone of contention for so many years, in the major out-of-hours agreement signed in 1978.

The success was followed by negotiations on a far reaching pay and structure claim at the NJB culminating in a final session lasting 12 hours on 28 February 1974, the day that the Heath Government, faced with the threat of further industrial action by the miners announced a General Election. The agreement reached was a complex one, entailing both improvements in pay to the maximum likely to be sanctioned by the Pay Board (although in the event following the return of the Labour Party to power the Board was abolished) and making structural changes in the Schedules intended to improve the career structures and prospects offered in the supply industry. It was not until the autumn that agreement to assimilate power station staffs into the new NJB Schedule was reached, although it was to be effective from the same date, 1 February 1974, as for other NJB posts.[19] The 1974 settlement embodied the most radical and far-reaching changes made for EPEA members for more than fifty years; in fact the agreement represented the greatest change since the Stoker Award and the first NJB Schedule of 1920. In place of the 17 separate grades and scales the agreement introduced a common six grade structure with six scales. By integrating all Headquarters posts into the new structure the agreement resolved the vexed question of Headquarters staff being paid on column X of the old Schedule by its abolition. The Trained Engineer Agreement established a career path for suitably trained engineers to the second engineer grade. And, of fundamental importance to the Association's future pay strategy, the 1974 Agreement established for the first time (if not irrevocably as far as the employers were concerned – see p 204) a specific pay link between NJB and NJIC salary Schedules.

With the settlement went an agreement to introduce a system of job evaluation to decide the grading of posts in the new structure. While many members had unhappy memories of the Urwick Orr exercise (see p 187), the fundamental and different concept behind this agreement was that the job evaluation scheme to be introduced was to be a *joint* system; equal involvement of both sides of the NJB meant the end of the old method when management decisions on grading were then followed by Association appeals. The scheme took a long time to work out and implement; introduced in 1981, some 28,000 NJB posts have been evaluated and the initial implementation phase with its appeal mechanism will be completed in 1989[20] (see also Chapter 10). In the following year the pay agreement reached at the end of May – overnight on 24 May – gave an average increase of more than 30% on NJB salaries.

While there were, as ever, some who did not like the new militancy of the Association, for most EPEA members the effect of the successful industrial action of 1973 and the unprecedented settlements of 1974 and 1975 not only improved considerably their financial position but also was morale boosting of the kind that was most needed. In a speech made at Birmingham in June 1973 John Lyons gave his first impressions of the EPEA.

I find an Association of engineers, scientists, many other specialists and managers ... with a prevailing sense of grievance, even bitterness and intensively distrustful of their higher management.[21]

This was, he recognised, the product of the previous five years, but the pattern of improving pay and the flexing of industrial muscle contributed to a change in the mood of the Association and the increase in membership which also took place.

The ADC becomes the supreme governing body

The revision of the Association's constitution to provide the more flexible, responsive and professional organisation demanded by the Reform Movement could not be achieved overnight. But the changes initiated and implemented in 1973 and 1974 went far enough for the Movement to decide to suspend itself indefinitely in 1974.[22] The Association's complex structure of committees which had accounted for some of the delays in the past – most issues were discussed at least three times – was simplified; the most important change was the introduction of the annual delegate conference and the transfer to it, from the old NEC, of the responsibility for policy-making. As Arthur Palmer noted in the *Electrical Power Engineer*,

An annual conference was first advocated in the pages of the *Electrical Power Engineer* roughly 27 years ago. [In fact it was mooted some years before that.] No one can complain that reform is an over-hasty process within the EPEA.[23]

At the same time the new National Executive Committee was to be a smaller body, meeting regularly and concerned with carrying out the policy as laid down at annual conference. The proposals for these structural changes were approved by the old NEC in November 1973 and in the course of 1974 the necessary changes made to the rules so that the new structure and constitution could come into effect at the beginning of 1975. The inaugural ADC was therefore held in April 1975.

Addressed by Eric Varley, the Secretary of State for Energy, Len Murray, the General Secretary of the TUC and Sir Arthur Hawkins, the Chairman of the CEGB, (who drew attention to the fact that he was a long standing and paid up member of the EPEA), the first ADC established its precedents and what were hoped would become its traditions. Delegates were all elected directly or indirectly by the sections, thus giving the rank and file member more direct access to the policy-making body than under the old system of elections to the National Executive Council.

The retiring President, M Greenbat, pointed out the contrast between the old and the new systems:

> The ADC takes over from the old NEC the function of Supreme Governing Body of the Association. As such it will determine the policy of the Association – its Rules and its rates of subscription. It will also adopt or otherwise the statement of accounts form and the report of the National Executive Committee. It is the latter body not the ADC itself which is charged with the execution of Association policy. That is just as well since in my view the old NEC palpably failed in its executive role as a consequence of its size and its infrequency of meetings. But, that is not to say that it did not try. As it hopelessly contrived to regulate the activities of its General Purposes Committee and the separately appointed National Joint Board staff side its debates produced at times an exciting atmosphere of cut and thrust that will be remembered by many. For me the unending efforts of the floor to upend the chairman which occupied so much of its time, is a matter of nostalgia rather than regret.[24]

He went on to draw attention to the increased number

of permanent officials at Chertsey; in response to the membership's demand for greater professionalism, and following the appointment of John Lyons, a Research Department had been set up in 1973 and Simon Petch (later EPEA Deputy General Secretary and now General Secretary of the Society of Telecom Executives) was recruited to head it. New Area Secretaries were appointed, including Harry Page (a former President) who later became a National Officer and an acknowledged authority on safety in the industry and R Blackburn, who had just completed his term of office as President. (The new officials joined the then existing cadre of Area Secretaries amongst whom Sid Alger and Harry Brocklesby (both past Presidents), Sam Wallace and Bob Score were already widely known to the members.) From outside the industry Dennis Bound was recruited. He was later to become Secretary of the NJB Staff Side, in succession to John Lyons, and then the Association's deputy General Secretary.

Revising the Managerial Machinery

Some Association members had never been happy with the managerial grades as fellow-members; the hostility went a long way back (see page 164) and in 1972 there were discussions with the EETPU about a possible transfer. But on the advice of the new General Secretary, these were abandoned and the EPEA turned its attention to the problems in the managerial machinery. Each of the three Associations had three representatives and, early in 1973 at the NJMC meeting to discuss the annual round claim, the EPEA was outvoted by the AMEE and NALGO acting in concert. It was for the EPEA an

> intolerable position whereby the union which represented the majority of the managerial staff in the industry only had one third of the staff side seats on the negotiating body.[25]

The Association therefore gave a year's notice in June 1973 of its intention to withdraw from the machinery as constituted. In the discussions that followed, a merger with the AMEE was considered by both sides (as it had been in the previous decade) but once again it proved impossible for the much smaller AMEE to agree to join ranks with the major managerial union in the industry. (A few years later AMEE decided to throw in its lot with the EETPU, which had not, until then, represented any managers.) The Electricity Council referred the matter to ACAS who after investigation recommended that in order to represent the respective strengths in the industry more fairly the EPEA should have six seats, and the AMEE and NALGO two each. This solution proved acceptable and came into effect at the beginning of 1976, enabling the Association to take the lead in negotiating better terms and conditions for the 1700 jobs covered by the NJM.[26] In the wake of this relations between NJB and NJM members improved and the latter moved to greater participation in EPEA affairs.

Northern Ireland – keeping the lights on

The Association's members in Northern Ireland faced a difficult time in the 1970s as sectarian strife and urban terrorism increased in the province. In 1973 attempts to agree a system of government to replace direct rule from Westminster, imposed the previous year, were accompanied by bombing and indiscriminate murders fuelled by sectarian hatred. In May 1974, to demonstrate their opposition to power-sharing, the Ulster Workers' Council called a national strike, to include electricity workers, in the hope and with the intention of shutting down the Northern Ireland electricity system. Against tremendous hostility, EPEA members kept the system going through the strike, an undertaking they were prepared to carry out as long as troops were not brought in to run the power stations, as the General Secretary had advised the Prime Minister. Later the same year an unofficial dispute between the employers and the NJIC workers in Northern Ireland led to the withdrawal of the manual workers and staff.

The problems of the province continued and in the spring of 1977 Ian Paisley, on behalf of the Ulster Unionist Action Council (UUAC) made a call for a general strike on the issue of government security policy in the province. Ballylumford Power Station, which supplied 60% of the province's electricity, became the focus of intense political and public pressure. Working with the NJIC staff, Association members insisted that all who worked at the power station should participate in the decision whether to strike or not. The result of a secret ballot was a decisive and substantial majority against joining the strike, a decision which undoubtedly played a key part in the collapse of the UUAC's attempt to impose its authority by a general strike.

The Association and the TUC

The Association and its General Secretary were not oblivious to the wider trade union world. Although the Association had, since it affiliated to the TUC, always sent a delegation to the Annual Conference, its participation in TUC affairs had been minimal. John Lyons adopted a more active role in representing the Association at the TUC. At the 1975 conference he vigorously attacked the lack of democracy in the decision made by the General Council, without further consultation, to endorse the extension of the social contract with the Labour government. This decision involved the imposition of a £6 a week ceiling for pay rises for the duration of a year. In the following year there were further consultations by the General Council of the TUC before it agreed Phase 11 of the Government's anti-inflation policy.[27]

It was felt by some members – although only a few with regret – that from 1973 onwards the Association became more of a trade union and less an association. For many, this was symbolised by the Association's decision in 1973 to withdraw its registration under the Industrial Relations Act of 1971. This had required trade unions to register, but as part of its opposition to the Act in the first instance, the TUC advised its affiliated members not to register. However, in 1971 the EPEA's NEC, fearing that it might find itself in a 'no-man's land', had decided that it would register – with one NEC member only, D Laing, a supporter of the Reform Movement, opposing the decision.[28] As the TUC's opposition hardened it had threatened to expel 32 unions for registering (in the event it actually expelled 20 of them);[29] and in June 1973, after an extensive debate, the NEC decided (by 53 votes to 11) to deregister.[30] In fact the Association, preoccupied with its own turbulent affairs at the time, had played no part in the furore which had followed the 1971 Act and the issue of registration died away when the Act was repealed by the Labour government which was returned to power in the 1974 election.

There was also the recurring problem of whether the supply industry should be reorganised. Although there had been reorganisation of the CEGB in 1971, following criticism of its failure to keep to cost estimates on major capital projects, the industry's move into deficit in 1974-5 again raised questions about its efficiency. Fierce competition from the gas industry, with its supplies of North Sea gas, compounded the problems and in the winter of 1975-6 the industry, for the first time since before the war, had spare capacity – a margin of 42%.[31] At the Association's first ADC Arthur Hawkins had told members, 'The short term outlook for the future is bleak. The accent for the next few years will be on retrenchment not expansion.'[32] It was in these circumstances that the Government asked Lord Plowden to head a committee to enquire into the structure of the supply industry. The Association's evidence to Plowden came down in favour of the establishment of a strong central authority, with the existing Generating Board continuing with responsibility for generation and transmission, but with the setting up of a new Central Electricity Distribution Board to counter-balance it, which would take over the statutory authority of the Area Boards.[33] In fact when Plowden reported in 1976 its major recommendation was that the supply industry in England and Wales should be unified, with a single statutory board taking over the responsibilities of the CEGB, the Electricity Council and the Area Boards.[34] As the then Secretary of State for Energy, Tony Benn's response was to announce that a period of discussion would encourage all views about the shape of the industry to be canvassed, but major differences between the Minister on the one hand and the unions and management on the other delayed the drafting of the Bill. When it was introduced in 1978 it failed to gain support from the Liberal party which at this stage in the declining fortunes of the government was crucial for the passage of any legislation. By the time the Conservatives came to power in 1979, the CEGB chairman no longer supported the Plowden recommendations and the Area Board chairmen were divided.

A wider federation of professional engineers

In the mid-1970s, as trade union membership grew, engineers outside the supply industry began to look for an organisation which could take on a protective function for them. Many of them found the non-political stance of the EPEA attractive, in contrast to the more partisan position taken by TASS and ASTMS, and approached the Association to see whether it could extend its membership. There were, it was estimated, 200,000 engineers working in manufacturing industry, of whom less than 10,000 were members of an effective trade union. The issue of whether the EPEA should embark on wider recruitment came before the 1976 ADC. At the outset the General Secretary told the conference that there was only one way in which the Association could proceed if conference chose to recruit members in industry: the provision of a federal structure so that the EPEA would not find itself submerged, losing its identity and ultimately being a minority in a large organisation over which it had no control.

There was considerable hostility to the idea and to the members of the NEC who appeared to support it. George Fisher (President in 1973-74, a man whose 'boldness, gritty determination and common sense adaptability' had sustained him in the Presidency at a time when the 'tide of events [was] sweeping [the Association] inexorably onwards to a head-on collision with everyone in sight in the negotiating field'[35]) was driven to deploring the way in which speakers described the NEC as 'a bunch of schemers who are out to hoodwink you at every opportunity'.[36]

Some members complained that they had not had
sufficient time to consider the matter (the motion had
been in circulation for three months) and some were
worried about the expense involved. Two speeches, both
from managerial members, carried the day. M P Ault from
the Midlands argued strongly for wider recruitment:

> We are small fish but we are in the TUC and we have some
> influence in the TUC and it is up to us to try to strengthen
> that influence as much as we can...If we neglect the
> opportunity to recruit professional engineers, technical and
> managerial staff from outside our particular sphere ... they
> will organise themselves outside the TUC and as such they
> will produce an antagonistic situation and we as professional
> people will be identified with them and the TUC will not
> shout for us. Our influence must be stronger if we are to
> represent a very substantial body of professional people in
> this country.
>
> Whatever we do today we cannot stand still. If we reject this
> motion the influence of the EPEA will diminish. If we support
> the motion, which I believe we should, we shall strengthen the
> influence of the EPEA...Our job is to lead the membership,
> not necessarily to reflect a gut feeling that is not rationalised
> in any way. Courage is needed.[37]

On the same lines J Newell argued:

> We now find ourselves in the position of being one relatively
> strong association amongst a very weak outside structure. We
> have the opportunity of being the leaders in setting up such a
> federal structure. Let us be realistic about what is going to
> happen if we don't. We are going to see more dithering, more
> weakness, and before long a number of other little petty
> organisations will flounder and the engineers will find
> themselves in essentially non-professional unions, as a
> minority in unions committed to the removal or at least
> minimisation of differentials.[38]

In a card vote conference voted by a majority of nearly
5,000 to embark on wider recruitment.

The Association's interest in engineers outside the
supply industry was not confined to the issue of wider
recruitment. The Association was increasingly aware of
the shortage of engineers in Britain and that 'Neither in

industry nor in society is the qualified engineer recognised for what he is – the single most important figure in the development of modern technology based industry'.[39] Accordingly it pressed for a Committee of Inquiry into the supply and use of qualified engineering manpower; after its first proposal in 1975, the Association was able to carry a resolution at the TUC urging the appointment of such an inquiry in 1976. Subsequently the Association's activities were instrumental in the appointment of the Finniston committee (see Chapter 10).

But there were still many in the Association who doubted the wisdom of its expansion and feared that the deployment of its resources and energies to wider recruitment would damage its ability to carry on its essential functions in the supply industry for its existing membership. Many of these doubts and fears were expressed at the special conference which met in November 1976 to consider the NEC's report on creating a new organisation to handle wider recruitment. It was a stormy meeting but at the end 23,504 voted for the NEC's report and only 7,352 against.[40] The launch of the Engineers and Managers Association as a federal body followed at the ADC held at York in 1977.

Pay negotiations 1976-79

As inflation accelerated in the mid 1970s (to 16% in 1974 and 24% in 1975) some of the ground gained in the early years of the decade was lost. The Association's calculations in January 1977 showed that, assuming a 15% rate of inflation in the coming year, as predicted, by the beginning of 1978 members would be suffering a reduction in living standards varying from 25% to 36% since February 1975.[41] Indeed when inflation was running at 25%, the Association – with overwhelming membership support – specifically supported the TUC in accepting the restrictive pay limitations of 1976 and 1977, which had undermined the value of the differential pay relationship established in the 1974 and 1975 settlements. But, with the virtual collapse of the Labour government's attempts to control incomes, the EPEA was able to set about recovering some of the position for members in the 1978 annual pay round negotiations.

In the course of those negotiations, however, the Association was disturbed to find that the Electricity Boards' members at the NJB sought to take advantage of the Association's goodwill over the previous two years, arguing that relationships between NJB and NJIC scales had changed over the last few years and the relativities which the EPEA thought had been established by the NJB/NJIC pay link in 1974-75 were no longer appropriate. The Association pointed out that its members had 'deliberately and voluntarily allowed erosion of those differentials, to help deal with the country's inflationary problems, but this had always been without prejudice to their basic position'.[42] It was not until the following year's negotiations that, after a breakdown of the talks and a threat of EPEA industrial action, an interim settlement based on restoration of the 1974-5 link was reached. Further sanction of the link came at the end of 1979 when outstanding differences went to arbitration. The arbitration award noted 'we could see no reason of substance why this relationship should not be restored ... we are convinced that this relationship should be continued'.[43] A similar pay link was also established between NJB and NJMC salary Schedules, although in the case of managerial salaries an unwelcome ceiling was provided by the salaries of Area Board chairmen and deputy chairmen. These were, it was widely believed, partly restrained by government pressure, and the 1979 Arbitration Award noted, on the basis of evidence presented to it, that the Boyle review of top salaries had treated 'the electricity industry less than fairly'.[44]

The EPEA's success in 1978-79, at a time when the industry was facing increasingly difficult conditions, is indicative of the strength and professionalism it had developed since 1973. Its General Secretary had defined its position then:

'As an Association we have developed a markedly defensive attitude of mind, which seems to have been based on the belief that the Association was helpless before the wiles and stratagems of the management, and that the only way we could look after ourselves was by a policy of near total immobility.'[45]

By 1979 that was no longer the case and at the start of the new decade the Association was better equipped to meet the challenges of the 1980s than it had been when facing the 1970s.

Notes

1. Hannah, *op cit*, p 282.
2. Information from H Page.
3. Presidential Statement (J Forrester), NEC June 1971.
4. Campbell Report, Cmnd 4410 July 1970.
5. Letters from G Darby to Editor, *EPE*, 9 January 1989, and from H Page, 26.1.89.
6. *Ibid*.
7. *EPE*, 1971 Reports of section meetings.
8. Memorandum, 1 October 1970. I am grateful to Paul Thompson for the loan of papers connected with the Reform Movement as well as information. Other Association members involved to a greater or lesser extent in the RM have helped greatly by talking about it.
9. Reform Movement file – Paul Thompson.
10. Reform Movement Manifesto, September 1971.
11. Reform Movement Newsletter, February 1972.
12. P Thompson; letter to author 27 June 1987.
13. *EPE*, May/June 1972.
14. NEC Minutes, January 1972.
15. *EPE*, June 1972.
16. NEC Minutes, November 1972.
17. R J Davies, 'Incomes and Anti-Inflation Policy', in *Industrial Relations in Britain*, G S Bain (ed), Blackwell 1983, p 454.
18. *Daily Telegraph*, 29 December 1973, quoted in *EPE*, Jan 1974.
19. *EPE*, March 1974, November 1974.
20. EPEA Archives, TR/74-16. *EPE*, May 1974.
21. *EPE*, June 1973.
22. *EPE*, October 1974.
23. *EPE*, September 1973.
24. *EPE*, May 1975.
25. NEC Minutes, March 1973.
26. ACAS Report Number 4, December 1975.
27. TUC Conference Reports. See also R Taylor, *The Fifth Estate*, Routledge and Kegan Paul 1978, p 39.
28. NEC Minutes, November 1971.
29. H Clegg, *The Changing System of Industrial Relations in Great Britain*, Blackwell 1979, p 335.
30. NEC Minutes, June 1973.

31. Hannah, *op cit*, p 286–7.
32. *EPE*, May 1975.
33. EPEA evidence to the Plowden Committee.
34. Plowden Report, Cmnd 6388, January 1976.
35. Obituary of George Fisher, *EPE*, January 1977.
36. *EPE*, May 1976.
37. *Ibid*.
38. *Ibid*.
39. J Lyons, 'The Engineer in a Changing Society', Address to the IEE, 10 March 1977.
40. *EPE*, January 1977. Verbatim report of Special Conference.
41. *Ibid*.
42. NJB Minutes, 17.1.78, 14.3.78, 16.5.78, 18.7.78 and 17.10.78.
43. Arbitration Award 1979.
44. *Ibid*.
45. *EPE*, Jan 1975.

Chapter 10

The Association at 75 years old

> 'We shall continue unremittingly to look after members' security of employment, and not only to protect, but improve their salaries and conditions ... We shall maintain the high standard of professional service we give our members ...'
>
> John Lyons, *Electrical Power Engineer*, 1989.

It is difficult if not impossible to see the events of recent years in perspective but, to complete the account of the Association's first 75 years, some attempt to summarise what has been happening and its effects on the industry and the Association is necessary. For those living through the 1980s the changes in the economic and social climate seem to have created an environment significantly different from that which existed before, with the recession into which the British economy moved in 1980 marking the divide. In the previous decade the sterling crisis of 1976 marked the lowest point for the economy and, although there were nearly 1½m people unemployed at the beginning of 1977, there were signs of recovery later in that year and in 1978. As inflation dropped to single figures it was hoped that North Sea oil would reduce the balance of payments deficit and stimulate the economy. But in 1979 Callaghan's 'winter of discontent', and the rise of inflation again into double figures presaged the 1980 recession. It fell to the Conservative government of Margaret Thatcher to preside over unemployment reaching the 2m mark and still rising in 1980 as the effects of the worst depression since the 1930s were felt in almost every industrial sector.

Contraction in the electricity supply industry

The electricity supply industry was no exception to the rule and in 1980, against all post-war experience, the demand for electricity fell for the second successive year. In response the CEGB increased its power station closure programme (announced in 1980 to be implemented from 1982 onwards) from the 1583MW already planned to 3402MW. For the same reasons the two Scottish Boards announced a reduction of 1592MW capacity.

In these circumstances the EPEA had to face the reality of a greater decline in the number of jobs in the industry for its members than it had previously anticipated. From the mid 1970s on the Association had actively pursued the philosophy that changes in the industry should be carried out by agreement between itself and the employers, a policy accepted by Harold Spear, the Member for Industrial Relations at the Electricity Council, and by the Boards' side of the NJB in 1975. The formula that 'neither side should impose its will upon the other' served the industry well in the difficult conditions of 1980 and 1981. Clause 'j' of the 1980 Agreement had provided that management should make proposals to adjust staffing to workload, and the implementation of the clause enabled staff reductions to be made in an orderly fashion. The Association successfully resisted compulsory redundancy and on that basis negotiated agreed reductions and members accepted voluntary severance terms.

An inevitable corollary of this was the contraction of Association membership and an increase in the number of retired members. The EPEA's NJB membership fell by almost 4,000 (from 28,879 to 24,795) between 1980 and 1985 while over the same period the number of NJM members fell to under 1,000.[1] At the same time the number of retired members increased by nearly 1,600. Many of them were in their 50s and remained active in their sections and in some areas they have also developed extensive social programmes. While it might have been anticipated that compensation for the loss of members in the supply industry would come from wider recruitment following the establishment of the EMA in 1977, in the short term that did not prove to be the case. The effect of the recession on the engineering and shipbuilding industries was severe and and EMA was handicapped by other difficulties.

The EMA struggles for survival

The major problem which faced the EMA in its early years was one of recognition. Employers were reluctant to recognise the new Association – the Engineering Employers' Federation (EEF) would not recognise it – partly because of the hostility of other TUC trade unions and partly because it feared the EMA would be too successful. Both AUEW (TASS) and ASTMS established, within two years of the EMA's foundation, new organisations to provide for the professional engineers, as also did the EETPU. In the TUC the 'Bridlington' rules were designed to prevent inter-union conflict over membership among affiliated unions and the EMA lost the two cases brought against it although it had acted fully within the Bridlington rules. When the Association initiated legal action against the TUC it was threatened with expulsion.

The Employment Protection Act of 1975 had given the Advisory, Conciliation and Arbitration Service (ACAS) a statutory constitution, and independent trade unions were given the right to refer recognition issues to ACAS which had powers to investigate, report and make recommendations. Between 1977 and 1980 the EMA referred a succession of cases to ACAS, one of which became the subject of extensive litigation. Every ballot carried out by ACAS on the EMA references showed that the majority of the staff wanted the EMA to represent them but ACAS refused to recommend recognition in any of them. It also refused to carry out any further investigations into references made by the EMA while litigation was going on. A reference on behalf of EMA members at GEC Whetstone was the subject of legal proceedings against ACAS by the EMA. The Association lost its case in the High Court but when the case went to appeal in May 1979 the Appeal Court judges found in favour of the EMA.

Lord Denning did not mince his words of judgement:

> We have heard arguments on behalf of EMA, UKAPE and
> ACAS. But in the midst of it all the persons who are most
> concerned of all – the 300 professional men at Whetstone –
> have not been heard at all. They have been caught in the
> crossfire between TASS, EMA and UKAPE. The evidence in
> this case shows that most of them urgently desire to be
> represented by some union or other for the purpose of
> collective bargaining. Everyone of them has a right which is
> recognised by the European Court of Human Rights 'to form
> and to join trade unions for the protection of their interests'.
> Yet they are being hindered or prevented from exercising
> this right by the failure of ACAS to ascertain their options – as
> ACAS is by statute enjoined to do. I am tempted to remind
> ACAS of the words of Magna Carta: 'To none will we sell, to
> none will be delay or deny right or justice'. Let them get on
> with their appointed task – in justice to the workers
> themselves.[2]

The Appeal Court judgement however was overturned in
the House of Lords (by a decision of three votes to two)
when ACAS took the case there.

There was no doubt in the EMA's mind that ACAS,
under Jim Mortimer's chairmanship, was determined to
block and frustrate its attempts to gain recognition with
new employers. It clearly preferred a situation where no
union at all should be recognised, rather than to give its
support to the EMA. But the responsibility of ACAS for
recognition matters was abolished by the Conservative
government's 1980 Employment Act, with the EMA's cases
still unresolved. By then the hostility in the TUC was
starting to fade and the 'Bridlington rules' were changed,
partly as a direct result of the EMA's criticisms of their
misuse against them. The EMA had also achieved a major
victory early in 1979 when, in the teeth of fierce
opposition from TASS and ASTMS, it gained official
recognition for the 2000 managers employed by British
Shipbuilders. It was not, however, until 1985 that the
EMA was able to achieve the crucial breakthrough when it
became affiliated to the Confederation of Shipbuilding
and Engineering Unions (CSEU), the body recognised for

purposes of negotiating and consultation within the engineering, aerospace and shipbuilding industries. This success, for which the Association had been working since 1979, came cruelly late, for by that time the political climate for trade union recruitment had changed decisively for the worse. Nevertheless membership of the CSEU consolidated the EMA's position, taking it beyond further argument and giving it a firmer platform on which to base its activities in the future.

The Association role in the TUC

The struggle within the TUC over the EMA had brought home to the Association that might equals right and that the most important rule in the TUC is force and numbers. From the start the EMA was conscious of the need for the smaller trade unions in the TUC, particularly those representing professional staff, to work together. In 1977 the Association had, with the British Airline Pilots Association (BALPA), organised an informal conference to discuss the problems common to associations of professional and managerial staffs.[3] In the TUC the EMA pushed for a change in the composition and election of the General Council dominated until then by the big brigades – the large general unions. 'Automaticity' as it became known – a system which gave an automatic seat on the General Council to all unions with 100,000 members or more, and at the same time provided 11 seats to be shared between unions with less than 100,000 members, which they would elect among themselves – was agreed in principle at the 1981 Blackpool Congress. 'Intensive politicking' and a rearguard action to defend its introduction followed, but at the 1983 Blackpool Congress there was a three to one vote in favour and the new system came into force.[4] Among the newcomers elected to the 11 seats for the smaller unions was John Lyons. That remote possibility, as it had been considered in 1942 (see p 145), became a reality.

The Association and its General Secretary continued to follow a policy of representing professional workers at the TUC, and of speaking its mind, not always popular moves, particularly in the strained atmosphere created by the miners' strike of 1984-5.

The coal strike of 1984-5

The strike which developed in March 1984, to protest at the NCB's plans to close down some 20 pits and eliminate around 20,000 jobs – 'savage butchery' as NUM President Arthur Scargill termed it – was seen from the start by many in the EPEA and, particularly its General Secretary, as being 'essentially a revolutionary strike' so far as the leadership was concerned, as well as having real industrial objectives.[5] The EPEA had always opposed the use of the supply industry as a battleground for the disputes of other industries and, between May and August 1984, acted in concert with the other unions in the industry in refusing to consider the appeal made by Peter Heathfield, Secretary of the NUM, to the Electricity Supply Unions' Council (ESUC – formerly the Employees' National Committee and subsequently the Electricity Supply Trade Unions' Council, ESTUC) to support the miners' actions and to 'act in solidarity'; on behalf of the ESUC, John Lyons advised the NUM to channel any proposals through the TUC.[6] It was not however until September that the NUM approached the TUC, bringing to the Congress at Brighton a request for total support and a blockade of coal and alternative fuels.

Although the motion won overwhelming support, it was opposed publicly by both Eric Hammond of the EETPU and John Lyons of the EPEA. Such were the emotions aroused, and the hostility engendered that the Association hired a bodyguard for its General Secretary. The latter's outspoken opposition to the TUC offering a support that it could not deliver, and warning that 'the electricity supply industry is not, and never has been, available to solve industrial disputes external to it, not even for the miners' was greeted with abuse.[7] Aware, however, that the government and the NCB had provoked the strike and that the strikers were making considerable sacrifices, John Lyons privately warned the Electricity Council that his members would not tolerate any dragging of the heels by either the Government or the NCB in reopening negotiations with the miners. The following day the NCB offered to reopen talks; but although these came near to a settlement they subsequently broke down. The strike dragged on until March 1985 and by the use of stocks built up by the CEGB before the strike, alternative fuels, and road transport for coal produced by the Nottingham coalfield, there were no power cuts and electricity supplies were maintained.[8]

An 'engine of change'

It was however not only in the TUC that the EMA and the EPEA sought to represent professional workers. In January 1980 the Association welcomed the long-awaited report of the Finniston Committee. Against considerable opposition from government departments and the engineering institutions, the EPEA had, after its success in demanding the enquiry at the 1976 TUC Congress, persisted in securing the implementation of their resolution urging the need for a far-ranging inquiry into the engineering profession. Through Bernard (now Lord) Donaghue, head of the Prime Minister's Policy Unit, John Lyons was able to engage the interest of James Callaghan, and in July 1977, Eric Varley, Secretary of State for Industry, announced the establishment of an inquiry under the chairmanship of Sir Monty Finniston, former head of the British Steel Corporation. The EPEA regarded this as a victory, not least because the inquiry's terms of reference were almost identical with those the Association had proposed. The committee was to review the manufacturing industry in the light of national economic needs and make recommendations on:

1. the requirements of British industry for professional and technician engineers, the extent to which these needs are being met, and the use made of engineers by industry
2. the role of the engineering institutions in relation to the education and qualifications of engineers at professional and technician level

3. the advantages and disadvantages of statutory registration and licensing of engineers in the UK
4. the arrangements in other major industrial countries, particularly in the EEC, for handling these problems, having regard to relevant comparative studies.

Finniston's recommendations also echoed those of the EMA, made in its evidence to the Committee.[9] The major recommendation was the establishment of a statutory body – the Engineering Authority – which would not only deal with the registration of engineers (first mooted, it should be noted, in the 1920s) but would also represent the profession.

For the 'formation of engineers', the phraseology adopted by the Committee, the report proposed three levels of qualification, to be the responsibility of the Engineering Authority rather than the professional institutions. In the event the Engineering Council, chartered not statutory, was the body established to act as 'an engine of change' in attitudes to engineers. John Lyons served as a founder member of the Council from 1982 to 1986. The training, use, supply and registration of engineers are the responsibility of the Council. There have been many criticisms of the Council and the Engineering Assembly it created as a means of communication. It is not what was intended by Finniston; but, in the circumstances of the time, as John Lyons noted in the *Electrical Power Engineer*:

> The Engineering Council, warts and all, is an organisation of the kind for which this Association campaigned in the 70s, and which we spent much time effectively helping to create in the early 1980s. It does not represent our ideal. But is is not an ineffectual body, and it is the only one in the field, or likely to be so, for years to come.[10]

For the Association, the implementation of Finniston was one of many important issues claiming its attention in the early 1980s.

The job evaluation exercise

The first half of the 1980s saw the completion of two sets of long drawn out and complex negotiations, set in train by the major restructuring agreement made in 1974 (see p 194). It took seven years for the two sides of the NJB to reach agreement on a comprehensive and detailed job evaluation scheme covering the 26,000 NJB posts then in existence. Not only was the scheme jointly devised at every stage (Tony Frith, an NEC member seconded from the London Electricity Board as job evaluation officer of the Association, played an indispensable role in bringing about the agreement), but it was to be jointly implemented. Assessment teams were established and trained jointly and undertook the initial allocation of posts in the context of the new scheme. This again took several years to work through. Although up to three years' back dating had been agreed for those whose posts suffered long delays in assessment, the total process of initial allocation took virtually six years to complete. The length of time the scheme took to implement, coupled with discontent among groups of Headquarters and specialist staffs at its outcome, led to growing discontent among Association members. At the 1986 Annual Delegate Conference at Bournemouth the National Executive Committee was instructed to negotiate the Association's withdrawal from the scheme. But that proved impossible: the Boards' side of the NJB would not agree to the Association's withdrawal, arguing that it was a joint scheme, that it had graded the entire NJB workforce and therefore both sides had to live with the results. The Association then sought a review of the scheme to iron out some of the deficiencies that members perceived in it but this also proved to be abortive.

The scheme therefore remains in operation; however it was agreed by the two sides of the NJB in 1986 that current claims for improved gradings made by members would be considered in the same way as before with the proviso that, in the event of a difference of principle that could not be resolved, the job evaluation scheme would be used as the final determinant of such claims.

The NJB job evaluation scheme is possibly the most comprehensive of such schemes introduced in this country. It produced directly some 2000 upgradings of NJB staff. No person was downgraded, although it was agreed that a few hundred posts would drop to a lower grade once their present occupants left them. In addition, approximately another 2000 posts were upgraded, either as a result of Boards (particularly Area Boards), reorganising and upgrading staff, in anticipation of the job evaluation scheme in the late 1970s, or as a result of the knock on effects of the scheme itself – as for example in the power station agreements (see below).

The scheme automatically replaced the old classification system for power station and distribution staffs thus lifting the ceiling previously imposed on the grading of shift charge engineers in the largest power stations and of district engineers in the largest distribution districts. Once the six grade structure had been introduced across the country, a consistent system of evaluation of the posts between those six grades was essential and the job evaluation scheme went a long way to meet that demand. The fact that ultimately it did not fully succeed in meeting its own criteria of being a 'felt fair' scheme by the entire NJB staff is perhaps not surprising given the complexities involved.

The other major negotiation completed in the early 1980s concerned the structure and grading of managerial and NJB posts in the largest conventional power stations, known as the 2000 MW stations. It had been agreed in 1974 that the grading and organisation of the 2000 MW and AGR power stations would be jointly reviewed by the CEGB and the Association. (The South of Scotland Electricity Board was not party to the review.) The CEGB wanted to reorganise and restructure the staffing of its power stations, abolishing the post of deputy station manager and introducing instead, under the station manager, a new three-headed management structure covering production, engineering and resources. The Association intended to increase the grading levels in the large stations, an increase it believed to be justified by both the size and the responsibilities devolving on the staff.

This was only possible once the introduction of job evaluation had lifted the classification ceilings that had previously held down the grading levels. While that was still the case, the Association had steadily improved the grading levels in the smaller stations, leading to substantial disaffection among the members who had moved to staff the large stations and felt the extra responsibilities they had undertaken were not being properly rewarded.

The negotiations began in 1975 and were completed for the 2000 MW stations in 1982. At the start the CEGB resisted the upgrading of shift charge engineers and other shift staff in these stations. It was several years before the Board realised that the Association regarded upgrading as an essential part of the reorganisation package which the Board proposed; the negotiations also became enmeshed with the job evaluation exercise.

The CEGB was adamant that the job evaluation scheme should not lead to automatic upgrading of any key staff in these stations. Finally it was agreed that the points score for, for example, the shift charge engineers would fall just below the minimum necessary for automatic upgrading (in what was termed the 'grey area' under the job evaluation scheme) but the Board undertook to use the discretion which this 'grey area' point score would give them to lift the posts into the next grade, provided the Association agreed to the restructuring the CEGB wanted. This turned out to be the essential component and on this basis an agreement was finally reached in 1982 – an agreement which also raised the grading and salary of the station managers, by then long overdue. However, even then, the path was not easy. The Association actually reached agreement with the Board in 1981 and its negotiating team visited every 2000 MW power station to explain the terms to a highly critical membership. The Association's negotiators were left in no doubt that the 1981 agreement did not carry the members' support. Early in 1982, therefore, they proposed a number of changes to the 1981 agreement with the Board, to most of which the Board agreed. The agreement was introduced on a station by station basis over the next 18 months or so.

Soon afterwards the Association opened negotiations

with the Board to bring the AGR (nuclear) stations into line with the gradings in the 2000 MW conventional stations. Although the AGR stations had a megawatt capacity of 1300 MW as against the 2000 MW of the large conventional station, similar grading standards were justified in the Association's view by the particular responsibilities associated with running a large and complex nuclear station. Agreement was reached covering AGR stations at the end of 1985.

These two sets of negotiations effectively improved the career structure available to all power station staff; although the agreements had their critics – as do most agreements – they represented a major negotiating success for the Association.

Pay and conditions in the 1980s

The introduction of the job evaluation scheme, combined with the effects of the 1978 Agreement on out of hours payments and the cementing of the NJB/NJIC link by the 1979 arbitration tribunal (see Chapter 9), together established NJB pay and conditions on a new footing. On a comparative basis, the technical staff in the supply industry achieved a position in the top six non-manual occupational groups, which they have maintained since 1973; their ranking has varied but in 1988 they were number three, preceded only by medical practitioners and finance, insurance and tax specialists.[11]

Annual pay settlements in the 1980s have preserved the NJB staffs' position in relation to the NJIC – the most important differential – but also in relation to other earnings. Throughout the period 1975 to 1988 the increase in NJB earnings has outstripped the increase in NJIC earnings and, except between 1980 and 1984, the increase in NJB earnings has been greater than the increases in other non-manual earnings and in all male earnings.[12] Although working hours have only been reduced once – in 1981 from 38 to 37 – it has been Association policy, determined at the ADC, to prefer pay increases to further reductions in working hours.

The clarification and simplification of pay matters,

particularly the resolution of shift and out of hours payment problems and the apparently interminable grading problems before job evaluation, meant that the Association's NEC and officials had more time to devote to other issues (see below). The problem of the NJB/NJIC interface, however, remained unresolved in these years.

The NJB–NJIC interface

The Association devoted a lot of effort in the 1980s in trying to resolve the problems of the NJB/NJIC interface, that is the jobs and responsibilities which lie where the bottom of the NJB structure and the top of the NJIC structure meet. In 1980 the NJIC was on the point of agreeing on the introduction of revised duties for Band IV and Band V craftsmen, a number of which were currently undertaken by NJB staff. Upon learning of this the Association informed the Boards' side of the NJB that it would in no circumstances accept that either the management or the NJIC unions had a right to reallocate duties of NJB staff without its agreement; if the revision went ahead, the Association would instruct its members to oppose the prospective agreement by all means at their disposal. Consequently the NJIC made a modified agreement which did not involve any alteration to the duties of NJB staff. The Association then offered to discuss the duties across the interface between the two groups of staff with a view to agreeing to any necessary changes, but subject to a number of conditions the Association wished to see incorporated in any resulting agreement.

Thus started the negotiations on the NJB/NJIC interface which continued intermittently through the 1980s and are still unconcluded. The Association's initiative was important because it recognised that there was a problem, but it was only prepared to seek a solution in the context of a properly structured agreement binding on all three parties. Delays occurred in the early years, firstly because the Electricity Boards seemed uncertain what they actually wanted, and then because the subject was inevitably shelved for the year long duration of the miners' strike. Discussions were eventually resumed leading to tripartite meetings between the Boards, the Association and the NJIC unions in 1987 and 1988. At the 1988 meeting an outline of a possible agreement between the three parties finally emerged, although it seemed as if the industrial unions would not be satisfied with it. However, by this time the Government had announced its plans to privatise the industry. Since then the industry has been diverted into dealing with privatisation and it now seems unlikely that all three parties will wish to conclude any agreement before the industry is privatised.

New coordinating machinery

Although the advisory machinery established at nationalisation (see p 166) served the industry well for two decades, by the early 1970s it had, in the Association's view, degenerated into more or less a talking shop. Nationally increasing demands for greater participation in management decisions led to the appointment of the Bullock Committee, whose report on industrial democracy in the private sector was published in 1977. The Government announced that it intended to introduce legislation to implement Bullock's recommendations for employee representation on Boards in both the private and public sectors. But by that time the supply industry had already formulated and agreed proposals for new machinery to reform and revitalise the existing advisory processes, along the lines agreed by the EPEA's 1976 Annual Delegate Conference.

The National Joint Coordinating Council (for England and Wales – Scotland had a separate council) held its inaugural meeting in May 1977, some ten months after it had started work on an interim basis. Its formation and functions were intended to provide for greater participation, giving the trade unions in the industry a more influential voice in policy matters, as indicated by the ten subjects given as examples of the kind of topics the Council might consider; these included fuel policies, financial matters and corporate planning as well as matters relating to efficiency.

A National Joint Negotiating Committee was also set up with the power to negotiate for the common interest of two or more negotiating machines if they so wished (for example the NJB and NJC). Superannuation matters were, for the first time, accepted as being capable of negotiation by the new Committee. Local coordinating machinery was to be established at Area Board and CEGB regional and divisional level.[13] The Association's interest and expertise in health and safety matters was recognised by all the unions in the supply industry, when it was elected to hold the joint secretaryship of the new Health and Safety Committee (HESAC). Over the past decade the Association's contribution on health and safety in the industry has been recognised as a valuable one, as it was too in another area – nuclear power.

The nuclear debate

The last decade has seen increasing public concern about the environment, which, in the supply industry, focuses on the questions of nuclear power and acid rain. The Association's commitment to the use of nuclear fuel in the electricity supply industry has been consistent – as reaffirmed at the 1987 ADC: civil nuclear power should be developed as part of a balanced policy for the supply of electricity, but it must be on a safe and socially acceptable basis. The Association has never been slow to criticise the industry where members felt that safeguards were inadequate, and in recent years, as public concern developed, the expertise of EPEA members on nuclear matters has been used to examine critically incidents in the industry, and issues and policies. Management at Sellafield, where accidental discharges caused mounting public concern, was blamed for a 'lack of attention to the stringent requirements of a major nuclear plant', by Stan Dean, President elect at the 1984 ADC.[14] In 1981 the Association brought pressure to bear on the CEGB when the NJCC were offered an 'unsatisfactory' paper on nuclear waste transport and disposal. This led to the CEGB staging the spectacle of a high speed train crash to demonstrate (successfully) that the nuclear flask it was carrying would be undamaged.

In the same year the Government gave approval in principle to the sale of civil plutonium to the USA. Although it was stated that the plutonium was for civil uses, the announcement coincided with an expansion of the US nuclear weapons programme, causing considerable public concern as to whether plutonium exported from the UK might be diverted from civil to military use. Since then the Association has campaigned vigorously, partly through the TUC, for assurances, which were forthcoming from the CEGB and the US administration, that the plutonium would only be used for civil nuclear power.

Public fears about accidents with nuclear installations were fuelled by the incident at Three Mile Island, Harrisburg in March 1979. The Association monitored the accident closely and, as part of a delegation sent by the CEGB (but representing the industry's trade unions), John Lyons went to Washington to be briefed by the US Nuclear Regulatory Commission. Although the accident took place at a PWR station, and there were then no PWR stations in the UK, there were, the General Secretary and the NEC reported, lessons to be learned. On the EPEA's recommendations, the CEGB subsequently made changes in its training programmes for those concerned with nuclear installations.

Similarly an Association representative (Ms Jackie Norfolk) was part of a UK delegation to the USSR after the explosion in April 1986 at Chernobyl. The effects of Chernobyl, which spread its contamination through the northern hemisphere, gave added ammunition to the anti-nuclear power campaigners. In the trade union movement this focussed in a motion from the NUM at the 1986 TUC conference demanding the closure of the UK's nuclear power stations. Speaking against the motion John Lyons made clear the Association's stance:

> What Chernobyl established for ever is that even a civil nuclear disaster is an event with international consequences. That is why for the first time there is now an intense drive to bring under international control the design operation and safety requirements of all nuclear reactors, military as well as

civil, in every country. We not only agree with that: we demand
it. For whatever we do in this country, the rest of the world is
not going to turn its back on nuclear power...[15]

The motion was defeated and, with the Association's full
support, the TUC embarked on a review of nuclear
power.

The future of the industry

After the Plowden proposals sank, almost without trace, in
1983 the CEGB announced a major reorganisation
consultation exercise while through the early 1980s the
Area Boards reorganised themselves

> at frequent intervals. Indeed, in the opinion of members in
> those Boards which have been in a more or less continuous
> state of reorganisation throughout recent years, too
> frequently.[16]

From the end of 1983, however, privatisation of the
industry was on the agenda as a possibility. After the
return of the Conservative party to power again in 1987,
privatisation became a reality.In cooperation with the
other trade unions in the supply industry through the
Electricity Supply Trade Union Council (ESTUC), the
FUSE anti-privatisation campaign was launched. (The
Association sent a fact-finding mission to the USA to
investigate and report on the regulation of a privately-
owned utilities system. The report it subsequently
published was widely recognised as breaking new ground.)
But against the doctrinaire determination of the Conservative government, it was difficult to make much impact.
Over the last year, while reaffirming its intrinsic
opposition to the principle of privatisation, the NEC has
identified key issues on which it has taken a firm stand and
consistently brought them to the attention of the public.

Continuity and change

As in any organisation, change is a continuous process;
over the last decade many of the Association's officials and

active members mentioned in previous chapters have
retired. In 1983 Arthur Palmer left the House of
Commons and the EPEA, and after more than 30 years,
the Association had to find a new voice in Parliament.
'AMP's' contributions have been many; the Annual School
which he introduced has expanded and become an EPEA
institution; the Technical Representatives too now have a
school. The Technical Groups have dwindled to two but
they still have busy programmes. There is no doubt that
over the last 15 years the Association has developed

> from an important but nevertheless rather inward looking
> organisation, into one which has rightly earned the respect of
> those with whom we deal, and one which is continually
> engaged in a wide range of important activities which
> recognise the authoritative role that our members fill within
> the ESI.[17]

On nuclear power and on the structure of the industry, to
name only two issues, that authoratitive role can be clearly
seen. The stand taken by the Association in 1977 during
an NJIC unofficial dispute, both in maintaining supplies
and in standing up to the then Secretary of State for
Energy, Tony Benn, provides ample illustration of this.[18]
Over the last two decades the Association has been
continually involved in a wide range of complex issues
inside and outside the supply industry. In 1919 one of the
founders wrote of his vision of the Association 50 years on:

> You must understand that in fifty years the world makes
> great progress, in electrical matters no less than in others. I
> am ...the President of the IEE. I am also a chief engineer of
> one of the largest Government power stations. More than that
> I am a member and a Past President of the Electrical
> Association... the modern development and direct offspring
> of the EPEA.... Nowadays the most cordial and happy
> relations exist between all chiefs and their staffs. All without
> exception belong to the same Association, their interests
> being identical. This profession is the most highly paid in the
> country, and in the street an electrical engineer can always be
> picked out by reason of the air of serene happiness he
> habitually wears.... As to the EPEA, incorporated under royal
> charter in 1929, membership of its present day descendant is

considered one of the highest honours to which any man can aspire. The original function and *raison d'être* of the EPEA have under modern conditions become altogether unnecessary, but the spirit of its founders still survives among us. A special order of knighthood has been instituted by the King which is conferred on every president of the Association on the vacation of his term of office ...[19]

Seventy years later reality differs from the 'fantasy'; far from 'withering away' the 'original function and *raison d'être*' of the Association remains as vital now as then: the maintenance of an efficient, independent and non-political protective organisation for the technical staff in the electricity supply industry. At the same time the dream of W H Simpson in 1919 has come true in some respects, for in the last decade the engineers in the supply industry have been among the best paid engineers in the country.

But the Association's activities and prestige have moved much further beyond anything that could have been envisaged in 1919. Much of the credit for the appointment of Finniston must go to the EPEA and Finniston has helped to promote the national importance of engineers. In the TUC the Association is now well-known and, over the last 15 years it has come to exert an influence within the TUC and the wider trade union world which was thought impossible in its first 30 years of affiliation. The Association has projected the professional knowledge of its members in the nuclear field in a way that has won respect, even from environmentalists. In creating the EMA, its responsibilities and ambitions now range more widely than electricity; and with the privatisation of the supply industry, EPEA members are realising how important and relevant the EMA is to them. The engineers in the EPEA have demonstrated clearly over the last two decades that they are the key people in the supply industry, whose interests can no longer be treated with disdain and whose cooperation has to be won by management; over the same period they have demonstrated equally clearly that their commitment to the future is the protection of the electricity system against all external threats.

Notes

1. EPEA Annual Report 1986.
2. EMA v ACAS, Appeal Court 1979. Quoted in EMA:BDC Report 1977-79.
3. *EPE*, August/September 1977.
4. *EPE*, November/December 1981. F Chapple, *Sparks Fly!* Michael Joseph 1985.
5. *EPE*, October/November 1984. P Wilsher, D Macintyre, M Jones, (eds), *Strike*, Coronet 1985, p 266.
6. EPEA Archives. Correspondence between ESUC and Peter Heathfield, May–June 1984.
7. Wilsher etc, *op cit*, pp 157–9, Chapter 12. See also M Adeney and J Lloyd, *The Miners' Strike 1984–5*, Routledge and Kegan Paul 1986, p 284.
8. *Ibid*.
9. Finniston Report: Engineering Our Future, January 1980; *EPE*, February 1980.
10. *EPE*, September 1988.
11. Department of Employment, New Earnings Surveys 1973-1988.
12. *Ibid*.
13. NJCC Agreement, *EPE*, August/September 1977.
14. S Dean, President-elect's speech at the 1984 ADC.
15. TUC Congress 1986.
16. EPEA Annual Report 1986.
17. R Smith in *EPE*, April 1988.
18. *EPE*, December 1977.
19. *EPE*, November 1919.

Appendix 1: A technical note

AC   **Alternating current** an electric current which reverses alternately the direction of its flow.

DC   **Direct current** an electric current flowing in one direction.

Hz   **Hertz or cycles per second** the number of cycles of AC per second. In the early years there was a great variety of Hz used, with 25 Hz and 40 Hz the most common. Subsequently the UK standardised on 50 Hz.

KW   **Kilowatt** 1,000 watts.

Load factor   The ratio of the amount of electricity produced or supplied in a year to the amount that would have been produced if maximum demand had been maintained for the year.

MW   **Megawatt** 1 million watts

V   **Volt** the unit of pressure causing a current to flow.

W   **Watt** the unit in which current flowing in an electrical circuit is measured.

Appendix 2: Presidents of the Association

1913–18	W A Jones
1918–19	A L Lunn
1919–20	A L Lunn
1920–21	J H Parker
1921–22	J F Heslop
1922–23	W J Jeffery
1923–24	W J Oswald
1924–25	T A Margary
1925–26	R R Telford
1926–27	A J Ostler
1927–28	A W Crompton
1928–29	A C Stewart
1929–30	T D Martin
1930–31	A V Sendell
1931–32	A E Ricketts
1932–33	H J Taylor
1933–34	D J Duffy
1934–35	R H Toynbee
1935–36	C Cooper
1936–37	J F Sarvent
1937–38	H J Cox
1938–39	L Hoskison
1939–40	P S Jolin
1940–41	G Gunn
1941–42	H A Gray
1942–43	P L Weir
1943–44	E Laming
1944–45	S Gough
1945–46	G E Moore

1946–47	J A Welburn
1947–48	G O James
1948–49	F Lumby
1949–50	F Seddon
1950–51	W Ingledew
1951–52	I C Williams
1952–53	J L Moss
1953–54	J Jones
1954–55	E Hanson
1955–56	J Parr–Morley
1956–57	J E Stanton
1957–58	L Benallick
1958–59	C Donnellan
1959–60	R Johnson
1960–61	H Brockelsby
1961–62	H J Fraser
1962–63	S Fuller
1963–64	S Alger
1964–65	T Jackson
1965–66	F Pugh
1966–67	L Greenwood
1967–68	J J Bradley
1968–69	D R Taylor
1969–70	W A R South
1970–71	H R Page
1971–72	J Forrester
1972–73	R A Blackburn
1973–74	G T Fisher
1974–75	M Greenbat
1975–76	J Acklam
1976–77	E Busby
1977–78	J Ashford
1978–79	K Ashton
1979–80	R Colclough
1980–81	E Platt
1981–82	D C Williams
1982–83	A H Ives
1983–84	J Campbell
1984–85	S Dean
1985–86	J Kirby
1986–87	D Holland

1987–88   A Pendlebury
1988–89   R M Jones

Appendix 3: General Secretaries of the EPEA

1919–45   W A Jones
1946–52   J F Wallace
1953–72   H Norton
1973–   J Lyons

Appendix 4: A Note on Sources

Except for the early years, 1913–17, the Association's own archives are very full. This history therefore is mainly based on the records at Chertsey: National Executive Council Minutes 1918–74 and National Executive Committee Minutes 1975 – present; General Purposes Committee and other EPEA Committee Minutes. Since 1975 there have been the Proceedings of the Annual Delegate Conferences and the proceedings of the two Special Conferences. More recently there has been the EMA's Biennial Conference. NJB Minutes are extant from 1919 to 1945 at the Electricity Council and 1945 to the present at Chertsey where there are also NJMC Minutes from 1953.

There are a few surviving section committee records from the early days – the South East for example – but most of them have disappeared. The complete set of the *Electrical Power Engineer* from 1919 to the present has put much of the flesh on the bones.

Published sources are indicated in the notes to the chapters.

Index